JavaScript from Frontend to Backend

Learn full stack JavaScript development using the MEVN stack with quick and easy steps

Eric Sarrion

BIRMINGHAM—MUMBAI

JavaScript from Frontend to Backend

Copyright © 2022 Packt Publishing

All rights reserved. No part of this book may be reproduced, stored in a retrieval system, or transmitted in any form or by any means, without the prior written permission of the publisher, except in the case of brief quotations embedded in critical articles or reviews.

Every effort has been made in the preparation of this book to ensure the accuracy of the information presented. However, the information contained in this book is sold without warranty, either express or implied. Neither the author, nor Packt Publishing or its dealers and distributors, will be held liable for any damages caused or alleged to have been caused directly or indirectly by this book.

Packt Publishing has endeavored to provide trademark information about all of the companies and products mentioned in this book by the appropriate use of capitals. However, Packt Publishing cannot guarantee the accuracy of this information.

Associate Group Product Manager: Pavan Ramchandani

Publishing Product Manager: Jane D'souza

Senior Editor: Mark D'souza

Content Development Editor: Debolina Acharyya

Technical Editor: Shubham Sharma

Copy Editor: Safis Editing

Proofreader: Safis Editing

Indexer: Rekha Nair

Production Designer: Vijay Kamble

Marketing Coordinater: Marylou De Mello, Anamika Singh

First published: August 2022

Production reference: 2090822

Published by Packt Publishing Ltd.
Livery Place
35 Livery Street
Birmingham
B3 2PB, UK.

ISBN 978-1-80107-031-7

www.packt.com

Contributors

About the author

Eric Sarrion is a trainer, a developer, and an independent consultant. He has been involved in all kinds of IT projects for over 30 years. He is also a long-time author in web development technologies and is renowned for the clarity of his explanations and examples.

About the reviewer

Presently, **Kailash Ramanathan** works at Uber as a Senior Software Engineer. Since 2009, he has built several lean and powerful web-based applications using contemporary frameworks. Now, he enjoys working with Vue & React. When not at work, he enjoys music & a good-natured banter with friends and family.

> *First, I thank my parents for their incessant and unconditional support for every enterprise I undertake. Second, I thank God for this life & surrounding it with beautiful people I know - near and dear. Third, I thank my mentors & authors who I have read and learned from. And, to you who are reading these words and have chosen to know more and go beyond.*

Gabriel Bieules is an engineer with 18 years of experience in building software applications. He worked in various industries like telecommunication, eDiscovery, and the web. He got exposed to multiple programming languages, but his expertise is mostly around Java and JavaScript.

Table of Contents

Preface

Part 1: JavaScript Syntax

1
Exploring the Core Concepts of JavaScript

Technical requirements	4
Types of variables used in JavaScript	5
Numerical values	5
Boolean values	6
Character strings	6
Arrays	6
Objects	7
Running a JavaScript program	8
Running a JavaScript program in a browser	8
Running a JavaScript program on a Node.js server	13
Differences between JavaScript code written for the browser and the server	14
Declaring variables in JavaScript	15
Using the const keyword	15
Using the var keyword	17
Using the let keyword	20
What if we don't use var or let to define a variable?	22
What is an uninitialized variable worth?	23
Writing conditions for conditional tests	25
Forms of writing instructions	25
Expressions used to write conditions	27
Nested test suites	29
Creating processing loops	30
Loops with while()	30
Loops with for()	32
Using functions	33
Function displaying the list of the first 10 integers	34
Function calculating the sum of the first 10 integers	38
Function calculating the sum of the first N integers	39
Summary	40

2
Exploring the Advanced Concepts of JavaScript

Technical requirements	42	Adding items to the array	64
Classes and objects	42	Deleting array elements	66
Defining a class	42	Filtering elements in an array	69
Creating an object by using a class	43	**Character strings**	**72**
Creating an object without using a class	45	Creating a character string	72
Adding properties to a class	46	Accessing characters in a string	75
Adding methods to a class	47	Modifying a character string	77
Changing an object's property values	49	Using regular expressions	78
Using the class constructor	50	**Multitasking in JavaScript**	**82**
Merging one object with another	53	Using the setTimeout() function	83
Arrays	**55**	Using the setInterval() function	86
Creating an array	55	Using the clearInterval() function	87
Accessing array elements	57	**Using promises**	**89**

Part 2: JavaScript on the Client-Side

3
Getting Started with Vue.js

Technical requirements	96	Defining methods in the methods section	111
Using Vue.js in an HTML page	96	Defining computed properties in the computed section	112
Creating our first Vue.js application	97	**Using attributes in components**	**114**
Using reactivity	99	**Using directives**	**117**
Creating our first component	103	The v-if and v-else directives	118
Inserting a component in the application file	104	The v-show directive	120
Inserting a component from an external file	107	The v-for directive	120
		The v-model directive	123
Adding methods in components	110	**Summary**	**126**

4
Advanced Concepts of Vue.js

Technical requirements	128	When the element appears	144
Managing events	128	When the element disappears	151
Using the $event parameter	130	Using a name for the effect	154
Checking that the entered value is less than 100	130	Producing an effect on several elements	156
Allowing only digits to be entered	132	Examples of commonly used effects	157
Assembling components	134	The shrink effect	157
Using $emit() to communicate with a parent component	136	The opacity effect	159
Using props to communicate with children	140	The move-down effect	160
Using visual effects	143	Summary	163

5
Managing a List with Vue.js

Technical requirements	166	Removing an element from the list	178
Displaying application screens	166	Modifying an element in the list	183
Splitting the application into components	169	Transforming the <span> element into an <input> element	183
Adding an element to the list	173	Exiting from the input field	185
Using the <Element> component	174	Giving focus to the input field	188
Changing the appearance of the list using CSS code	177	Summary	191

Part 3: JavaScript on the Server-Side

6
Creating and Using Node.js Modules

Technical requirements	196	Reading the contents of a file	206
Creating and using our own modules	196	Displaying file contents as strings	207
		Using non-blocking file reading	208
Creating a module	196	**Using downloaded modules with npm**	**210**
Using the node_modules directory	198		
Using the package.json file	199	Using the npm command	210
Adding functionalities to the module	201	Using a downloaded module with npm	211
Using internal Node.js modules	**206**	**Summary**	**214**

7
Using Express with Node.js

Technical requirements	216	Different types of routes possible	225
Using the Node.js http module	216	Analyzing routes defined in the app.js file	226
Installing the Express module	219		
The MVC pattern used by Express	222	Adding a new route in the app.js file	229
Using routes with Express	223	**Displaying views with Express**	**231**
The initial content of the app.js file	223	**Summary**	**235**

8
Using MongoDB with Node.js

Technical requirements	238	**Creating documents in MongoDB**	**243**
Installing MongoDB	238		
Using the mongo utility	239	Describing document structure using schemas and models	243
Installing the mongoose module	240		
Connecting to the MongoDB database	**241**	Creating the document	245

Searching for documents in MongoDB	251	Updating documents in MongoDB	258
Writing search conditions	252	Deleting documents in MongoDB	260
Retrieving and displaying the results	253	Summary	262

9
Integrating Vue.js with Node.js

Technical requirements	264	Using Axios with a GET type request (client side)	292
Displaying application screens	264	GET type request processing (server side)	294
Building the app with Express	272		
MongoDB database structure	274	Modifying an element in the list	297
Installing the Axios library	277	Using Axios with a PUT type request (client side)	297
Inserting a new element in the list	280	PUT type request processing (server side)	300
Replacing the text and index attributes with the element attribute	280	Removing an element from the list	302
Description of the Axios library for communicating between the client and the server	285	Using Axios with a DELETE type request (client side)	302
Using Axios with a POST type request (client side)	286	DELETE type request processing (server side)	305
POST type request processing (server side)	288	Summary	308
Verifying the correct operation of the insertion in the database	291	Thanks	308
Displaying list elements	292		

Index

Other Books You May Enjoy

Preface

JavaScript is the most widely used programming language in the world. It has numerous libraries and modules and a dizzying array of need-to-know topics. Picking a starting point can be difficult. This concise, practical guide will get you up to speed in next to no time.

Who this book is for

This book is for JavaScript developers looking to strengthen their core JavaScript concepts and implement them in building full stack apps.

What this book covers

Chapter 1, *Exploring the Core Concepts of JavaScript*, is where you discover how to use variables, conditions, and loops in JavaScript.

Chapter 2, *Exploring the Advanced Concepts of JavaScript*, is where you learn how to use object-oriented programming in JavaScript.

Chapter 3, *Getting Started with Vue.js*, is where you learn the basics of Vue.js, with components and directives.

Chapter 4, *Advanced Concepts of Vue.js*, is where you explore in-depth Vue.js with communication between components and visual effects.

Chapter 5, *Managing a List with Vue.js*, is where you learn how to build a full project with Vue.js.

Chapter 6, *Creating and Using Node.js Modules*, is where you learn the basics of Node.js programming with modules.

Chapter 7, *Using Express with Node.js*, is where you explore the main library used to build Node.js applications.

Chapter 8, Using MongoDB with Node.js, is where you learn how to use the MongoDB database with Node.js using the Mongoose module.

Chapter 9, Integrating Vue.js with Node.js, is where you learn how to build a full project integrating Vue.js and Node.js.

To get the most out of this book

Prior knowledge of HTML and CSS is a must for this book.

Software/hardware covered in the book	Operating system requirements
JavaScript	Windows, macOS, or Linux
Vue.js	
Node.js	

If you are using the digital version of this book, we advise you to type the code yourself or access the code from the book's GitHub repository (a link is available in the next section). Doing so will help you avoid any potential errors related to the copying and pasting of code.

Download the example code files

You can download the example code files for this book from GitHub at `https://github.com/PacktPublishing/JavaScript-from-Frontend-to-Backend`. If there's an update to the code, it will be updated in the GitHub repository.

We also have other code bundles from our rich catalog of books and videos available at `https://github.com/PacktPublishing/`. Check them out!

Download the color images

We also provide a PDF file that has color images of the screenshots and diagrams used in this book. You can download it here: `https://packt.link/xdibe`

Conventions used

There are a number of text conventions used throughout this book.

`Code in text`: Indicates code words in text, database table names, folder names, filenames, file extensions, pathnames, dummy URLs, user input, and Twitter handles. Here is an example: "So `{ lastname: "Clinton" }` can also be written `{ "lastname":,"Clinton" }` by surrounding the `lastname` property with single or double quotes."

A block of code is set as follows:

```
var p = { lastname : "Clinton", firstname : "Bill" };
console.log("The person is", p);
```

When we wish to draw your attention to a particular part of a code block, the relevant lines or items are set in bold:

```
class Person {
    firstname;
    lastname;
    age;
}

var p = new Person;
console.log(p);
```

Bold: Indicates a new term, an important word, or words that you see onscreen. For instance, words in menus or dialog boxes appear in **bold**. Here is an example: "This writing format is also called **JavaScript Object Notation (JSON)** format."

> **Tips or Important Notes**
> Appear like this.

Get in touch

Feedback from our readers is always welcome.

General feedback: If you have questions about any aspect of this book, email us at `customercare@packtpub.com` and mention the book title in the subject of your message.

Errata: Although we have taken every care to ensure the accuracy of our content, mistakes do happen. If you have found a mistake in this book, we would be grateful if you would report this to us. Please visit `www.packtpub.com/support/errata` and fill in the form.

Piracy: If you come across any illegal copies of our works in any form on the internet, we would be grateful if you would provide us with the location address or website name. Please contact us at `copyright@packt.com` with a link to the material.

If you are interested in becoming an author: If there is a topic that you have expertise in and you are interested in either writing or contributing to a book, please visit `authors.packtpub.com`.

Share Your Thoughts

Once you've read *JavaScript from Frontend to Backend*, we'd love to hear your thoughts! Scan the QR code below to go straight to the Amazon review page for this book and share your feedback.

`https://packt.link/QUTSC`

Your review is important to us and the tech community and will help us make sure we're delivering excellent quality content.

Part 1: JavaScript Syntax

This part explains the basics you need to know to use JavaScript on the client or on the server. It explains the syntax and the main data types that can be used in JavaScript.

This section comprises the following chapters:

- *Chapter 1, Exploring the Core Concepts of JavaScript*
- *Chapter 2, Exploring the Advanced Concepts of JavaScript*

1
Exploring the Core Concepts of JavaScript

The JavaScript language was created (in the mid-1990s) to be executed in internet browsers, in order to make websites more fluid. It was originally used to control what was entered into input forms. For example, it was used to do the following:

- Allow the entry of numeric characters in a field – and only numeric ones. Other characters, for example, letters, had to be rejected in this case. This made it possible, thanks to the JavaScript language included in the browser, not to validate the entry of the form and avoid sending data to the server, which would have indicated an entry error in this case.

- Check that the mandatory fields of the form were all entered, by checking all the fields before sending the form fields to the server.

These two examples (among many others) show that it is desirable to have a language that checks the validity of the data entered by the user before sending this data to the server. This avoids data transfers from the browser to the server, in the event that the data entered is not correct. For more complex checks, such as checking that two people do not have the same identifier, this can continue to be done on the server because it has access to all existing identifiers.

The goal was, therefore, at the beginning of JavaScript, to have the browser check as many things as possible and then transmit the information entered to the server in order to process it.

For this, an internal browser language was created: the JavaScript language, whose name contained a very popular word at the time – "Java" (even though the two languages Java and JavaScript had nothing to do with each other).

Over the years, developers have had the idea of also associating it with the server side, to use the same language on the client side and on the server side. This allowed the creation of the Node.js server, which is widely used today.

Whether client-side or server-side, the JavaScript language uses a basic syntax that allows you to write your own programs. This is what we are going to discover in this chapter.

In this chapter, we will cover the following topics:

- Types of variables used in JavaScript
- Running a JavaScript program
- Declaring variables in JavaScript
- Writing conditions for conditional tests
- Creating processing loops
- Using functions

Technical requirements

To develop in JavaScript, and write and then run the programs in this book, you will need the following:

- A text editor for computer programs, for example, Notepad++, Sublime Text, EditPlus, or Visual Studio.
- An internet browser, for example, Chrome, Firefox, Safari, or Edge.

- A PHP server, for example, XAMPP or WampServer. The PHP server will be used to execute JavaScript programs containing `import` statements in HTML pages because these `import` statements only work on an HTTP server.

- A Node.js server: The Node.js server will be created through Node.js installation. We will also install and use the MongoDB database to associate the Node.js server with a database.

- You can find the code files for this chapter on GitHub at: `https://github.com/PacktPublishing/JavaScript-from-Frontend-to-Backend/blob/main/Chapter%201.zip`.

Let's now begin our discovery of JavaScript, by studying the different types of variables it offers us.

Types of variables used in JavaScript

Like any language, JavaScript allows you to create variables that will be used to manipulate data. JavaScript is a very simple language so, for example, data types are very basic. We will thus have the following as the main data types:

- Numerical values
- Boolean values
- Character strings
- Arrays
- Objects

Let's take a quick look at these different types of data.

Numerical values

Numerical values can be positive or negative and even in decimal form (for example, 0, -10, 10.45). All mathematical numbers called real numbers comprise numerical values or data points.

Boolean values

These are of course the two Boolean values—true or false—that are found in most languages. These values are used to express conditions: if the condition is true, then we perform a particular process, otherwise, we perform an alternative one. The result of the condition is therefore a true or false value, which is symbolized by the two values `true` and `false`.

We will see how to express conditions in the *Writing conditions* section, later in this chapter.

Character strings

Character strings refer to values such as `"a"`, `"abc"`, or `"Hello, how are you?"`. An empty character string will be represented by `""` (consecutive quotes with nothing inside). Note that you can use double quotes (`"`) or single quotes (`'`). Thus, the string `"abc"` can also be written as `'abc'` (with single quotes).

Arrays

Arrays, such as `[10, "abc", -36]`, can contain values of any type, like here where we have both numeric values and character strings. An empty array will be represented by `[]`, which means that it contains no value.

The values stored in an array are accessed by means of an index, varying from 0 (to access the first element placed in the array) to the length of the array minus 1 (to access the last element of the array). So, if the array `[10, "abc", -36]` is represented, for example, by the variable `tab`, the following occurs:

- `tab[0]` will allow access to the first element of the array: `10`.
- `tab[1]` will allow access to the second element of the array: `"abc"`.
- `tab[2]` will allow access to the third and last element of the array: `-36`.

> **Note**
> Note that it is possible to add elements to an array, even if it is empty. So, if we access index 3 of the previous array `tab`, we can write `tab[3] = "def"`. The array `tab` will therefore now be `[10, "abc", -36, "def"]`.

Objects

Objects are similar to arrays. They are used to store arbitrary information, for example, the values `43`, `"Clinton"`, and `"Bill"`. But unlike arrays that use indexes, you must specify a name to access each of these values. This name is called the key, which thus allows access to the value it represents.

Let's suppose that the previous value `43` is that of a person's age, while `"Clinton"` is their last name, and `"Bill"` is their first name. We would then write the object in the following form: `{ age: 43, lastname: "Clinton", firstname: "Bill" }`. The definition of the object is done by means of braces, and what is indicated inside is pairs of data of the form `key: value` separated by commas. This writing format is also called **JavaScript Object Notation (JSON)** format.

So, if the previous object is associated with the variable `person`, we can access their age by writing `person["age"]` (which will therefore be `43` here), but we can also write `person.age`, which will also be `43`. Similarly, we can also write `person.lastname` or `person["lastname"]` and `person.firstname` or `person["firstname"]` to access the person's last name and first name, respectively.

The key is also called a property of the object. Thus, the `age` key is also called the `age` property. We can choose any name for the key; you just have to indicate the key and then use it under this name. So, if you specify `age` as a property in the `person` object, you must use the term `age` in the expressions `person.age` or `person["age"]`; otherwise it will not work.

Note that if you write `person[age]` instead of `person["age"]`, JavaScript considers `age` to be a variable with a previously defined value, which it is not here and therefore cannot work in this case. You would have to set the `age` variable to have the value `"age"` for this to work.

The elements of an array are ordered according to their index (starting from 0, then 1, and so on), while the elements contained in an object are ordered according to the keys indicated for each element. But even though the `lastname` key is listed in the `person` object before the `firstname` key, this does not differentiate the object `{ age: 43, lastname: "Clinton", firstname: "Bill" }` from the object `{ firstname: "Bill", lastname: "Clinton", age: 43 }` because the order in which keys are written to an object is irrelevant.

Finally, there are empty objects, such as those containing no key (therefore no value). We write an empty object in the form `{ }`, indicating nothing is inside. We can then add one or more keys to an object, even if it is initially empty.

Now that we have seen the main variable types used in JavaScript, let's see how to use them to define variables in our programs.

Running a JavaScript program

JavaScript is a language that can be executed in a browser (Edge, Chrome, Firefox, Safari, and so on) or on a server with Node.js installed. Let's see how to write JavaScript programs for these two types of configurations.

Running a JavaScript program in a browser

To run a JavaScript program in a browser, you must insert the JavaScript code into an HTML file. This HTML file will then be displayed in the browser, which will cause the execution of the JavaScript code included in the file.

JavaScript code can be specified in the HTML file in two different ways:

- The first way is to write it between the `<script>` and `</script>` tags, directly in the HTML file. The `<script>` tag indicates the beginning of the JavaScript code, while the `</script>` tag indicates the end of it. Anything written between these two tags is considered JavaScript code.
- The second way is to write the JavaScript code in an external file and then include this external file in the HTML file. The external file is included in the HTML file by means of a `<script>` tag in which the `src` attribute is indicated, the value of which is the name of the JavaScript file that will be included in the HTML page.

Let's take a look at these two ways of writing the JavaScript code that will run in the browser.

Writing JavaScript code between the <script> and </script> tags

A file with an `.html` extension is used; for example, the `index.html` file. This file is a traditional HTML file, in which we have inserted the `<script>` and `</script>` tags, as shown in the following code snippet:

index.html file

```
<html>
  <head>
    <meta charset="utf-8" />
    <script>
```

```
      alert("This is a warning message displayed by
      JavaScript");
    </script>
  </head>
  <body>
  </body>
</html>
```

We have inserted the `<script>` tag (and its ending `</script>`) in the `<head>` section of the HTML page. The `<meta>` tag is used to indicate the encoding characters to use. In the preceding code, we have used `utf-8` so that accented characters can be displayed correctly.

The JavaScript code inserted here is rudimentary. We use the `alert()` function, which displays a dialog box on the browser screen, displaying the text of the message indicated in the first parameter of the function.

To run this HTML file, simply move it (by dragging and dropping) from the file manager to any browser; for example, Firefox. The following screen is then displayed:

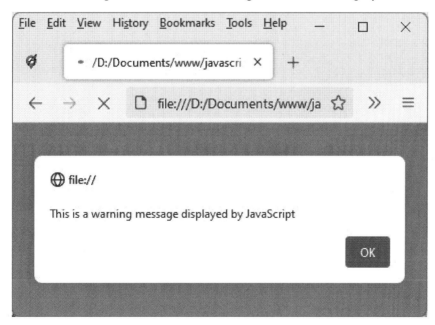

Figure 1.1 – Displaying a message in the browser window

The JavaScript code present in the `<script>` tag ran when the HTML page was loaded. The message indicated in the `alert()` function is therefore displayed. A click on the **OK** button validates the message displayed and continues the execution of the JavaScript code. As we can see, there is nothing more in the program; the program ends immediately by displaying a blank page on the screen (because no HTML code is inserted into the page).

Writing JavaScript code to an external file

Rather than integrating the JavaScript code directly into the HTML file, we can put it in an external file, then insert this file into our HTML file by indicating its name in the `src` attribute of the `<script>` tag.

Let's first write the file that will contain the JavaScript code. This file has the file extension `.js` and will be named `codejs.js`, for example, and will be coded as follows:

codejs.js file (in the same directory as index.html)

```
alert("This is a warning message displayed by JavaScript");
```

The `codejs.js` file contains the JavaScript code that we had previously inserted between the `<script>` and `</script>` tags.

The `index.html` file is modified to include the `codejs.js` file using the `src` attribute of the `<script>` tag as follows:

index.html file

```
<html>
  <head>
    <meta charset="utf-8" />
    <script src="codejs.js"></script>
  </head>

  <body>
  </body>
</html>
```

> **Note**
> Notice the use of the `<script>` and `</script>` tags. They are contiguous (that is, they have no spaces or newlines between them), which is necessary for this code to work.

In the rest of our examples, we will mainly use the insertion of the JavaScript code directly in the code of the HTML file, but the use of an external file would produce the same results.

Let's now explain another way to display messages, without blocking the program as before with the `alert(message)` function.

Using the console.log() method instead of the alert() function

The `alert()` function used earlier displays a window on the HTML page, and the JavaScript program hangs waiting for the user to click the **OK** button in the window. Thus, the function requires the intervention of the user to continue the execution of the program.

An alternative makes it possible to use a display without blocking the execution of the program. This is the display in the console, using the `console.log()` method.

> **Note**
> The `console.log()` form of writing means that we use the `log()` method, which is associated with the `console` object. This will be explained in detail in the following chapter.

Let's write the program again using the `console.log()` method instead of the `alert()` function. The `index.html` file will be modified as follows:

index.html file using console.log() method

```html
<html>
  <head>
    <meta charset="utf-8" />
    <script>
      // display a message in the console
      console.log("This is a warning message displayed by
      JavaScript");
    </script>
  </head>

  <body>
  </body>
</html>
```

12　Exploring the Core Concepts of JavaScript

> **Note**
> The use of comments in the JavaScript program requires placing `//` before what needs to be commented out (on the same line). You can also comment out several lines by enclosing them with `/*` at the beginning and `*/` at the end.

Let's run this program by pressing the *F5* key on the keyboard to refresh the window. A white screen will appear, with no message.

Indeed, the message is only displayed in the console. The console is only visible if you press the *F12* key (and can be removed by pressing *F12* again).

> **Note**
> You can go to the site `https://balsamiq.com/support/faqs/browserconsole/`, which explains how to display the console in the event that the *F12* key is inoperative.

The following is what you will see when the console is displayed:

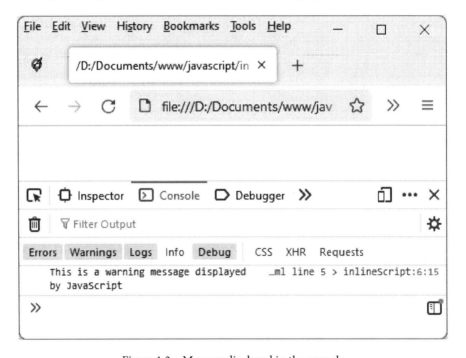

Figure 1.2 – Message displayed in the console

The message is displayed in the lower part of the browser window.

Now that we have learned how to run a JavaScript program in a browser, let's move on to learning how to run a JavaScript program on a Node.js server.

Running a JavaScript program on a Node.js server

To run a JavaScript program on a Node.js server, you must first install the Node.js server. To install, simply go to `https://nodejs.org/` and download and install the server. Note that if you are using macOS, Node.js is already installed.

We can verify the correct installation of Node.js by just opening a shell and typing the command `node` -h in it. Node.js is correctly installed if the command help appears as follows:

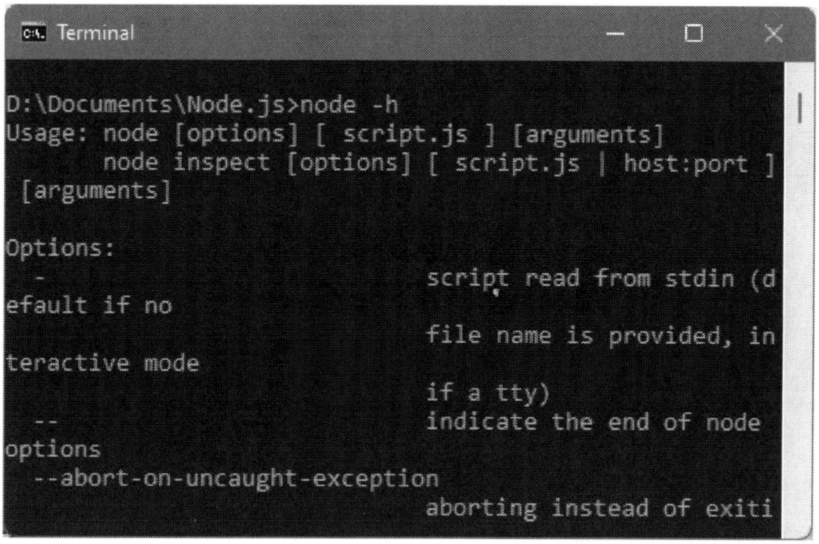

Figure 1.3 – node -h command that displays help

Once Node.js is installed, it can run any JavaScript program you want. All you have to do is create a file containing JavaScript code, for example, `testnode.js`. The contents of this file will be executed by the server using the `node testnode.js` command.

Here is a very simple example of a JavaScript file that can be executed by Node.js:
It displays a message in the server console. The server console here represents the
command interpreter in which you type the command to execute the testnode.js file:

testnode.js file

```
console.log("This is a warning message displayed by
JavaScript");
```

Let's type the command node testnode.js in the preceding terminal window.

Figure 1.4 – Running a Node.js program

We see that the message is displayed directly in the command interpreter.

In the previous examples, we have written JavaScript code that runs both on the client side
(the browser) and on the server side. The question that can be asked is: can the same code
run in exactly the same way on the client side and on the server side?

Differences between JavaScript code written for the browser and the server

Although the two pieces of code are similar, we cannot say that they are the same, because
the issues to be managed are different in the two cases. Indeed, on the client side, we will
mainly want to manage the user interface with JavaScript, while on the server side, we will
rather want to manage files or databases. So, the libraries to use in these two cases will not
be the same.

On the other hand, we find in both cases the same basic language, which is the JavaScript
language that we will be describing now.

Declaring variables in JavaScript

Variables of the types previously described under the *Types of variables used in JavaScript* section, as we know, consist of numerical values, Boolean values, character strings, arrays, and objects.

JavaScript is a weakly typed language, which means that you can change the type of a variable at any time. For example, a numeric variable can be transformed into a character string, or even become an array.

Of course, it is not advisable to make such voluntary changes in our programs, and it is prudent to maintain the type of a variable throughout the program, for comprehension. However, it is important to know that JavaScript allows changing variable types. A variant of JavaScript called *TypeScript* provides more security by preventing these type changes for variables.

Now let's learn how to define a variable. We will do so using one of the following keywords: `const`, `var`, or `let`.

Using the const keyword

The `const` keyword is used to define a variable whose value will be constant. Any subsequent attempt to change the value will produce an error.

Let's define the constant variable `c1` having the value `12`. Let's try to modify the value by assigning it a new value: an error will be displayed in the console:

> **Note**
> To say that we are defining a constant variable is an abuse of language.
> We should rather say that we are defining a constant value.

Defining a constant value (index.html file)

```html
<html>
  <head>
    <meta charset="utf-8" />
    <script>
      const c1 = 12;
      console.log(c1);
      c1 = 13;   // attempt to modify the value of a
                 // constant: error
```

```
        console.log(c1);   // no display because an error
                           // occurred above
    </script>
  </head>

  <body>
  </body>
</html>
```

After implementing the preceding code, we will also see the error displayed in the console (if the console is not visible, it can be displayed by pressing the *F12* key) of the browser as follows:

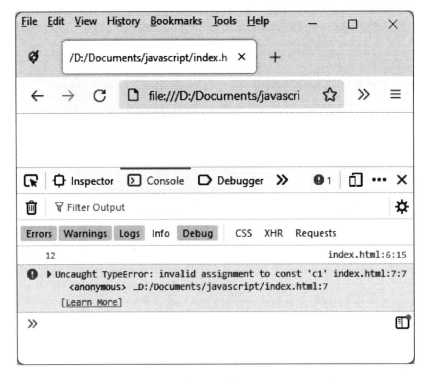

Figure 1.5 – Error when modifying a constant value

As we can see from the preceding figure, the first display of the constant `c1` displays the value **12**, while the second display does not occur because an error occurred before (while trying to change the value of a constant). Therefore, a value defined by the `const` keyword should not be modified.

Using the var keyword

Another way to define a variable (whose value can be modified) is to use the `var` keyword. Let's see how using the following code example:

Definitions of several variables

```html
<html>
  <head>
    <meta charset="utf-8" />
    <script>
      var a = 12;
      var b = 56;
      var c = a + b;
      var s1 = "My name is ";
      var firstname = "Bill";
      console.log("a + b = " + a + b);
      console.log("c = " + c);
      console.log(s1 + firstname);
    </script>
  </head>

  <body>
  </body>
</html>
```

We defined the variables `a`, `b`, `s1`, and `firstname` by preceding them with the keyword `var` and assigning them a default value. The variable `c` corresponds to the addition of the variables `a` and `b`.

18   Exploring the Core Concepts of JavaScript

> **Note**
> The name of a variable consists of alphanumeric characters but must start with an alphabetic character. Lowercase and uppercase are important in writing the variable name (variables' names are case sensitive). Thus, the variable a is different from the variable A.

The result of the previous program is displayed in the browser console (if it is not visible, it must be displayed by pressing the *F12* key):

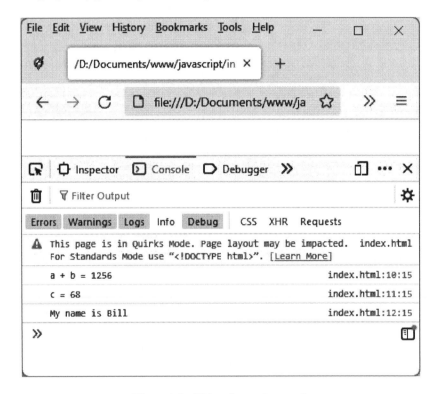

Figure 1.6 – Using the var keyword

In the preceding figure, we can see a result that may seem surprising. Indeed, the direct calculation of a + b produces the display of **1256** the first time, then **68** the second time.

Indeed, when we write `console.log("a + b = " + a + b);` the fact that we've started to display characters by writing "a + b = " means that JavaScript will interpret the rest of the display in the form of a character string; in particular, the values a and b, which follow on the line. So, the values a and b are no longer interpreted as numeric values, but as the character strings 12 and 56. When these character strings are connected by the + operator, this does not correspond to addition but to concatenation.

Conversely, the calculation of the variable c does not involve character strings, so the result of a + b here is equal to the sum of the values of the variables a and b, therefore **68**.

Note that the same program can be run on the Node.js server. To do so, we would write it in our testnode.js file as follows:

testnode.js file

```
var a = 12;
var b = 56;
var c = a + b;
var s1 = "My name is ";
var firstname = "Bill";
console.log("a + b = " + a + b);
console.log("c = " + c);
console.log(s1 + firstname);
```

We can then execute the preceding code with the node testnode.js command. The result displayed under Node.js is similar to that displayed in the browser console:

Figure 1.7 – Running the program under Node.js

We learned about the const and var keywords for defining variables; all that remains is for us to learn how to use the let keyword.

Using the let keyword

To understand the use of the `let` keyword and see the difference from the `var` keyword, we must use braces in our programs. Braces are used to create program blocks in which instructions are inserted, in particular after the conditional `if` and `else` instructions (which we will see in the *Writing conditions* section).

Let's write a simple `if(true)` condition that is always `true`: the code included in the braces following the condition is therefore always executed:

index.html file including a condition

```html
<html>
  <head>
    <meta charset="utf-8" />
    <script>
      var a = 12;
      if (true) {   // always executed (because always true)
        var b = 56;
        let c = 89;
        console.log("In the brace:");
        console.log("a = " + a);
        console.log("b = " + b);
        console.log("c = " + c);
      }

      console.log("After the brace:");
      console.log("a = " + a);
      console.log("b = " + b);
      console.log("c = " + c);
    </script>
  </head>

  <body>
  </body>
</html>
```

In the preceding code, we have defined the variable a outside of any braces. This variable will therefore be accessible everywhere (in and out of braces) as soon as it is defined.

The variables b and c are defined within braces following the condition. Variable b is defined using var, while variable c is defined using the let keyword. The difference between the two variables is visible as soon as you exit the block of braces. Indeed, the variable c (defined by let) is no longer known outside the block of braces where it is defined, unlike the variable b (defined by var), which is accessible even outside.

This can be checked by running the program in the browser as follows:

Figure 1.8 – The variable c defined by let is inaccessible outside the block where it is defined

Note that the same program gives a similar result on the Node.js server, as can be seen in the following screen: the variable c defined by `let` in a block becomes unknown outside the block.

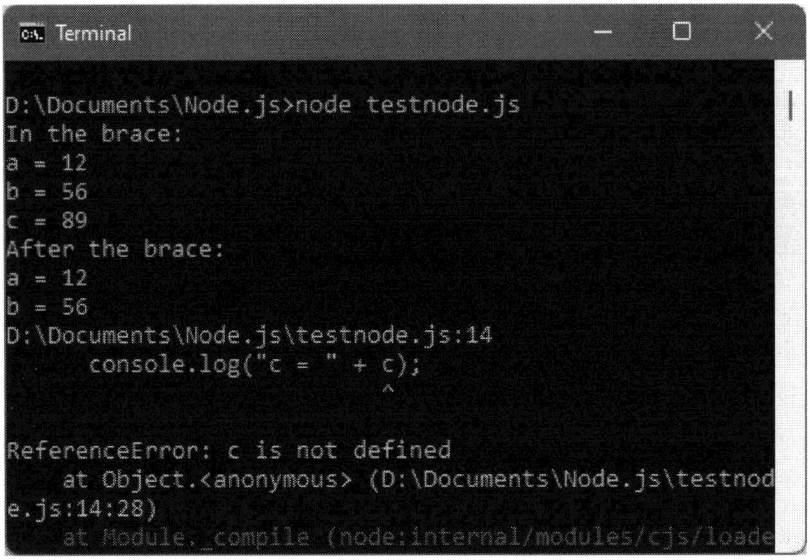

Figure 1.9 – The same results on the Node.js server

As we can see in the preceding screen, the variable c, defined by `let` in a block, becomes unknown outside the block.

What if we don't use var or let to define a variable?

It is possible not to use the `var` or `let` keywords to define a variable. We can simply write the variable's name followed by its value (separated by the sign =). Let's see how using the following example:

Creating variables without specifying var or let

```
a = 12;
b = 56;
console.log("a = " + a);    // displays the value 12
console.log("b = " + b);    // displays the value 56
```

In the preceding example, where the variables are initialized without being preceded by `var` or `let`, these variables are global variables. As soon as they are initialized, they become accessible everywhere else in the program. This will become apparent when we study the functions in the *Using functions* section of this chapter.

> **Note**
> It is strongly advised to use as few global variables as possible in the programs, as this complicates the design and debugging of the programs that contain them.

What is an uninitialized variable worth?

Each of the preceding variables was declared by initializing its value, with the = sign, which is the assignment sign. Let's see what happens if we don't assign any value to the variable, but just declare it using `var` or `let` as follows:

Declaration of variables without initialization

```html
<html>
  <head>
    <meta charset="utf-8" />
    <script>
      var a;
      let b;
      console.log("a = " + a);    // displays the value
                                  // undefined
      console.log("b = " + b);    // displays the value
                                  // undefined
    </script>
  </head>

  <body>
  </body>
</html>
```

In the preceding code, we have defined two variables, a and b – one using `var`, the other using `let`. Neither of the two variables has an initial value (that is, they're not followed by an = sign).

The result displayed in this case for these uninitialized variables is a JavaScript value called `undefined`. This corresponds to the value of a variable that does not yet have a value. The `undefined` value is an important keyword in the JavaScript language.

> **Note**
>
> The variables a and b are not initialized, and it is necessary to declare them using `var` or `let`. Indeed, you cannot simply write `a;` or `b;` as this would cause a runtime error.

Let's run the preceding program in the browser and observe the results displayed in the console:

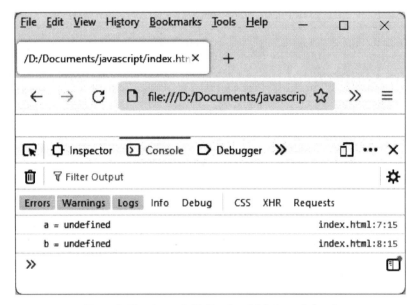

Figure 1.10 – An uninitialized variable is undefined

> **Note**
>
> The `undefined` value is also associated with an uninitialized variable if using server-side JavaScript with Node.js.

We now know how to define variables in JavaScript. To create useful JavaScript programs, you have to write sequences of instructions. One of the most used instructions allows you to write conditional tests with the `if` statement, which we will talk about next.

Writing conditions for conditional tests

JavaScript obviously allows you to write conditions in programs. The condition is expressed through the `if (condition)` statement:

- If the condition is `true`, the statement (or block in braces) that follows is executed.
- If the condition is `false`, the statement (or block) following the `else` keyword (if present) will be executed.

Forms of writing instructions

We can use the following forms to express the conditions:

Forms of conditional expressions with if (condition)

```
// condition followed by a statement
if (condition) statement;   // statement executed if condition
                            is true

// condition followed by a block
if (condition) {
  // block of statements executed if condition is true
   statement 1;
   statement 2;
   statement 3;
}
```

Forms of conditional expressions with if (condition) ... else ...

```
// condition followed by a statement
if (condition) statement 1;   // statement 1 executed if
                              // condition is true
  else statement 2;           // statement 2 executed if
                              // condition is false

// condition followed by a block
if (condition) {
  // block of statements executed if condition is true
   statement 1;
```

```
    statement 2;
    statement 3;
}
else {
    // block of statements executed if condition is false
    statement 5;
    statement 6;
    statement 7;
}
```

> **Note**
> If the process to be executed includes several instructions, these instructions are grouped together in a block surrounded by braces. A block can consist of only one statement, even if, as in this case, the block is optional (no need for braces).

Let's write the following program in the `testnode.js` file, which we will execute using the `node testnode.js` command in a command interpreter, as follows:

testnode.js file

```
var a = 12;
console.log("a = " + a);
if (a == 12) console.log("a is 12");
else console.log("a is not 12");
```

In the preceding code, the condition is expressed in the form `a == 12`. Indeed, it is customary to test the equality between two values by means of the sign = repeated twice successively (hence ==).

> **Note**
> We use == for equality, != for difference, > or >= to check superiority, and < or <= to check inferiority.

In the preceding code, since the variable a is 12, the following result can be seen:

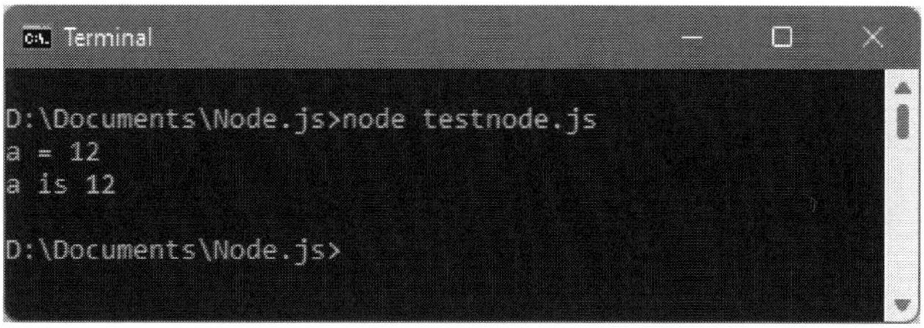

Figure 1.11 – Using conditional tests

If we assign the value 13 to the variable a, the else part of the statement will be executed:

Figure 1.12 – Running the else part of the test

We have seen how to execute one part of the code or another depending on a condition. Let's now study how to write more complex conditions than those written previously.

Expressions used to write conditions

The condition written previously is a simple test of equality between two values. But the test to write can sometimes be more complex. The goal is to have the final result of the condition, which is true or false, which will then make it possible for the system to decide the next course of action.

The condition is written in Boolean form with the *OR* keyword (written as ||) or with the *AND* keyword (written as &&). Parentheses between the different conditions may be necessary to express the final condition as follows:

Condition expressed with "or"

```
var a = 13;
var b = 56;
console.log("a = " + a);
console.log("b = " + b);
if (a == 12 || b > 50) console.log("condition a == 12 || b > 50 is true");
else console.log("condition a == 12 || b > 50 is false");
```

In the preceding code, since the variable b is greater than 50, the condition is true, as seen in *Figure 1.13*.

> **Note**
>
> In an *OR* condition, it suffices that one of the conditions is true for the final condition to be true.
>
> In an *AND* condition, all the conditions must be true for the final condition to be true.

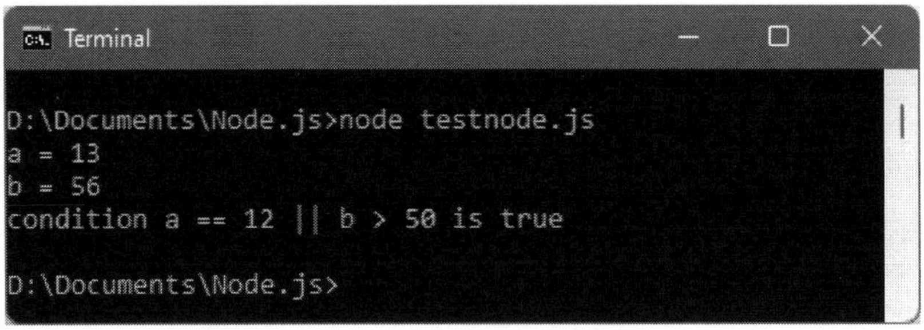

Figure 1.13 – Condition with or

By default, the condition expressed in if (condition) is compared with the value true. We can sometimes prefer to compare with the value false. In this case, it suffices to precede the condition with the sign !, which corresponds to a negation of the following condition.

It is sometimes necessary to chain several tests in a row, depending on the results of the previous tests. We then have a succession of tests, called cascade tests.

Nested test suites

It is possible to chain tests in the processes to be performed. Here is an example:

Test nesting

```
var a = 13;
var b = 56;
console.log("a = " + a);
console.log("b = " + b);
if (a == 12) console.log("condition a == 12 is true");
else {
  console.log("condition a == 12 is false");
  if (b > 50) console.log("condition b > 50 is true");
  else console.log("condition b > 50 is false");
}
```

The `else` part is composed of several statements and is grouped in a block surrounded by braces:

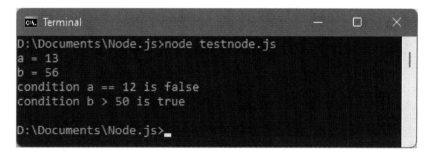

Figure 1.14 – Test nesting

We learned about writing conditions in JavaScript programs. We are now going to learn how to write processing loops, which make it possible to write the instructions in the program only once. These instructions can, however, be executed as many times as necessary.

Creating processing loops

It is sometimes necessary to repeat an instruction (or a block of instructions) several times. Rather than writing it several times in the program, we put it in a processing loop. These instructions will be repeated as many times as necessary.

Two types of processing loops are possible in JavaScript:

- Loops with the `while()` statement
- Loops with the `for()` statement

Let's take a look at these two types of loops.

Loops with while()

The `while(condition)` instruction allows you to repeat the instruction (or the block of instructions) that follows. As long as the condition is `true`, the statement (or block) is executed. It stops when the condition becomes `false`.

Using this `while()` statement, let's display the numbers from 0 to 5:

Displaying numbers from 0 to 5

```
var i = 0;
while (i <= 5) {
   console.log("i = " + i);
   i++;
}
```

The preceding `console.log()` instruction is written only once in the program, but as it is inserted in a loop (`while()` instruction), it will be repeated as many times as the condition is `true`.

The variable `i` allows you to manage the condition in the loop. The variable `i` is incremented by 1 (by `i++`) at each pass through the loop, and we stop when the value 5 is exceeded:

Figure 1.15 – Displaying numbers from 0 to 5

We can verify that this program works in a similar way on the client side, that is to say in a web browser, as follows:

Displaying digits 0–5 in a browser console

```
<html>
  <head>
    <meta charset="utf-8" />
    <script>
      var i = 0;
      while (i <= 5) {
        console.log("i = " + i);
        i++;
      }
    </script>
  </head>

  <body>
  </body>
</html>
```

The result is displayed similarly in the browser console:

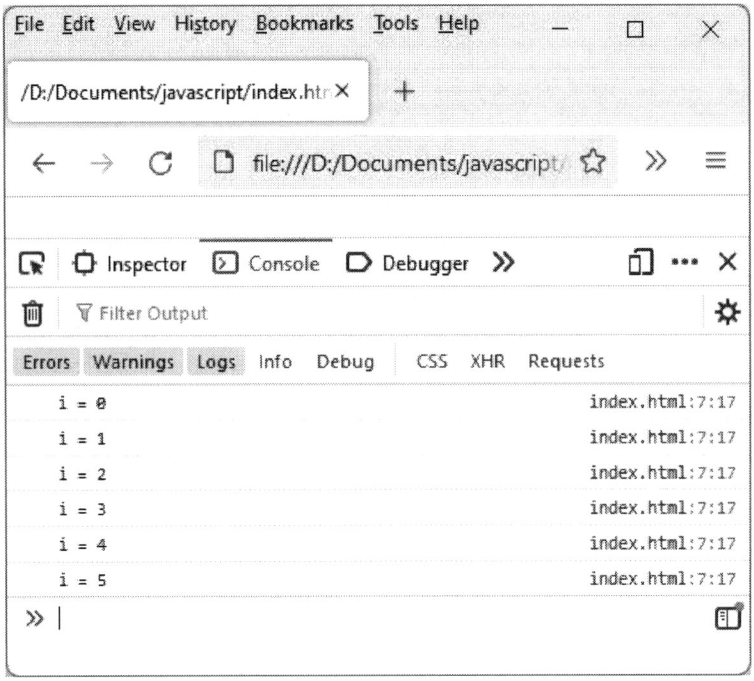

Figure 1.16 – Displaying numbers from 0 to 5 in the browser console

Loops with for()

Another widely used form of loop is one with a `for()` statement. It simplifies the writing of the previous loop by reducing the number of instructions to write.

Let's write the same program as before to display the numbers from 0 to 5 using a `for()` statement instead of the `while()` statement:

```
for (var i=0; i <= 5; i++) console.log("i = " + i);
```

As we can see in the preceding code, a single line replaces several lines as in the previous instance.

The `for()` statement has three parts, separated by a `;`:

- The first corresponds to the initialization instruction. Here, it is the declaration of the variable `i` initialized to `0` (which is the beginning of the loop).
- The second corresponds to the condition: as long as this condition is `true`, the statement (or the block that follows) is executed. Here, the condition corresponds to the fact that the variable `i` has not exceeded the final value `5`.

- The third corresponds to an instruction executed after each pass through the loop. Here, we increment the variable i by 1. This ensures that at some point, the condition will be `false`, in order to exit the loop.

Let's verify that it works identically to the `while()` statement:

Figure 1.17 – Loop with the for() statement

In this section, we learned how to write sequences of statements that will be executed multiple times, using the `while()` and `for()` statements. Now let's look at how to group statements together, using what are called functions.

Using functions

A function is used to give a name to a block of instructions so that it can be used in different places in the program. In general, in a function, we group a set of instructions that are used to carry out a particular task, for example:

- Display the list of the first 10 integers.
- Calculate the sum of the first 10 numbers (from 0 to 9).
- Calculate the sum of the first N numbers (from 0 to N-1). In this case, N would be a parameter of the function because it can change with each call (or use) of the function.

The functions described above are very simple but show that the role of functions is to encapsulate any process by summarizing in one sentence what is expected of this process. The name given to the function symbolizes the action expected in return, which allows the developer to easily understand the sequence of instructions (including for an external developer who has not participated in the development). Let's discuss the three functions we listed one by one.

Function displaying the list of the first 10 integers

Let's write the first function, which displays the list of the first 10 integers. We will call this function `display_10_first_integers()`. The name must be as explicit as possible because a JavaScript program is composed of many functions whose names must be unique in the program (if two function names are the same, only the last one is taken into account because it overwrites the former).

A function is defined using the keyword `function`, followed by the name of the function, followed by parentheses. Then, we indicate in the braces that follow the instructions that make up the function. It is this instruction block that will be executed each time the function is called in the program.

Let's write the function `display_10_first_integers()`, which displays the first 10 integers:

Display first 10 integers with a function (testnode.js file)

```
function display_10_first_integers() {
   for (var i=0; i <= 10; i++) console.log("i = " + i);
}
```

The function is defined using the `function` keyword, followed by the function name and parentheses.

The function statements are grouped in the block that follows between the braces. We find as instructions the previous `for()` loop, but it could also be the `while()` loop, which works in the same way.

Let's run this program assuming it's included in the `testnode.js` file:

Figure 1.18 – Using a function to display numbers from 1 to 10

As we can see in the preceding figure, the screen remains blank as no display is registered in the console.

Indeed, we have simply defined the function, but we must also use it, that is, call it in our program. You can call it as many times as you want – this is the purpose of functions: we should be able to call (or use) them at any time. But it must be done at least once; otherwise, it is useless, as seen in the preceding figure.

Let's add the function call following the function definition:

Definition and call of the function

```
// function definition
function display_10_first_integers() {
   for (var i=0; i <= 10; i++) console.log("i = " + i);
}

// function call
display_10_first_integers();
```

The result of the preceding code can be seen in the following figure:

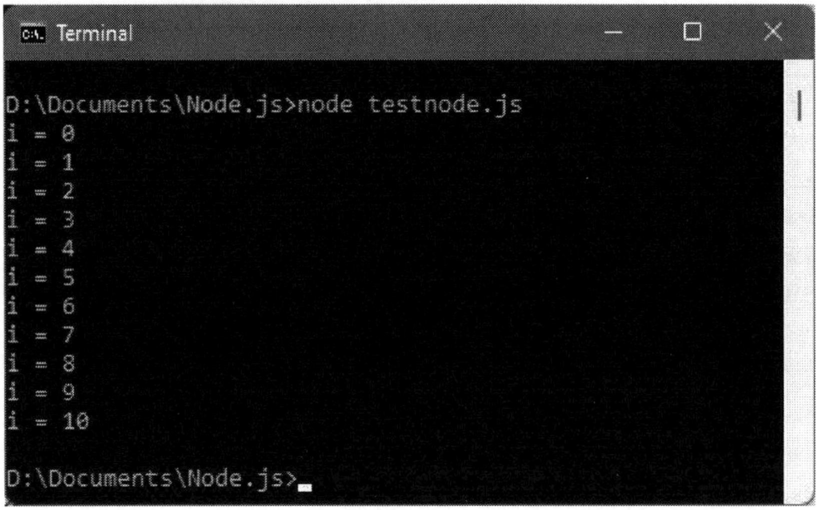

Figure 1.19 – Call of the display_10_first_integers() function

Interestingly, the function can be called in several places of the program. Let's see how in the following example:

Successive calls to the display_10_first_integers() function

```
// function definition
function display_10_first_integers() {
  for (var i=0; i <= 10; i++) console.log("i = " + i);
}

// function call
console.log("*** 1st call *** ");
display_10_first_integers();

console.log("*** 2nd call *** ");
display_10_first_integers();

console.log("*** 3rd call *** ");
display_10_first_integers();
```

In the preceding code, the function is called three times in succession, which displays the list of the first 10 integers as many times. The order of the calls is indicated before each list as follows:

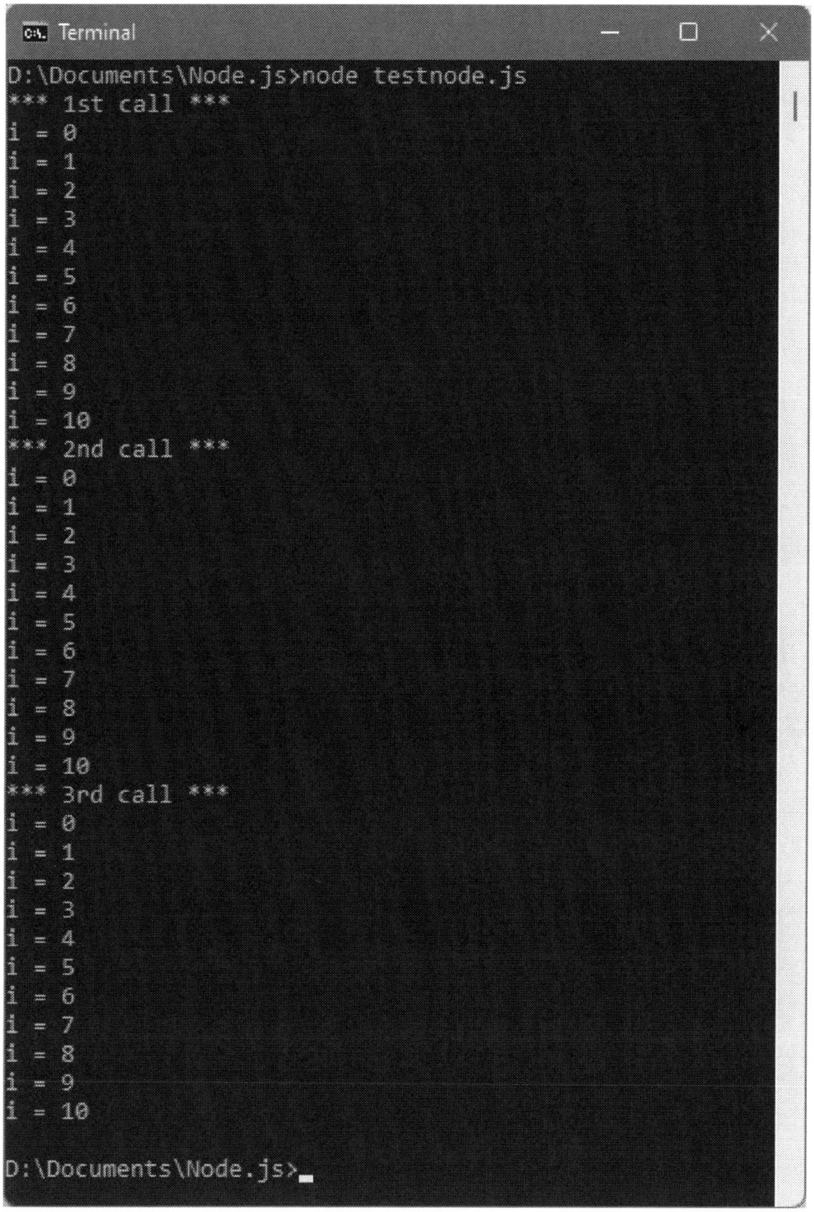

```
D:\Documents\Node.js>node testnode.js
*** 1st call ***
i = 0
i = 1
i = 2
i = 3
i = 4
i = 5
i = 6
i = 7
i = 8
i = 9
i = 10
*** 2nd call ***
i = 0
i = 1
i = 2
i = 3
i = 4
i = 5
i = 6
i = 7
i = 8
i = 9
i = 10
*** 3rd call ***
i = 0
i = 1
i = 2
i = 3
i = 4
i = 5
i = 6
i = 7
i = 8
i = 9
i = 10

D:\Documents\Node.js>
```

Figure 1.20 – Successive calls to the display_10_first_integers() function

Function calculating the sum of the first 10 integers

We now want to create a function that calculates the sum of the first 10 integers, that is, 1+2+3+4+5+6+7+8+9+10. The result is 55. This will allow us to show how a function can return a result to the outside (that is, to the program that uses it). Here, the function should return 55.

Let's call the function `add_10_first_integers()`. This can be written as follows:

Function that adds the first 10 integers

```
// function definition
function add_10_first_integers() {
  var total = 0;
  for (var i = 0; i <= 10; i++) total += i;
  return total;
}

// function call
var total = add_10_first_integers();
console.log("Total = " + total);
```

We define the `total` variable in the function. This variable is a local variable to the function because it is defined using the `var` or `let` keyword. This allows this `total` variable to not be the same as the one defined outside the function, even if the names are the same.

> **Note**
>
> If the `total` variable in the function was not defined using the `var` or `let` keyword, it would create a so-called global variable that would be directly accessible even outside the function. This is not good programming because you want to use global variables as little as possible.

The function uses a `for()` loop to add the first 10 integers, then returns that total using the `return` keyword. This keyword makes it possible to make accessible, outside the function, the value of any variable, in our example, the `total` variable.

Let's run the previous program. We should see the following output:

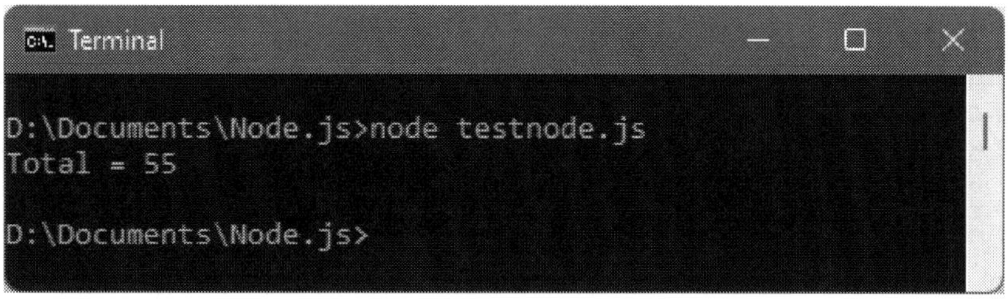

Figure 1.21 – Calculation of the sum of the first 10 integers

Function calculating the sum of the first N integers

The previous function is not very useful because it always returns the same result. A more useful function would be to calculate the sum of the first N integers, knowing that N can be different each time the function is called.

N would in this case be a parameter of the function. Its value is indicated in parentheses when using the function.

Let's call the add_N_first_integers() function to calculate this sum. The N parameter would be indicated in parentheses following the function name. A function can use several parameters, and it suffices to indicate them in succession, separated by a comma. In our example, a single parameter is enough.

Let's write the add_N_first_integers(n) function and use that to calculate the sum of the first 10, then 25, then 100 integers. The values 10, 25, and 100 will be used as parameters during successive calls to the function and will replace the parameter n indicated in the definition of the function:

Function that adds the first N integers

```
// function definition
function add_N_first_integers(n) {
  var total = 0;
  for (var i = 0; i <= n; i++) total += i;
  return total;
}


// calculation of the first 10 integers
var total_10 = add_N_first_integers(10);
```

```
console.log("Total of the first 10 integers = " + total_10);


// calculation of the first 25 integers
var total_25 = add_N_first_integers(25);
console.log("Total of the first 25 integers = " + total_25);


// calculation of the first 100 integers
var total_100 = add_N_first_integers(100);
console.log("Total of the first 100 integers = " + total_100);
```

The `add_N_first_integers(n)` function is very similar to the `add_10_first_integers()` function written earlier. It uses the parameter n indicated between the parentheses and does not loop from 0 to 10 as before, but from 0 to n. Depending on the value of n that will be used when calling the function, the loop will thus be different, and the result returned by the function as well.

When calling the function, it passes the parameters 10, 25, then 100 as desired. The result is returned by the function's `total` variable, and then used by the `total_10`, `total_25`, and `total_100` variables outside the function:

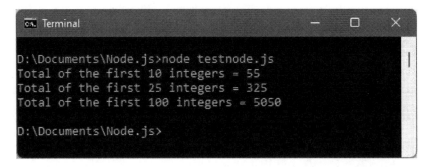

Figure 1.22 – Calculation of the sum of the first 10, then 25, then 100 integers

Summary

The basic features of JavaScript have been covered in this chapter: variables with different types, conditional tests, loops, and functions. They are used on the client side and on the server side.

In the next chapter, we'll take a look at some more in-depth features of JavaScript, such as object-oriented programming with JavaScript.

2
Exploring the Advanced Concepts of JavaScript

In this chapter, we will explore the advanced features of JavaScript, such as object-oriented programming. We will also study two types of objects that are widely used in JavaScript: arrays and strings. Finally, we will see how JavaScript allows you to trigger deferred processing, using so-called callback functions.

In this chapter, we'll be covering the following topics:

- Classes and objects
- Arrays
- Character strings
- Multitasking
- Using promises

All these topics are fundamental to building JavaScript applications. Let's start now!

Technical requirements

You can find the code files for this chapter on GitHub at: `https://github.com/PacktPublishing/JavaScript-from-Frontend-to-Backend/blob/main/Chapter%202.zip`.

Classes and objects

The notion of classes and objects is fundamental to programming languages. JavaScript allows them to be used as well.

A class is used to represent any type of data. For example, people, customers, cars, and so on. We can define a class to represent each of these types of elements, for example, a `Person` class to represent people, a `Client` class to represent customers, and a `Car` class to represent cars.

> **Note**
> Note that the class name traditionally begins with an uppercase letter.

An object, on the other hand, will be a particular element of a class (this element will be also called an instance). For example, among all the people of the class `Person`, the person identified by his name "Clinton" and his first name "Bill" represents a particular object of the class `Person`. This object can be associated, for example, with the variable p in the program. We can thus create variables to identify each object associated with the class.

Defining a class

The question to ask yourself when creating a class is what actions you want to perform on the type of data it represents.

For example, if we create the `Person` class, we should ask what characterizes a person and what action can we perform on this class. We could, for example, say that the `Person` class is characterized by the last name, first name, and age of the person. You can also add an address, phone number, email, and so on.

As for the possible actions on people, we can imagine, for example, the action of getting married to another person, the action of moving to another city, the action of changing employers, and so on.

> **Note**
> Characteristics such as last name, first name, age, and so on are called properties of the class, while actions such as getting married, moving, and so on are called methods of the class. A class will therefore group together a set of properties and a set of methods.

A JavaScript class is created using the keyword `class` followed by the name of the class, followed by braces describing the content. For example, the `Person` class will be created as follows:

Person class

```
class Person {
}
```

This definition of the `Person` class will not be very useful for now, because no properties or methods are defined inside it. We will see later how to improve it.

Creating an object by using a class

Once the class is defined, we can create objects associated with this class. For this, we use the keyword `new` followed by the name of the class. This creates a variable that represents an object of that class:

Creating an object p of class Person

```
// define the Person class
class Person {
}

// create an object of class Person
var p = new Person;   // object p of class Person
console.log(p);
```

This is what you will see:

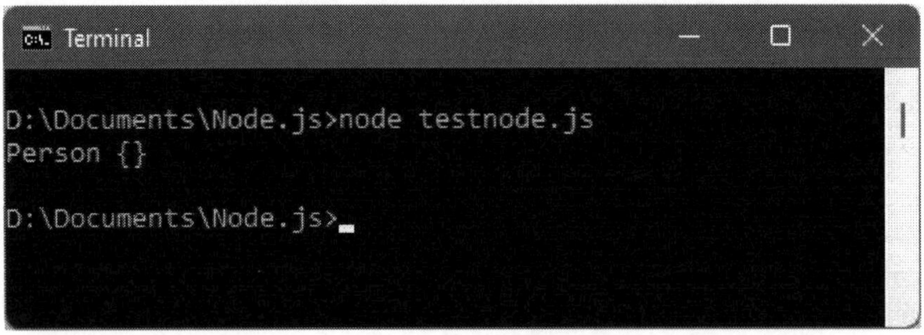

Figure 2.1 – Creating a Person class object

The p object is displayed in the console. We are told that it is a `Person` class object and that it is empty { }. The representation of an object in the form of braces is traditional in JavaScript, as we saw in the *Type of variables used in JavaScript* section of the previous chapter.

We can verify that it also works on the client side, in a browser. The HTML file is as follows:

index.html file

```
<html>
  <head>
    <meta charset="utf-8" />
    <script>
      class Person {
      }
      var p = new Person;
      console.log(p);
    </script>
  </head>

  <body>
  </body>
</html>
```

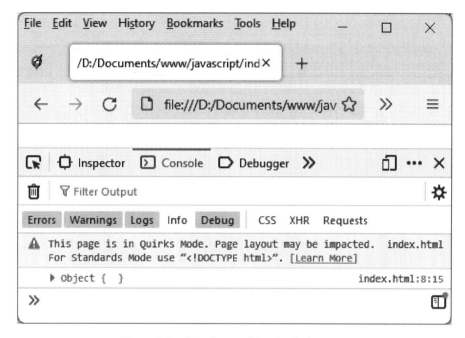

Figure 2.2 – Creating an object in the browser

We find the display of braces, which symbolizes the display of a JavaScript object.

Creating an object without using a class

It is possible to create an object without having created a class first. All you have to do is use the notation with the braces { and }.

For example, we can write the following:

Creating an object using the braces notation

```
var p = { lastname : "Clinton", firstname : "Bill" };
console.log("The person is", p);
```

This will create the object p with the `lastname` and `firstname` properties. Note that you can indicate the names of the properties by enclosing them in quotation marks, or not. So { `lastname: "Clinton"` } can also be written { `"lastname": "Clinton"` } by surrounding the `lastname` property with single or double quotes.

Now let's see how to improve the `Person` class previously created by adding properties and methods to it.

Adding properties to a class

A person has, in our example, a last name, a first name, and an age. We will create these three properties for people of the `Person` class.

All you have to do is indicate each of these properties, by name, in the body of the `Person` class. Above all, do not use the `var` or `let` keywords to define them:

Adding firstname, lastname, and age properties in Person class

```
class Person {
  firstname;
  lastname;
  age;
}

var p = new Person;
console.log(p);
```

```
D:\Documents\Node.js>node testnode.js
Person { firstname: undefined, lastname: undefined, age: undefined }

D:\Documents\Node.js>
```

Figure 2.3 – Creation of lastname, firstname, and age properties in the Person class

The `Person` class object p now has the properties added in the class. Any other object of this class will also have them.

Note that the values of the added properties are `undefined`. This is normal because no values have been specified for these properties in the p object or the `Person` class.

Let's modify the `Person` class so that the properties have default values, rather than `undefined`:

Properties with default values

```
class Person {
  firstname = "";
  lastname = "";
  age = 0;
}

var p = new Person;
console.log(p);
```

Each property is initialized with its default value. The `lastname` and `firstname` properties are initialized with an empty string `""`, while `age` is initialized by default to 0.

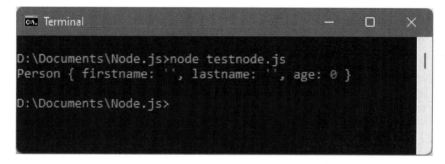

Figure 2.4 – Properties with default values

A class has properties, but also methods. Now let's see how to add methods to a class.

Adding methods to a class

You can add methods to a class. Objects created from the class (with `new`) will be able to use these methods directly.

For example, let's create the `display()` method, which displays a line of text containing the person's first and last name. The instruction `p.display()` (assuming that p is a `Person` class object) is used to display the last name and first name of the person related to the object p:

Creating the display() method in the Person class

```
class Person {
  // class properties
  firstname = "";
```

```
    lastname = "";
    age = 0;

    // class methods
    display() {
      console.log("The person's lastname is = " +
                  this.lastname +
                  ", firstname = " + this.firstname);
    }
  }

  var p = new Person;
  console.log("Variable p = ", p);
  p.display();    // use of the display() method on the p object
```

The properties of the class are accessible in the methods of the class by prefixing them with the keyword `this`. For example, `this.lastname` provides access to the `lastname` property of the class.

The `this` keyword refers to the object itself that uses the `display()` method, so here, the p object.

If you omit the `this` keyword and use the `lastname` property directly, you will get a syntax error because the property is only accessible with the `this` keyword.

The output of the preceding code snippet is displayed here:

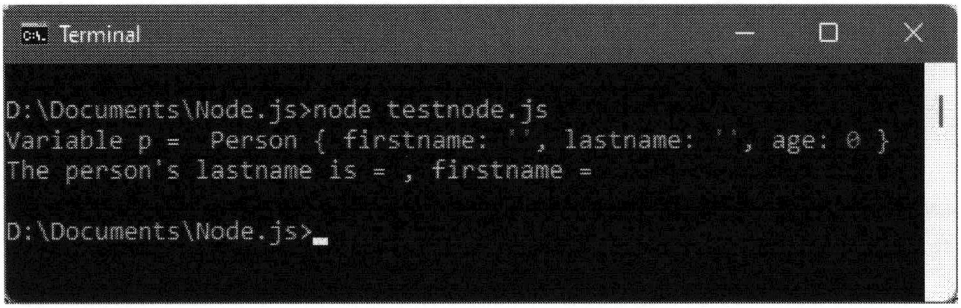

```
D:\Documents\Node.js>node testnode.js
Variable p =  Person { firstname: '', lastname: '', age: 0 }
The person's lastname is = , firstname =

D:\Documents\Node.js>
```

Figure 2.5 – Using the display() method

The `display()` method displays `firstname` and `lastname` of the person associated with the variable p, but since `lastname` and `firstname` have been initialized to an empty string, no last name or first name is displayed. Let's look at how to modify the value of a property.

Changing an object's property values

You can modify the value of the properties of an object by using these properties directly, for example, `p.lastname` allows you to read or modify the value of the `lastname` property for the object p:

Initialization of the lastname and firstname of the person

```
class Person {
  // class properties
  lastname = "";
  firstname = "";
  age = 0;

  // class methods
  display() {
    console.log(" The person's lastname = " + this.lastname +
                ", firstname = " + this.firstname);
  }
}

var p = new Person;
p.lastname = "Clinton";   // initialization of the lastname
                          // property of the object p
p.firstname = "Bill";     // initialization of the firstname
                          // property of the object p
console.log("Variable p = ", p);
p.display();
```

This is what you will see:

```
D:\Documents\Node.js>node testnode.js
Variable p =  Person { lastname: 'Clinton', firstname: 'Bill',
 age: 0 }
 The person's lastname = Clinton, firstname = Bill

D:\Documents\Node.js>
```

Figure 2.6 – The lastname and firstname properties are initialized

Once the object p has been created by the new operator, we initialize its `lastname` and `firstname` properties to the values indicated. The `age` property is not modified here, and will therefore remain equal to the value 0.

We modified the value of the `lastname` and `firstname` properties of the object p created using `p.lastname` and `p.firstname`.

This modification of property values is done after the object p is created. It is possible to do this modification during the very creation of the object, in the new instruction. This requires defining a method called `constructor()`, which allows this initialization.

Using the class constructor

The `constructor()` method is called the constructor of the class. It is automatically called during each new statement if the `constructor()` method exists in the class. We define it in a class if we want to perform a specific process each time an object is created in this class.

The `constructor()` method can have any number of parameters or none at all. The parameters indicated here will be used to initialize the `lastname` and `firstname` properties of the person:

Using a constructor for the Person class

```
class Person {
  // class properties
  lastname = "";
  firstname = "";
  age = 0;
```

```
    // class methods
    constructor(lastname, firstname, age) {
        this.lastname = lastname;
        this.firstname = firstname;
        this.age = age;
    }
    display() {
        console.log(" The person's lastname = " + this.lastname +
                    ", firstname = " + this.firstname);
    }
}

var p = new Person("Clinton", "Bill");
console.log("Variable p = ", p);
p.display();
```

The constructor() method is defined by giving it the three parameters lastname, firstname, and age. They are transferred into the properties of the object by means of this.lastname, this.firstname, and this.age.

Finally, the object p is now created by passing as parameters the values of lastname, firstname, and age of the person created with new. Here, age is not specified in parameters in the new instruction; it will therefore be an undefined value that will be transmitted to the constructor.

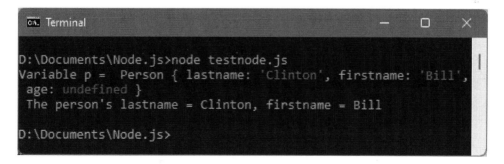

Figure 2.7 – Using a constructor

We find the `lastname` and `firstname` properties initialized, but the `age` property is now initialized to the value `undefined` instead of `0`. To assign it another value, simply pass an additional value when creating the object with `new`. This additional value will represent the person's age, for example:

Using age when creating Person class object

```
class Person {
  // class properties
  lastname = "";
  firstname = "";
  age = 0;

  // class methods
  constructor(lastname, firstname, age) {
    this.lastname = lastname;
    this.firstname = firstname;
    this.age = age;
  }
  display() {
    // the age of the person is also displayed
    console.log("The person's lastname = " + this.lastname +
                ", firstname = " + this.firstname +
                ", age = " + this.age);
  }
}

var p = new Person("Clinton", "Bill", 33);    // age is now
                                              // transmitted
console.log("Variable p = ", p);
p.display();
```

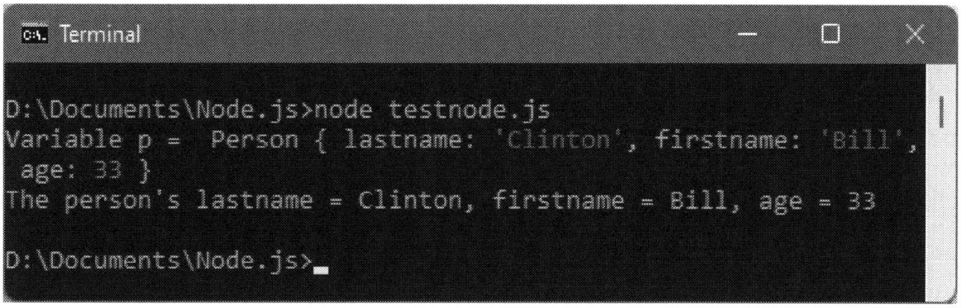

Figure 2.8 – The person's age is now transmitted

We have seen how to create an object, by directly defining its properties and methods using a class. However, we can also create an object from another object. Let's see how to do it.

Merging one object with another

There may be cases when you want to create a new object from an old object. Let's see how to do this.

If the object p contains a value, the statement `var p2 = p` does not create a new object p2 distinct from the object p, but only a reference p2 that points to the same value as the reference p. So any modification of the properties of the object p will also be visible in the object p2 because both point to the same memory location.

This can be verified using the following example:

Modifying an object in memory

```
var p = { lastname : "Clinton", firstname : "Bill" };
console.log("p (before modification of p2) =", p);
        // p = { lastname : "Clinton", firstname : "Bill" }

var p2 = p;
p2.city = "Washington";

console.log("p (after modification of p2) =", p);
        // p = { lastname : "Clinton", firstname : "Bill",
        // city : "Washington"}

console.log("p2 =", p2);
```

```
                // p2 = { lastname : "Clinton", firstname : "Bill",
                // city : "Washington"}
```

Even if only the p2 object is modified, the p object is also modified because they are memory references that point to the same location. If the contents of the memory location are changed, both references see the same change.

To avoid this situation, it would not be necessary to write p2 = p, but rather to copy the properties of the object p into those of the object p2, thus creating a new memory location. For this, JavaScript offers the spread operator, used in the form ..., which allows it:

Using the spread operator ...

```
var p = { lastname : "Clinton", firstname : "Bill" }
console.log("p (before modification of p2) =", p);

var p2 = { ...p};    // copy the properties of object p into
                     // object p2
p2.city = "Washington";

console.log("p (after modification of p2) =", p);
console.log("p2 =", p2);
```

The spread operator is used by surrounding the original object with braces { and }, and preceding the object with the spread operator (for example, {...p}).

```
D:\Documents\Node.js>node testnode.js
p (before modification of p2) = { lastname: 'Clinton', firstna
me: 'Bill' }
p (after modification of p2) = { lastname: 'Clinton', firstnam
e: 'Bill' }
p2 = { lastname: 'Clinton', firstname: 'Bill', city: 'Washingt
on' }

D:\Documents\Node.js>
```

Figure 2.9 – Using the spread operator...

Object p is no longer modified when object p2 is modified.

It is also possible to write it in shortened form:

Creating object p2 from object p, adding the city

```
// to avoid writing p2.city = "Washington"
var p2 = { ...p, city : "Washington" };
```

Now that we have looked at classes and objects and how to work with them, let's take a look at an important class object: the `Array` class.

Arrays

Arrays store a collection of data, ordered according to their index. The index is also called the index of the array. It starts at 0 and scales up to the total number of elements in the array, minus 1 (0 to n-1).

Let's learn how to create an array first.

Creating an array

An array corresponds in JavaScript to an `Array` class object. We therefore create an array using the `new Array` instruction.

However, since arrays are widely used in JavaScript programs, it is also possible to create them using a bracket notation `[ and ]`. This is an easier way to use them without going through the `Array` class.

Let's take a detailed look at these two ways to create an array (with brackets and with the `Array` class).

Creating an array using square brackets [and]

The easiest and fastest way to create an array is to use the bracket notation:

Creating an array using square brackets

```
var tab = ["Element 1", "Element 2", "Element 3", "Element 4", "Element 5"];
console.log(tab);
```

The array begins with an opening square bracket [and ends with a closing square bracket
]. The elements of the array are separated by a comma. We have inserted elements here as
strings, but in fact, any type of element can be inserted into an array.

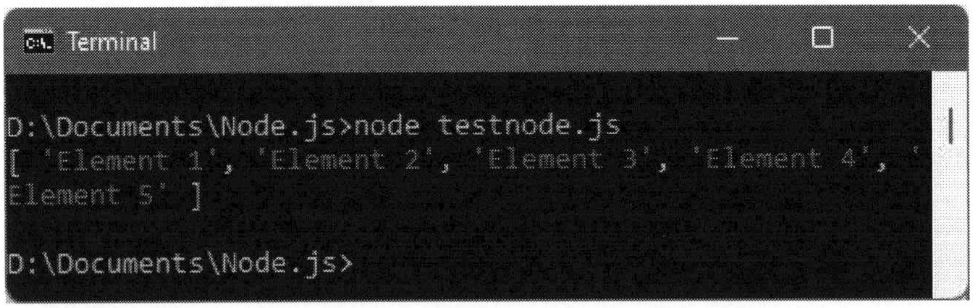

Figure 2.10 – Elements inserted into an array

Note that it is possible to create an empty array (without any elements). We write this as
[], without indicating any element inside the square brackets. It will then be possible to
add elements to this array.

Creating an array using the Array class

You can also use the Array class to create an array. The Array class includes
a constructor in which we indicate the list of array elements, each separated from the
next by a comma.

The same array as before can be created by the new Array statement by writing
the following:

Creating an array using new Array

```
var tab = new Array("Element 1", "Element 2", "Element 3",
"Element 4", "Element 5");
console.log(tab);
```

Figure 2.11 – Creation of the array using new Array

The array created is the same as before.

To create an empty array, simply pass no parameters to the constructor by writing the following:

Creating an empty array using new Array()

```
var tab = new Array();     // or new Array;
console.log(tab);
```

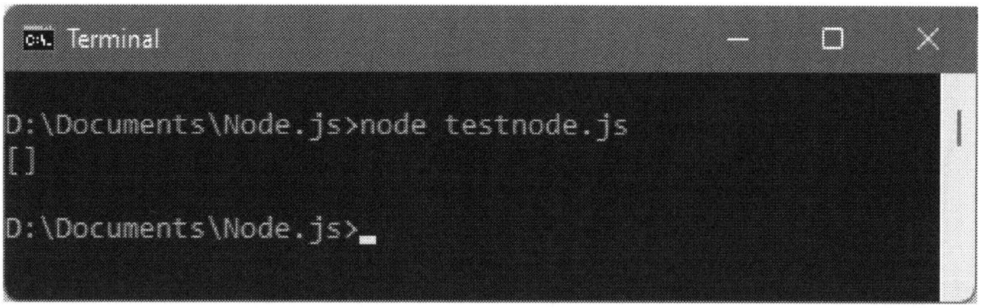

Figure 2.12 – Creating an empty array [ ]

Now that we've seen how to create an array, let's see how to access each of its elements.

Accessing array elements

In previous programs, we displayed the entire array, using the `console.log(tab)` statement. It is possible to access each element of the array separately. Each element can be accessed as follows:

- By its index
- With a `for()` loop
- With the `forEach()` method

Let's take a look at each of these three ways.

Accessing an element by index

Let's take the previous array of five elements, that is, `tab = ["Element 1", "Element 2", "Element 3", "Element 4", "Element 5"]`:

- The first element can be accessed by its index 0, that is, `tab[0]`.
- The next one, with index 1, will be accessed by `tab[1]`.
- The last one, with index 4, will be accessed by `tab[4]`.

This is how you will display each element:

Displaying each element of the array by its index

```
var tab = ["Element 1", "Element 2", "Element 3", "Element 4",
"Element 5"];
console.log("tab =", tab);
console.log("tab[0] =", tab[0]);
console.log("tab[1] =", tab[1]);
console.log("tab[2] =", tab[2]);
console.log("tab[3] =", tab[3]);
console.log("tab[4] =", tab[4]);
console.log("tab[5] =", tab[5]);
```

The result is displayed in the following figure:

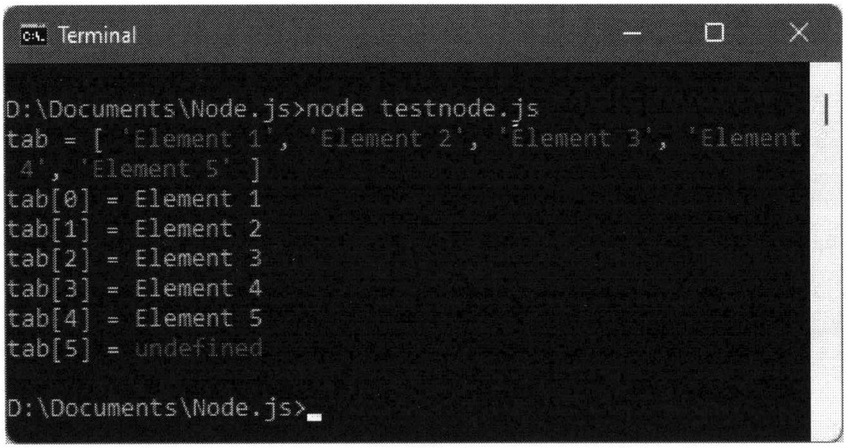

Figure 2.13 – Displaying each element by its index

The array contains five elements, which means the indices go from 0 to 4. However, to do a test, we also access the element with index 5. It is possible to access an index of an element that does not exist in the array. The result in this case is the JavaScript value `undefined`, which means that the value of this element has not yet been assigned.

Note that it is possible with this access method to modify the value of an array element – just give it a new value:

Modifying the value of the elements in indexes 2 and 3 of the array

```
var tab = ["Element 1", "Element 2", "Element 3", "Element 4",
"Element 5"];
console.log("Array before modification");
console.log("tab =", tab);

// modification of elements, index 2 and 3
tab[2] = "New element 3";
tab[3] = "New element 4";

console.log("Array after modification");
console.log("tab =", tab);
```

This is the result:

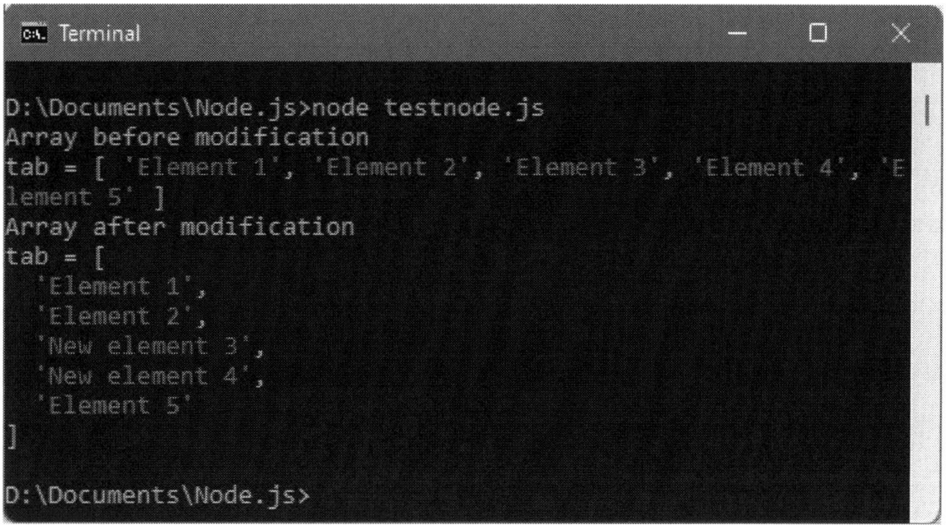

```
D:\Documents\Node.js>node testnode.js
Array before modification
tab = [ 'Element 1', 'Element 2', 'Element 3', 'Element 4', 'E
lement 5' ]
Array after modification
tab = [
  'Element 1',
  'Element 2',
  'New element 3',
  'New element 4',
  'Element 5'
]
D:\Documents\Node.js>
```

Figure 2.14 – Modifying array elements

Next, we will look at accessing an element with a `for()` or `while()` loop.

Accessing an element with a for() or while() loop

The `for()` and `while()` loops already studied in the previous chapter allow you to browse all the elements of an array. The index of the loop starts at 0 (to access the first element of the array, the one with index 0) and ends at the last index of the array.

To know this last index, JavaScript provides the `length` property in the `Array` class, which allows us to know the total number of elements of an array. The last index will be the one with the value `length - 1`:

Accessing array elements with a for() loop

```
var tab = ["Element 1", "Element 2", "Element 3", "Element 4", "Element 5"];
console.log("tab =", tab);
console.log("Access to each element by a for() loop");
for (var i = 0; i < tab.length; i++) console.log("tab[" + i + "]=", tab[i]);
```

Note that the end of the loop is written by testing the value `i < tab.length`. This is equivalent to writing `i <= tab.length - 1`.

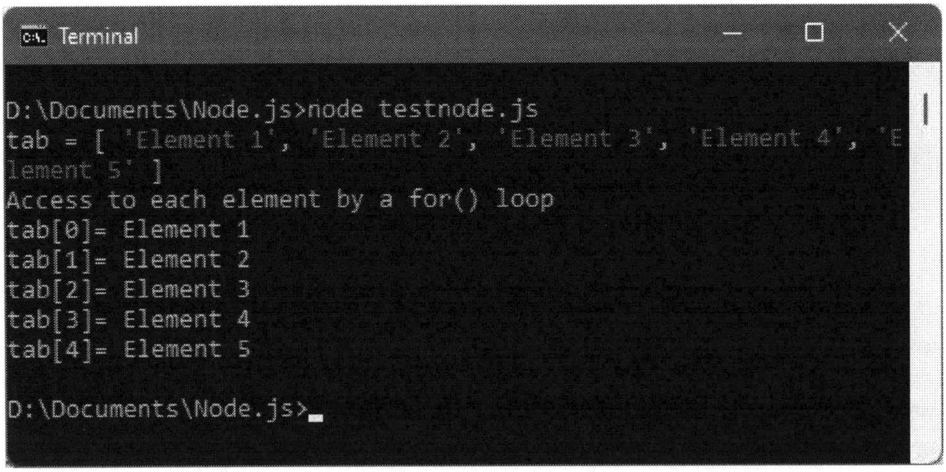

Figure 2.15 – Accessing array elements with a for() loop

Next, we will look at accessing an element with the `forEach(callback)` method.

Accessing an element with the forEach(callback) method

The `forEach(callback)` method is a method defined by JavaScript on the `Array` class. It is used to browse the elements of an array by transmitting each of the elements of the array to a function passed as a parameter. The function indicated as a parameter therefore has access to each element of the array (and to its index if necessary).

> **Callback Function**
> The principle of indicating a function in the parameters of a method is very common in JavaScript. The function in the parameters is known as a callback function, which means that the actual processing to be executed is that indicated in the callback function.

We show here how to use a callback function indicated in parameters of the `forEach(callback)` method.

We use the `tab` array of five elements seen previously, to which we apply the `forEach()` method:

Accessing array elements using the forEach() method

```
var tab = ["Element 1", "Element 2", "Element 3", "Element 4",
"Element 5"];
console.log("tab =", tab);
console.log("Access to each element by the forEach() method");
tab.forEach(function(elem, i) {
   console.log("tab[" + i + "]=", elem);
});
```

We indicate a function as a parameter of the `forEach()` method. This so-called callback function will be called automatically by JavaScript for each element of the `tab` array (which uses the `forEach()` method).

The callback function takes as its first parameter the element of the array for which the function is called (parameter `elem`), and its index (parameter `i`).

```
D:\Documents\Node.js>node testnode.js
tab = [ 'Element 1', 'Element 2', 'Element 3', 'Element 4', 'E
lement 5' ]
Access to each element by the forEach() method
tab[0]= Element 1
tab[1]= Element 2
tab[2]= Element 3
tab[3]= Element 4
tab[4]= Element 5

D:\Documents\Node.js>
```

Figure 2.16 – Accessing array elements using the forEach() method

The result is the same as that obtained by the `for()` loop. However, there is a (small) difference that we discover right away.

The difference between the for() loop and the forEach() method

The previous program did not show any difference between the `for()` loop and `forEach()` method results to access array elements.

To show the difference between these two approaches, let's introduce a new element in the array, at index 10, knowing that the last index used during the creation of the array was 4. We thus create a new element that is much further away than the current last element of the array. How will the array react to this enlargement?

Addition of an element at index 10

```
// original array
var tab = ["Element 1", "Element 2", "Element 3", "Element 4", "Element 5"];
// adding a new element in the array, at index 10
tab[10] = "Element 9";
console.log("tab =", tab);

// display the array with a for() loop
console.log("Access to each element by a for() loop");
for (var i = 0; i < tab.length; i++) console.log("tab[" + i +
```

```
"]=", tab[i]);

// display the array by the forEach() method
console.log("Access to each element by the forEach() method");
tab.forEach(function(elem, i) {
  console.log("tab[" + i + "]=", elem);
});
```

We add an element to the array using `tab[10] = "Element 9"`, then display the contents of the array using the `for()` loop and then the `forEach()` method.

The result is displayed in the following figure:

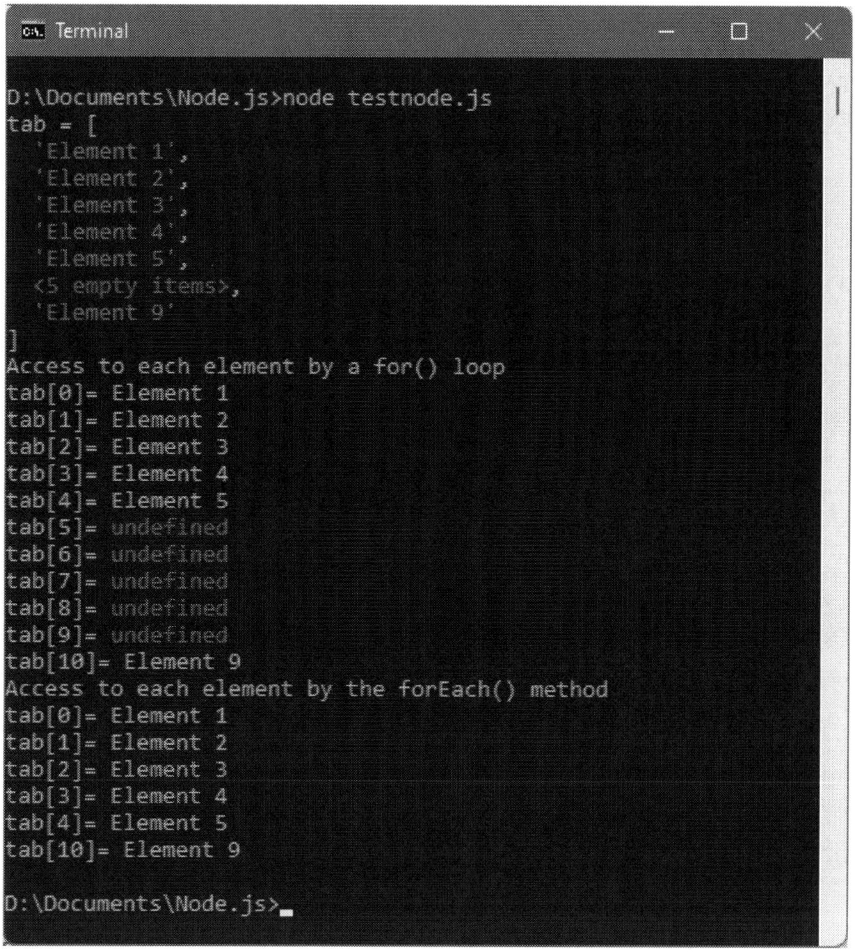

```
D:\Documents\Node.js>node testnode.js
tab = [
  'Element 1',
  'Element 2',
  'Element 3',
  'Element 4',
  'Element 5',
  <5 empty items>,
  'Element 9'
]
Access to each element by a for() loop
tab[0]= Element 1
tab[1]= Element 2
tab[2]= Element 3
tab[3]= Element 4
tab[4]= Element 5
tab[5]= undefined
tab[6]= undefined
tab[7]= undefined
tab[8]= undefined
tab[9]= undefined
tab[10]= Element 9
Access to each element by the forEach() method
tab[0]= Element 1
tab[1]= Element 2
tab[2]= Element 3
tab[3]= Element 4
tab[4]= Element 5
tab[10]= Element 9

D:\Documents\Node.js>
```

Figure 2.17 – Adding an element at index 10 of the array

The display of the `for()` loop shows that the elements with indices 5 to 9 exist but are of value `undefined`, because effectively, no values have been inserted for these indices of the array. However, the indices 5 to 9 with their `undefined` values are displayed by the `for()` loop.

Conversely, the `forEach()` method provides the callback function indicated in parameters with only the array elements that have actually been affected in the array. This therefore avoids the elements at indices 5 to 9, which have not been assigned in the program.

We have seen how to create an array, then how to access each of its elements. Let's look at how to add new elements to the array.

Adding items to the array

Once the array has been created (empty or not), it is possible to add elements to it. We will mainly use one of the two following techniques:

- Adding an element by its index in the array
- Adding an item using the `push()` method

Now let's take a look at these two techniques.

Adding an element by index

This corresponds to the assignment `tab[i] = value`. We used it in the previous section by writing `tab[10] = "Element 9"`.

Note simply that if the index used is greater than the current number of elements in the array, this enlarges the array by creating elements initialized to the value `undefined`. And if the index used is less than the number of elements in the array, it modifies the current value of the targeted element.

Adding an element using the push() method

The `push()` method is defined in the `Array` class. It allows you to add a new element to an array without worrying about the insertion index because it automatically inserts the element at the end of the array:

Inserting an element using the push() method

```
// original array
var tab = ["Element 1", "Element 2", "Element 3", "Element 4",
```

```
"Element 5"];
// insert an element using the push() method
tab.push("Element 6");
console.log("tab =", tab);

// display the array with a for() loop
console.log("Access to each element by a for() loop");
for (var i = 0; i < tab.length; i++) console.log("tab[" + i +
"]=", tab[i]);

// display the array by the forEach() method
console.log("Access to each element by the forEach() method");
tab.forEach(function(elem, i) {
   console.log("tab[" + i + "]=", elem);
});
```

The instruction tab.push("Element 6") inserts this element at the end of the array. The array is then displayed using the various methods seen previously.

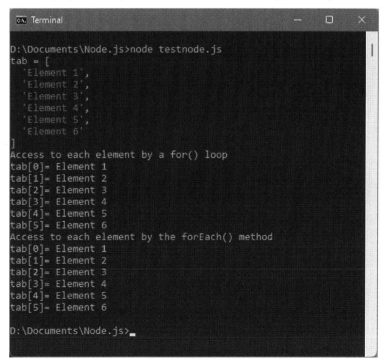

Figure 2.18 – Adding an element using the push() method

We know how to add and modify elements in an array. All that remains is to know how to delete elements from an array.

Deleting array elements

JavaScript allows us to delete array elements in two ways:

- Deleting the value of the element in the array, while retaining the element in the array with an `undefined` value
- Removing the element itself from the array

Let's examine these two possibilities now.

Deleting an element value (without deleting the element from the array)

We use the `delete` keyword to delete the value of an element in an array. For example, `delete tab[0]` deletes the value of the element with index 0 in the array `tab`, by assigning it the value `undefined`. The element is not removed from the array, which still has the same number of elements as before:

Deleting the value of the element with index 0

```
// original array
var tab = ["Element 1", "Element 2", "Element 3", "Element 4", "Element 5"];

// delete the value of the element with index 0
delete tab[0];
console.log("tab =", tab);

// display the array with a for() loop
console.log("Access to each element by a for() loop");
for (var i = 0; i < tab.length; i++) console.log("tab[" + i + "]=", tab[i]);

// display the array by the forEach() method
```

```
console.log("Access to each element by the forEach() method");
tab.forEach(function(elem, i) {
  console.log("tab[" + i + "]=", elem);
});
```

```
D:\Documents\Node.js>node testnode.js
tab = [ <1 empty item>, 'Element 2', 'Element 3', 'Element 4',
'Element 5' ]
Access to each element by a for() loop
tab[0]= undefined
tab[1]= Element 2
tab[2]= Element 3
tab[3]= Element 4
tab[4]= Element 5
Access to each element by the forEach() method
tab[1]= Element 2
tab[2]= Element 3
tab[3]= Element 4
tab[4]= Element 5

D:\Documents\Node.js>
```

Figure 2.19 – Deleting the value of the element with index 0

We see that the `for()` loop displays the `undefined` value of the element, while the `forEach()` method no longer displays the element because its value has been deleted.

> **Note**
>
> Note that if instead of using `delete tab[0]`, we use `tab[0] = undefined`, the `forEach()` method displays the element at index 0 as the first element of the array, because the value of the element has not actually been deleted but rather assigned to a new value, which here is `undefined`.

Now let's look at the second method for removing the element from the array.

Deleting an element from an array

Using the `delete` keyword does not delete the element from the array, which retains the same number of elements.

The `splice(begin, count)` method defined in the `Array` class allows you to physically remove the element from the array, which will therefore have at least one element less after its use.

The `splice(begin, count)` method includes the `begin` and `count` parameters, which allow you to indicate from which index you want to delete (`begin` parameter) the elements and the number of consecutive elements you want to delete (`count` parameter).

So, to remove the element with index 0 from the array `tab`, just write `tab.splice(0, 1)`:

Removing element with index 0 in array with splice() method

```
// original array
var tab = ["Element 1", "Element 2", "Element 3", "Element 4", "Element 5"];
// remove 1 element from index 0
tab.splice(0, 1);
console.log("tab =", tab);

// display the array with a for() loop
console.log("Access to each element by a for() loop");
for (var i = 0; i < tab.length; i++) console.log("tab[" + i + "]=", tab[i]);

// display the array by the forEach() method
console.log("Access to each element by the forEach() method");
tab.forEach(function(elem, i) {
   console.log("tab[" + i + "]=", elem);
});
```

This is what you will see:

```
D:\Documents\Node.js>node testnode.js
tab = [ 'Element 2', 'Element 3', 'Element 4', 'Element 5' ]
Access to each element by a for() loop
tab[0]= Element 2
tab[1]= Element 3
tab[2]= Element 4
tab[3]= Element 5
Access to each element by the forEach() method
tab[0]= Element 2
tab[1]= Element 3
tab[2]= Element 4
tab[3]= Element 5

D:\Documents\Node.js>
```

Figure 2.20 – Deletion of element with index 0

We have seen how to add and delete elements in an array. Now let's see how to extract a new array from the elements present in the current array.

Filtering elements in an array

It is common to filter the elements of an array, for example, to keep only certain elements or to return new ones. The Array class has two methods—filter(callback) and map(callback) —that allow us to return a new array according to our conditions.

Using the filter(callback) method

The tab.filter(callback) method returns a new array while keeping only the desired elements of the tab array.

The callback function of the form callback(element, index) is called for each of the elements of the array tab. It must return true if we decide to keep the element; otherwise, the element is excluded. A new array is returned as a result by the tab.filter() method, but the original tab array is not modified (unless it is assigned in return from the method, as in the following example).

Let's use the `filter()` method to keep only the elements of the array whose index is greater than or equal to 2:

Using the filter() method

```
// original array
var tab = ["Element 1", "Element 2", "Element 3", "Element 4",
"Element 5"];
console.log("initial tab =", tab);

// keep only items with index >= 2
tab = tab.filter(function(element, index) {
  if (index >= 2) return true;     // keep this element
});
console.log("\nfinal tab =", tab);
```

If the callback function returns `true`, the element is kept; otherwise, it is excluded. The callback function can also return `false`, or even return nothing, like here, and in this case, the element is excluded:

```
D:\Documents\Node.js>node testnode.js
initial tab = [ 'Element 1', 'Element 2', 'Element 3', 'Element 4', 'Element 5' ]

final tab = [ 'Element 3', 'Element 4', 'Element 5' ]

D:\Documents\Node.js>
```

Figure 2.21 – Using the filter() method

This brings us to the end of the filter() method.

Using the map(callback) method

The `tab.map(callback)` method is used to return a new array from the elements of the initial `tab` array. Each element of the initial array is passed to the callback function of the form `callback(element, index)`, which must return for each element a new element that will replace the original element.

Let's use the `map(callback)` method to return a new array in which all elements have been capitalized:

Using the map() method

```
// original array
var tab = ["Element 1", "Element 2", "Element 3", "Element 4",
"Element 5"];
console.log("initial tab =", tab);

// capitalize all elements
tab = tab.map(function(element, index) {
  return element.toUpperCase();
});
console.log("\nfinal tab =", tab);
```

The `toUpperCase()` method is a method defined on the `String` class (following screenshot), allowing you to capitalize the character string that uses the method.

The result is displayed in the following figure:

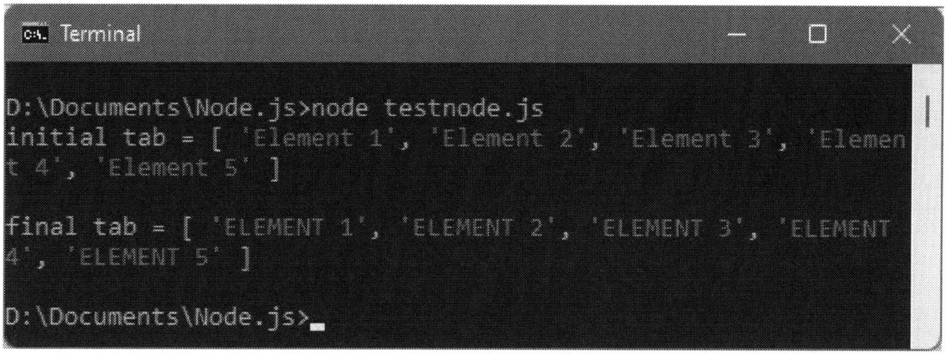

Figure 2.22 – Using the map() method

We have studied in this section the use of objects of the `Array` class. Another class of objects is also widely used with JavaScript: character strings, which are represented by the `String` class. Now let's see how to use objects of the `String` class.

Character strings

Strings are widely used in programming languages. They are used to represent text entered by a user or text that will be displayed to a user.

Creating a character string

A character string is represented by an object of class `String`. But since character strings are widely used in JavaScript, the language allows them to be used by surrounding them with double quotes " and " or single quotes ' and '. It is also possible, for certain uses, to use backticks (reverse quotation marks ' and ').

> **Note**
> The string literal must in this case begin and end with the same type of quotes.

Now let's see how to create a string using these various methods.

Creating a string literal using double or single quotes

The easiest way to create a string literal is to use the single or double quote notation:

Creating a string literal with double quotes

```
var s = "String 1";
console.log("s =", s);
```

Or, with single quotes:

Creating a string literal with single quotes

```
var s = 'String 1';
console.log("s =", s);
```

In both cases, the character string displayed is the same.

Figure 2.23 – Creating a character string

> **Advantage of Having the Option to Use Single/Double Quotation Marks**
> The advantage of having the possibility of using single or double quotes is visible if the string itself contains quotes. For example, if the string is `"I'll love JavaScript"`, using single quotes to create the string will produce an error because the string will be assumed to end with the apostrophe in the word `I'll`. In this case, you must use double quotes to avoid the error.

Creating a string literal using backticks

You can also use backticks. This is useful in special cases where you want to use the value of variables in character strings in a simpler way.

For example, suppose you want to display a string that uses a person's first and last name. The last name and first name are in variables named `lastname` and `firstname`:

Concatenating strings and variables

```
var lastname = "Clinton";
var firstname = "Bill";

// old way of concatenating strings and variables
var s1 = "lastname is " + lastname + ", firstname is " + firstname;

// new way of concatenating strings and variables
var s2 = `lastname is ${lastname}, firstname is ${firstname}`;
```

```
console.log("s1 =", s1);
console.log("s2 =", s2);
```

When using reverse quotes, the + symbol is no longer used to concatenate strings and variables. Everything is written in a single string, and the variables are identified by the "symbols" `${variable}`.

What is written between the braces `{ and }` can be a simple variable (like here), but also a more complex JavaScript expression that can be calculated (for example, `{a+b}`).

We can see that the two result strings are identical.

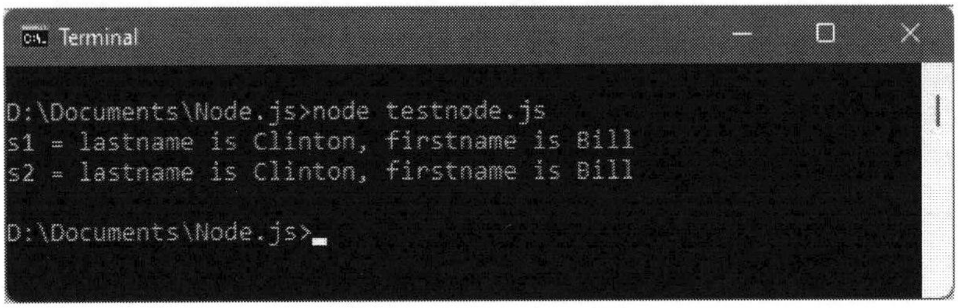

```
D:\Documents\Node.js>node testnode.js
s1 = lastname is Clinton, firstname is Bill
s2 = lastname is Clinton, firstname is Bill

D:\Documents\Node.js>
```

Figure 2.24 – Sequence of character strings and variables creating a string using the String class

Finally, it is possible to use the `String` class to create the character string. The `String` class has a constructor in which the string to be constructed is indicated as a parameter:

Using the String class

```
var s = new String("I'll love JavaScript");
console.log("s =", s);
```

The following figure displays the result:

```
D:\Documents\Node.js>node testnode.js
s = [String: "I'll love JavaScript"]

D:\Documents\Node.js>
```

Figure 2.25 – Using the String class

The `String` class has properties and methods. For example, the `length` property lets you know the number of characters in the string, and thus lets you compare, for example, the length of two character strings.

Let's use the `length` property to display the length of the two strings created using quotes and the `String` class:

Using the length property of the String class

```
var s1 = new String("I'll love JavaScript");
var s2 = "I'll love JavaScript";

console.log("s1 =", s1);
console.log("s2 =", s2);
console.log("s1.length =", s1.length);
console.log("s2.length =", s2.length);
```

This is the result:

Figure 2.26 – Using the length property of the String class

Regardless of how the string is created, its length is the same (here, 20 characters). We have seen how to create a character string, now let's see how to access the characters that compose it.

Accessing characters in a string

The `String` class defines methods for accessing characters in the string. These are, in particular, the `charAt(index)` and `slice(start, end)` methods. `charAt(index)` is used to retrieve the character located at the index indicated in the string, starting from index 0. The maximum index is that associated with the value of the `length` property, reduced by 1. `slice(start, end)` breaks the string into a substring, by extracting the characters that go from the `start` index (included) to the `end` index (excluded).

Using the charAt(index) method

Let's use the `charAt(index)` method to display the characters of a string, one by one:

Displaying characters from a string

```
var s = "Hello";

console.log("s =", s);
for (var i = 0; i <s.length; i++) console.log(`s.charAt(${i}) = ${s.charAt(i)}`);
```

Notice the use of reverse quotes to display the result string.

The result is displayed in the following figure:

Figure 2.27 – Using the charAt() method

Now, let's look at the `slice(start, end)` method.

Using the slice(start, end) method

The preceding `charAt(index)` method retrieves a single character from the string, while the `slice(start, end)` method can retrieve several consecutive ones:

> **Note**
> Note that the `slice(start, end)` method does not modify the string on which the method applies, but rather returns a new string. The original string is not modified, allowing it to remain intact.

Using slice() on the "Hello" string

```
var s = "Hello";

console.log("s =", s);
console.log(`s.slice(0,2) = ${s.slice(0,2)}`);
console.log(`s.slice(0,3) = ${s.slice(0,3)}`);
console.log(`s.slice(1,3) = ${s.slice(1,3)}`);
console.log(`s.slice(0,-1) = ${s.slice(0,-1)}`);
console.log(`s.slice(0,-2) = ${s.slice(0,-2)}`);
console.log(`s.slice(1,-2) = ${s.slice(1,-2)}`);
```

If the end index (second parameter) of the `slice(start, end)` method is negative, it means counting starts from the end of the string (instead of the beginning if it is positive).

We then obtain the following result:

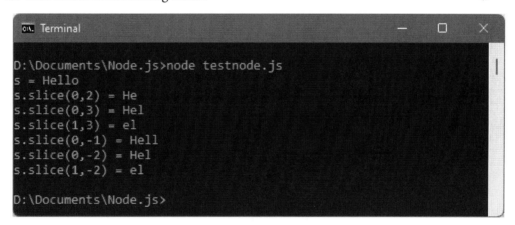

Figure 2.28 – Using the slice() method

Now that we have seen how to get the characters that make up the string, let's look at how to modify the string.

Modifying a character string

To modify a string, there is only one possibility: you have to construct a new one from it. The original string cannot be changed directly.

For this, we will use the previous `slice()` and `charAt()` methods, which will make it possible to extract parts of the original string, in order to build the resulting string.

But to search or modify parts of character strings, it is better to use regular expressions. We study them below.

Using regular expressions

Regular expressions are related to strings. They are used to check whether a string has a certain format (for example, the format of an email, of a telephone number, and so on), or to replace the characters that are in this format with others.

For this, the `String` class has the `match(regexp)` method to check whether a character string has a given format and the `replace(regexp, str)` method to replace the part of the string in this format with the new string `str`.

In both methods, the `regexp` parameter corresponds to a regular expression, the meaning of which we will study next.

Checking whether a string has a given format

The `match(regexp)` method is used to check whether the character string on which the method is used is in the format indicated in `regexp`. The `regexp` parameter is called a regular expression.

> **Regular Expressions**
>
> A regular expression is a sequence of characters surrounded by / and /, for example, `/abc/`. The regular expression `/abc/` means that we are looking for the sequence of characters `abc` in the character string. If the string contains the sequence `abc`, the `match(/abc/)` method returns this sequence of characters as a result, otherwise it returns the value `null`.
>
> A full description of regular expressions can be found at `https://developer.mozilla.org/fr/docs/Web/JavaScript/Reference/Global_Objects/RegExp`.

Here are some examples of regular expressions with the values returned when using the `match()` method on the string `"Hello"`:

Using match(regexp)

```
var s = "Hello";

console.log("s =", s);
```

```javascript
// search for "Hel"
console.log(`s.match(/Hel/) = ${s.match(/Hel/)}`);

// search for "hel"
console.log(`s.match(/hel/) = ${s.match(/hel/)}`);

// search for "hel" ignoring upper/lower case
console.log(`s.match(/hel/i) = ${s.match(/hel/i)}`);

// search for H followed by a or b or e followed by l
console.log(`s.match(/H[abe]l/) = ${s.match(/H[abe]l/)}`);

// search for He followed by 0 or 1 a followed by l
console.log(`s.match(/Hea?l/) = ${s.match(/Hea?l/)}`);

// search for He followed by 0 (min) to 1 (max) followed by l
console.log(`s.match(/Hea{0,1}l/) = ${s.match(/Hea{0,1}l/)}`);

// search for He followed 1 (min) to 2 (max) followed by l
console.log(`s.match(/Hea{1,2}l/) = ${s.match(/Hea{1,2}l/)}`);
```

When the regular expression is found in the "Hello" string, the part of the string found is returned by the match() method, otherwise it returns null.

The i sign at the end of the regular expression indicates that uppercase or lowercase letters must be ignored.

The square brackets [and] around a series of letters mean that only one of these letters is required.

The question mark ? means that the preceding character is optional (it can be present or not).

The braces {min,max} mean that the preceding character must be present at least min times and at most max times.

The result of the previous program is as follows:

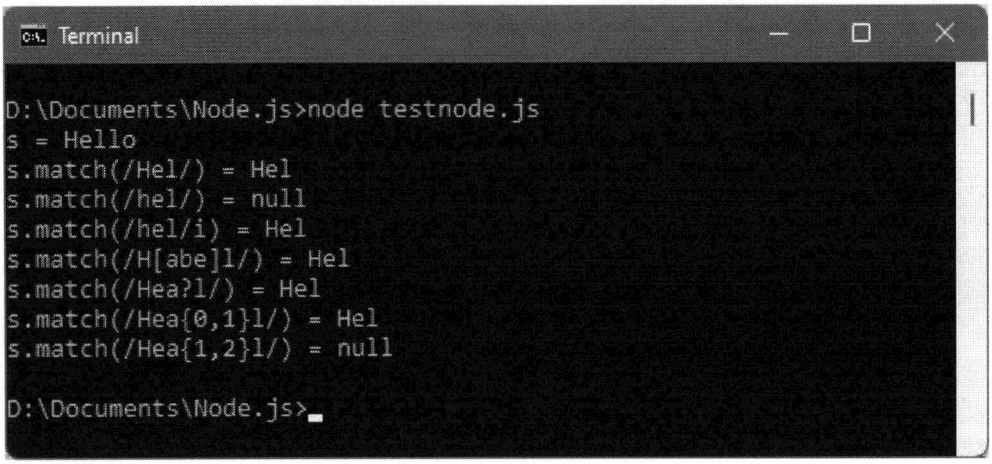

```
D:\Documents\Node.js>node testnode.js
s = Hello
s.match(/Hel/) = Hel
s.match(/hel/) = null
s.match(/hel/i) = Hel
s.match(/H[abe]l/) = Hel
s.match(/Hea?l/) = Hel
s.match(/Hea{0,1}l/) = Hel
s.match(/Hea{1,2}l/) = null

D:\Documents\Node.js>
```

Figure 2.29 – Using regular expressions

> **Note**
> Writing a regular expression can sometimes be complex to formulate. The site https://regex101.com/ allows you to test the regular expressions you want.

A regular expression can also modify parts of character strings, using the `replace()` method.

Replacing a part of a string with a given format

The `replace(regexp, str)` method is used to replace the part of the string having the format of the regular expression `regexp` with the string `str`. It returns a new string, and the original one is not modified. If the format indicated by the regular expression is not found, the original string is returned with no modifications.

Let's take the regular expressions from the previous example and replace the string found with the string "abc", thanks to the regular expressions:

Using the replace() method

```
var s = "Hello";

console.log("s =", s);
```

```javascript
// search for "Hel" and replace with "abc"
console.log(`s.replace(/Hel/, "abc") => ${s.replace(/Hel/, "abc")}`);

// search for "hel" and replace with "abc"
console.log(`s.replace(/hel/, "abc") => ${s.replace(/hel/, "abc")}`);

// search for hel ignoring upper/lower case and replacing with
// "abc"
console.log(`s.replace(/hel/i, "abc") => ${s.replace(/hel/i, "abc")}`);

// search for H followed by a or b or e followed by l and
// replace with "abc"
console.log(`s.replace(/H[abe]l/, "abc") => ${s.replace(/H[abe]l/, "abc")}`);

// search for He followed by 0 or 1 a followed by l and
// replaced by "abc"
console.log(`s.replace(/Hea?l/, "abc") => ${s.replace(/Hea?l/, "abc")}`);

// search for He followed by 0 (min) to 1 (max) followed by l
// and replaced by "abc"
console.log(`s.replace(/Hea{0,1}l/, "abc") => ${s.replace(/Hea{0,1}l/, "abc")}`);

// search for He followed by 1 (min) to 2 (max) followed by l
// and replaced by "abc"
console.log(`s.replace(/Hea{1,2}l/, "abc") => ${s.replace(/Hea{1,2}l/, "abc")}`);
```

The output is shown here:

```
D:\Documents\Node.js>node testnode.js
s = Hello
s.replace(/Hel/, "abc") => abclo
s.replace(/hel/, "abc") => Hello
s.replace(/hel/i, "abc") => abclo
s.replace(/H[abe]l/, "abc") => abclo
s.replace(/Hea?l/, "abc") => abclo
s.replace(/Hea{0,1}l/, "abc") => abclo
s.replace(/Hea{1,2}l/, "abc") => Hello

D:\Documents\Node.js>
```

Figure 2.30 – Using the replace() method

All executions of previous programs were executed immediately. We are now going to study how to perform deferred processing over time.

Multitasking in JavaScript

When you start coding in JavaScript, a question often comes up: is it possible to perform several processes simultaneously (what is called multitasking in computing)? This would be useful if a process to be executed will take a long time, so as not to block other equally urgent processes.

JavaScript does not allow several processing operations to be carried out simultaneously. On the other hand, it is possible not to block the program (both on the client side in the browser, and on the server side with Node.js) by using the callback function (which we have already talked about when studying the `forEach()` method in the *Accessing an element with the forEach(callback) method* section).

> **Callback Function**
> A callback function corresponds to a processing function used as parameters of a JavaScript method or function. The callback function will be executed at the desired time by the method or function that uses it.

Node.js makes extensive use of this feature. For example, when reading a file, the `readFile(callback)` method calls the callback function as a parameter when the file has been read, which allows the program not to block the pending processing of the file to be read.

JavaScript defines as standard two main functions that use this callback function concept: the `setTimeout()` and `setInterval()` functions. Both these use a callback function as a parameter. We'll describe these two functions next.

Using the setTimeout() function

The `setTimeout(callback, timeout)` function is used to position a processing function (the `callback` function) that will be executed when the time period expressed by `timeout` (in milliseconds) has elapsed.

This allows you, for example, to perform processing after 5 seconds (that is, 5,000 milliseconds). You can execute other instructions while waiting for this delay, so the program is not blocked during this time:

Processing instructions after a delay of 5 seconds

```
console.log("Before setTimeout()");
setTimeout(function() {
  console.log("In the callback function");
}, 5000);   // 5000 milliseconds, or 5 seconds
console.log("After setTimeout()");
```

We display a message (`"Before setTimeout()"`) in the console at the start of the program. We program a delay of 5 seconds, after which a callback function is triggered, which displays another message in the console (`"In the callback function"`). Finally, we end the program by displaying a new message (`"After setTimeout()"`).

Let's run this program with the `node testnode.js` command, for example. To test this program in a browser, simply place the preceding JavaScript code between the `<script>` and `</script>` tags of the `index.html` file.

The following screenshot shows the display after 1 second:

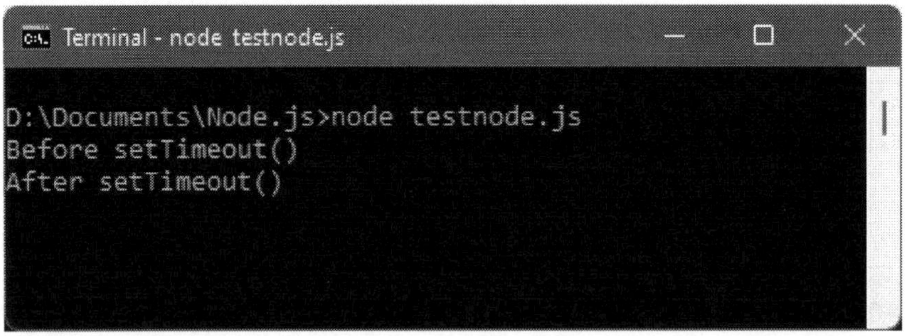

Figure 2.31 – Using setTimeout()

Note that the display message of the start and that of the end follow each other, even though the 5-second time limit has not elapsed. This shows that the program is not blocked, waiting for the timeout to expire.

The following screenshot shows the display after at least 5 seconds (when the delay used in the `setTimeout()` method has elapsed).

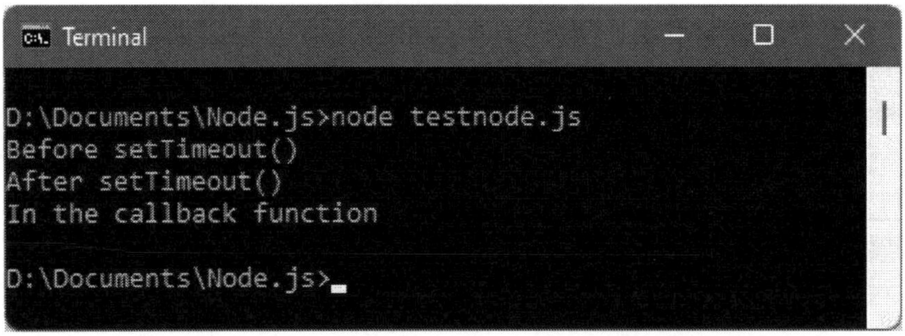

Figure 2.32 – Display when the 5-second delay has elapsed

We see that when the 5-second delay has elapsed, the callback function registered in the `setTimeout()` function is called automatically by the `setTimeout()` function.

Let's improve the program by displaying the time when the messages are displayed. This makes it possible to verify that the 5-second time limit is respected:

Displaying the time when messages are posted

```
console.log(time(), "Before setTimeout()");
setTimeout(function() {
  console.log(time(), "In the callback function");
}, 5000);   // 5000 = 5 seconds
```

```
console.log(time(), "After setTimeout()");

function time() {
 // return time as HH:MM:SS
 var date = new Date();
 var hour = date.getHours();
 var min = date.getMinutes();
 var sec = date.getSeconds();
 if (hour < 10) hour = "0" + hour;
 if (min < 10) min = "0" + min;
 if (sec < 10) sec = "0" + sec;
 return "" + hour + ":" + min + ":" + sec + " ";
}
```

The time() function is used to generate a character string that contains the time in the form HH:MM:SS. This time is displayed at the beginning of each message displayed in the console.

The Date class used here is a JavaScript class that allows you to manage dates and to extract hours, minutes, and seconds.

We now get the following:

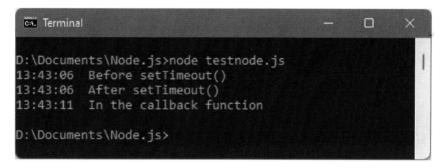

Figure 2.33 – Displaying the time when messages are displayed in the console

We can clearly see that the callback function is executed at the end of the 5-second period indicated in the parameter of the setTimeout() function.

Using the setInterval() function

The `setInterval(callback, timeout)` function is similar to the `setTimeout()` function seen previously. But instead of executing the callback function only once at the end of the delay (as the `setTimeout()` function does), the `setInterval()` function executes the callback function repeatedly by setting a new delay at the end of it. The callback function is therefore executed at regular intervals. The only way to stop this cycle is to use the `clearInterval()` function.

The `setInterval()` function is very useful for running processes at regular intervals.

Let's use the `setInterval()` function to display, every second, the value of a counter initialized to 1. The counter is incremented every second:

Incrementing a counter every second

```
console.log(time(), "Start of timer");
var count = 1;
setInterval(function() {
  console.log(time(), `count = ${count}`);
  count++;
}, 1000);     // 1000 = 1 second

function time() {
  // return time as HH:MM:SS
  var date = new Date();
  var hour = date.getHours();
  var min = date.getMinutes();
  var sec = date.getSeconds();
  if (hour < 10) hour = "0" + hour;
  if (min < 10) min = "0" + min;
  if (sec < 10) sec = "0" + sec;
  return "" + hour + ":" + min + ":" + sec + " ";
}
```

This is what you will see:

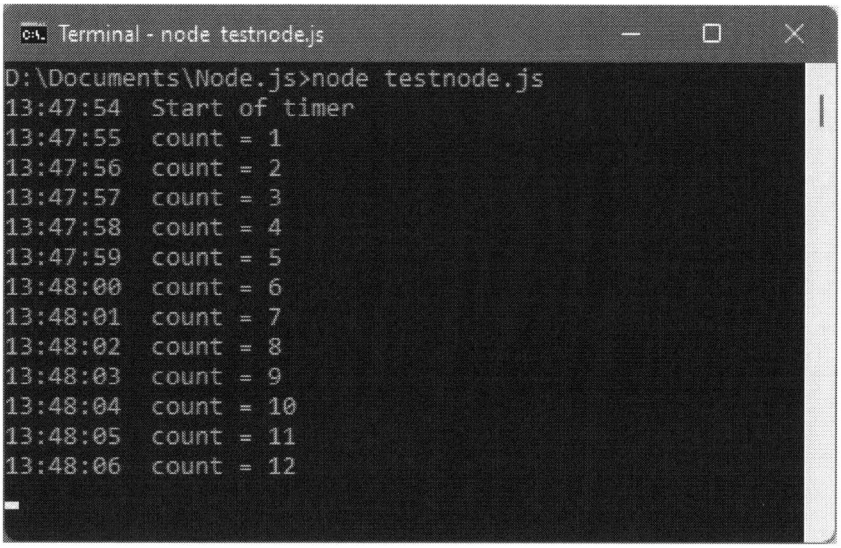

Figure 2.34 – Incrementing a counter every second

The counter increments every second, indefinitely. To stop this endless cycle, you have to use a new JavaScript function, which is `clearInterval()`.

Using the clearInterval() function

The `clearInterval(timer)` function is used to stop the cycle started during the `setInterval()` instruction.

> **Note**
> Note that multiple timers can be started by multiple calls to the `setInterval()` function. So the `clearInterval(timer)` function must specify which timer it wants to stop: the `timer` parameter is used to tell it.
>
> To do this, the `setInterval()` function returns the `timer` parameter that will be used when calling the `clearInterval(timer)` function.

Let's use the `clearInterval()` function to stop the timer when the `count` counter has reached the value 5:

Using the clearInterval() function to stop the timer

```
console.log(time(), "Start of timer");
var count = 1;
var timer = setInterval(function() {
  console.log(time(), `count = ${count}`);
  if (count == 5) {
     clearInterval(timer);   // timer stop
     console.log(time(), "End of timer");
  } else count++;
}, 1000);

function time() {
  // return time as HH:MM:SS
  var date = new Date();
  var hour = date.getHours();
  var min = date.getMinutes();
  var sec = date.getSeconds();
  if (hour < 10) hour = "0" + hour;
  if (min < 10) min = "0" + min;
  if (sec < 10) sec = "0" + sec;
  return "" + hour + ":" + min + ":" + sec + " ";
}
```

The program of the callback function is modified: as soon as the counter reaches 5, the timer is stopped. Otherwise, the counter is incremented by 1.

Check that the count stops after 5 times:

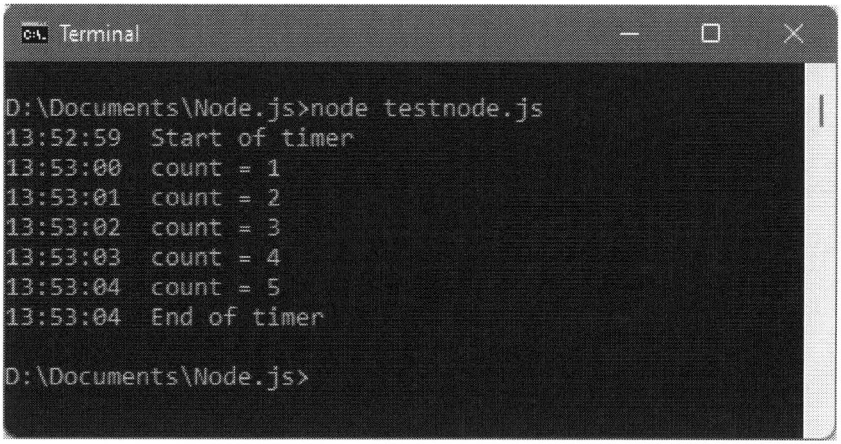

Figure 2.35 – Timer stops after 5 counts

The callback function that is used in the `setTimeout()` or `setInterval()` functions is included directly in the parameters of each function. JavaScript makes it easier to write callback functions by using a new type of object called a promise.

Using promises

Promises are another way to use callback functions. Rather than integrating the callback function into the method call (as a parameter), we use it as a parameter of the new `then(callback)` method. This simplifies the reading of JavaScript code in case it uses callback functions.

For an object to use the `then(callback)` method, it must be a `Promise` class object. The `Promise` class is a class defined in JavaScript language.

> **The Promise Class**
> A `Promise` class object uses a callback function of the form `callback(resolve, reject)` as a parameter of its constructor.

The `resolve` and `reject` parameters are functions, which will be called from the promise's callback:

- When the `resolve()` function is called, it triggers the `then(callback)` method.
- When the `reject()` function is called, it triggers the `catch(callback)` method.

90   Exploring the Advanced Concepts of JavaScript

The `resolve()` function must be called, otherwise the `then(callback)` method cannot be executed. On the other hand, calling the `reject()` function is optional, and if it is not used, the `catch(callback)` method will not be called (and therefore does not have to be present in the program).

Thanks to the `resolve` and `reject` parameters, we therefore have the possibility of executing the cases of success (with the `then(callback)` method) and the cases of failure (with the `catch(callback)` method). This way of writing ensures more readability of the JavaScript code.

To illustrate this, let's take the example of the `setTimeout(callback, timeout)` function seen previously. The callback function is included in the method call here, which we want to avoid with promises. Let's write the new `wait(timeout)` method that can be used in the form `wait(timeout).then(callback)`. The callback function is now externalized from the `wait()` method.

The callback function registered in the `then(callback)` method will be called when the timeout expires.

This form of writing is more readable than the previous one with `setTimeout()`, because it thus shows the delay before a process is executed.

To achieve this, the `wait(timeout)` method must return a `Promise` object:

Creating the Promise object, then using the then() method

```
function time() {
 // return time as HH:MM:SS
 var date = new Date();
 var hour = date.getHours();
 var min = date.getMinutes();
 var sec = date.getSeconds();
 if (hour < 10) hour = "0" + hour;
 if (min < 10) min = "0" + min;
 if (sec < 10) sec = "0" + sec;
 return "" + hour + ":" + min + ":" + sec + " ";
}

function wait(sec) {
  return new Promise(function(resolve, reject) {
    setTimeout(function() {
```

```
        resolve(sec);   // triggers the then() method
    }, sec*1000);
  });
}

console.log(time(), "Start of timer");
wait(2).then(function(sec) {
    console.log(time(), `End of timer of ${sec} seconds`);
});
```

The `wait()` method returns a `Promise` object thanks to the `return new Promise()` statement. In the `callback(resolve, reject)` function, we call the `resolve()` function when we consider that the `then()` method can execute, here at the end of the timeout.

It is possible to specify arguments for the `resolve()` and `reject()` methods. These arguments will be used in the callback functions used in the `then(callback)` or `catch(callback)` methods. For example, here, we call the `resolve(sec)` method, which allows us to use the `sec` parameter in the callback function of the `then()` method.

> **Note**
> Notice that the `reject()` function is not used in our example because no error cases can occur here. The `resolve()` function must, however, be called; otherwise, the `then()` method will never be executed.

The `time()` function is used to display the times of each process to check that the execution is correct.

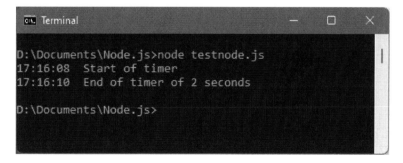

Figure 2.36 – Using the then() method

This brings us to the end of the chapter.

Summary

In this chapter, we went through advanced concepts related to JavaScript.

We learned how to use classes and objects, particularly the `Array` and `String` classes. We also saw how to delay the execution of instructions.

In the rest of the book, we will discover the use of the Vue.js JavaScript library associated with the client side of application development.

We will see how the knowledge obtained here will allow us to use this language in aspects of client-side and then server-side programming.

Part 2: JavaScript on the Client-Side

In this part, we discover the use of JavaScript in a browser (so-called client-side). We will learn how to use the Vue.js library to build JavaScript apps on the client-side. We also build a list management application (small but representative of the reality).

This section comprises the following chapters:

- *Chapter 3, Getting Started with Vue.js*
- *Chapter 4, Advanced concepts of Vue.js*
- *Chapter 5, Managing a list with Vue.js*

3
Getting Started with Vue.js

The JavaScript world is constantly changing. In recent years, a new concept has emerged: that of developing applications by creating components.

New JavaScript libraries for developing component-based apps have emerged, the main ones being Angular, React, Svelte, and **Vue.js**. Among all these libraries, which are quite similar to each other, we have chosen to present Vue.js to you because it is widely used and quite simple to implement. The other libraries mentioned operate according to the same principles.

> **Why Use Vue.js?**
> The main advantage of Vue.js is the possibility of developing an application using components. We cut the web application into a set of components (actually JavaScript files) and then assemble them to form the final application. Vue.js can test each component independently of the others and can also reuse them in other applications.

In this chapter, we will study how to build our first application with Vue.js, by creating and using our first component.

In this chapter, we will cover the following main topics:

- Using Vue.js in an HTML page
- Creating our first Vue.js application
- Using reactivity
- Creating our first component
- Adding methods in components
- Using attributes in components
- Using directives

Technical requirements

You can find the code files for this chapter on GitHub at: `https://github.com/PacktPublishing/JavaScript-from-Frontend-to-Backend/blob/main/Chapter%203.zip`.

Using Vue.js in an HTML page

To use Vue.js in an HTML page, simply insert the library file into it using the `<script>` tag.

To check that Vue.js is correctly integrated into the page, let's display the version number of the library in the `Vue.version` variable:

Displaying Vue.js version number (index.html file)

```
<html>
  <head>
    <meta charset="utf-8" />
    <script src="https://unpkg.com/vue@next"></script>
  </head>

  <body>
  </body>

  <script>
    alert(`Vue.version = ${Vue.version}`);
```

```
    </script>
</html>
```

If Vue.js is accessible in the page, the `Vue` object provides access to the version number in its `version` property as we can see in the following figure:

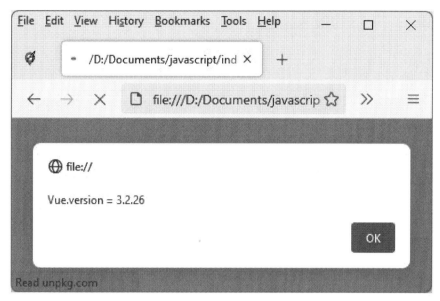

Figure 3.1 – Displaying the Vue.js version number

Now that we have integrated Vue.js into our HTML page, let's go about creating our first application.

Creating our first Vue.js application

Once Vue.js has been inserted into the HTML page, you must define the HTML elements of the page in which Vue.js will be used.

In general, you want to use Vue.js on the whole HTML page, but it is possible to use it only on certain elements of the page as well. This would allow us, for example, to manage an HTML page with jQuery, except for a particular `<div>` element, which would be managed with Vue.js.

To illustrate this, let us create an HTML page with two `<div>` elements, only the first of which will be managed by Vue.js:

Creating an HTML page partially managed by Vue.js

```
<html>
  <head>
    <meta charset="utf-8" />
    <script src="https://unpkg.com/vue@next"></script>
  </head>

  <body>
    <div id="app">First div</div>
    <div>The rest of the page is not managed by
    Vue.js</div>
  </body>

  <script>

    var app = Vue.createApp({
      template : "This div is managed with Vue.js"
    });

    // mount the Vue.js application on the <div> having the
    // id "app"
    var vm = app.mount("div#app");

  </script>

</html>
```

In the preceding code, we have used the `Vue.createApp(options)` method defined on the `Vue` object. The `options` object is used to set options for creating the Vue.js application. One of the options of `Vue.createApp(options)` is the `template` option, which allows us to define the view (that is to say the HTML display) that will be displayed on the page, thanks to the call of the `app.mount(element)` method:

- The `app` object is the one obtained as a result of the `Vue.createApp()` method call.
- The `element` parameter represents the HTML element on which Vue.js will act.

Let's run the previous program; we should see the following output:

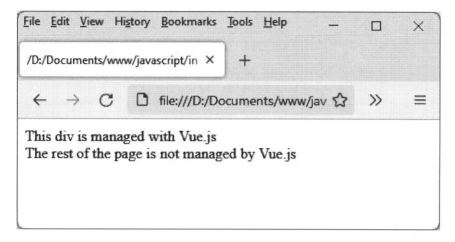

Figure 3.2 – First Vue.js app

On the preceding screen, we can see the result of using Vue.js on the page. The content of the first `<div>` is replaced by the template written in the `options` parameter of the `Vue.createApp(options)` method. The second `<div>` is not transformed.

Thus, to manage an entire HTML page with Vue.js, just indicate in the `<body>` part of the page a single `<div>` element, which will be the one on which Vue.js will be activated.

Now let's see how to use an important concept of Vue.js, which is the correspondence between the variables defined in the program and their display on the HTML page. This concept is called reactivity.

Using reactivity

One of the objectives of Vue.js is to separate the management of the display (the **view**) and that of the data (the **model**). This is the concept that is frequently found in what is called the **Model View Controller** (**MVC**) model.

To illustrate, suppose we want to display a counter that increments from 0. A good separation of view and model would be for the view to constantly display the value of the counter, even if that value is changed elsewhere. This concept makes it possible not to link the display with the management of the data displayed. For this, we use the reactivity offered by Vue.js, by creating so-called **reactive variables**.

> **Reactive Variables**
>
> A variable will be said to be reactive if its modification in memory causes it to be modified automatically wherever the variable is displayed.

Reactive variables are defined in the `options` object of the `Vue.createApp(options)` method. For this, we add in the `options` object, and the definition of the `data()` method, which will have to return an object containing the so-called reactive variables of the application.

Let's use a reactive variable named `count` in our Vue.js application:

Defining a count reactive variable

```html
<html>
  <head>
    <meta charset="utf-8" />
    <script src="https://unpkg.com/vue@next"></script>
  </head>

  <body>
    <div id="app"></div>
  </body>

  <script>

    var app = Vue.createApp({
      template : "The counter is: {{count}}",
      data() {
        // return an object containing the reactive
        // variables
        return {
          count : 0
        }
      }
    });

    var vm = app.mount("div#app");
```

```
    </script>

</html>
```

In the preceding code, the `count` reactive variable is defined in the `data()` method, which returns the `{ count : 0 }` object containing the program's reactive variable. Other variables can be defined afterward.

This reactive variable can then be used in the template by means of the notation with `{{` and `}}`. This notation is used to indicate a JavaScript expression, such as the value of a variable.

The definition of a so-called reactive variable makes it possible to link the display to the value of the variable. As soon as the variable is modified, the display is also modified. We can see the counter value in the following figure:

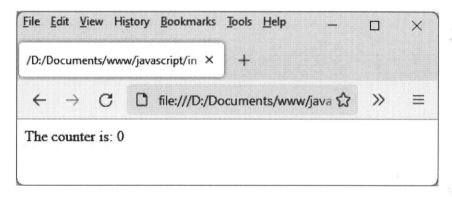

Figure 3.3 – Displaying a reactive variable

The counter remains positioned at its initial value: **0**. Reactivity is only visible when the variable is modified. The display will therefore be modified as soon as the `count` variable is modified.

To do this, let's increment the value of the variable every second as shown in the following code:

Incrementing count variable every second

```
<html>
  <head>
    <meta charset="utf-8" />
    <script src="https://unpkg.com/vue@next"></script>
```

```
    </head>

    <body>
      <div id="app"></div>
    </body>

    <script>

      var app = Vue.createApp({
        template : "The counter is: {{count}}",
        data() {
          // return an object containing the reactive
          // variables
          return {
            count : 0
          }
        }
      });

      var vm = app.mount("div#app");

      setInterval(function() {
        vm.count += 1;
      }, 1000);

    </script>

</html>
```

Using JavaScript's `setInterval()` function, we increment the value of the `count` variable every second. Vue.js provides access to the `count` variable using `vm.count`, where `vm` is the object returned by the `app.mount()` method. Reactive variables become properties of this `vm` object. In the preceding code, we can see the separation of view and data processing, as advocated by the MVC pattern. The incrementation of the variable is done outside the view, which would not have been possible with a library such as jQuery.

We can see the incrementation and the automatic update of the display, thanks to the reactivity offered by Vue.js, as evident in the following figure

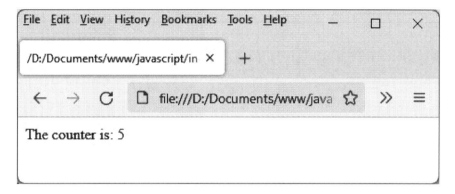

Figure 3.4 – Incrementing a reactive variable

The previous program is very simple, but in reality, applications are of course more complex. As such, it is necessary to break down an application into small pieces, which will then be assembled. Now let's learn how to write one of the small pieces of an application, called a component.

Creating our first component

Let's see how to use Vue.js to create our own components.

A Vue.js component will be similar to a new HTML element. It will be used in the form of HTML tags to which new attributes can be associated if necessary. To use the component, all you have to do is use the corresponding tag.

The components are therefore a means of enriching the HTML code by creating our own tags.

> **How to Discover the Components to Use to Build Our Application**
>
> All you have to do is visually cut the HTML page you want to display into the simplest possible elements (which will be the basic components of your application), then group several elements together to form a component that will group them, and so on until you have the main component, which will be your complete application.

For example, if a list of elements is displayed on the HTML page, each element's line of the list corresponds to a basic component, while the global list that groups these different components will be associated with another component. The set of all components of the HTML page corresponds to the main component, often named `<App>` or `<GlobalApp>`. Let's see how to create and use the `<counter>` component corresponding to the previous counter by first learning how to insert the component.

You can create the component directly into the HTML page or include it from an external file. Let's look at these two ways to do it.

Inserting a component in the application file

A component can simply be embedded in the main application Vue.js file. Just use the `app.component(name, options)` method to create it as follows. The variable `app` corresponds to the object returned by `Vue.createApp()`:

Creating the <counter> component directly in the application

```
<html>
  <head>
    <meta charset="utf-8" />
    <script src="https://unpkg.com/vue@next"></script>
  </head>

  <body>
    <div id="app"></div>
  </body>

  <script>

    var app = Vue.createApp({
      template : "<counter />"
    });

    app.component("counter", {
      template : "The counter is: {{count}}",
      data() {
        return {
          count : 0
```

```
        }
      }
    });

    var vm = app.mount("div#app");

</script>

</html>
```

In the preceding code, the variable app corresponds to the object returned by Vue.createApp().

The app.component(name, options) method works on the same principle as Vue.createApp(options):

- The name parameter corresponds to the name of the component, which will then be used as tags in HTML templates.
- The options parameter is similar in both cases. There is the template section, data, and so on.

The <counter> component can then be used in other templates, including the one defined for the application. When you run the preceding code, you will see the following screen:

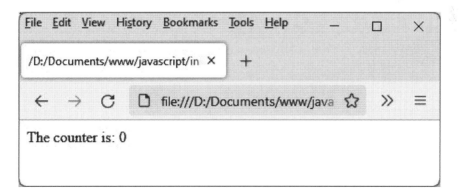

Figure 3.5 – The <counter> component

As we can see in the preceding figure, for the moment, the counter remains at 0. To increment the reactive variable count in the component, it is necessary to be able to write the instruction of incrementation once the component is created. For this, Vue.js provides internal methods allowing access to the life cycle of each component created.

One of the methods of a component's life cycle is the `created()` method. It is called when the component is created. You can use this method to write the increment of the variable `count` every second, using the `setInterval()` function.

Let's use the component's `created()` method as follows:

Using the component's created() method

```html
<html>
  <head>
    <meta charset="utf-8" />
    <script src="https://unpkg.com/vue@next"></script>
  </head>

  <body>
    <div id="app"></div>
  </body>

<script>

  var app = Vue.createApp({
    template : "<counter />"
  });

  app.component("counter", {
    template : "The counter is: {{count}}",
    data() {
      return {
        count : 0
      }
    },
    created() {
      setInterval(()=>{   // do not use the function()
                          // form here,
                          // otherwise the "this" object
                          // would not be the same
        this.count++;
      }, 1000);
```

```
        }
    });

    var vm = app.mount("div#app");

</script>

</html>
```

In the preceding code, we have used the notation `()=>` instead of `function()`. This notation (called a lambda function) was introduced in the latest versions of JavaScript in order to allow the value of `this` to be kept inside callback functions, which is necessary here. If you replace the lambda function `()=>` with the `function()` keyword, the program won't work, as the `this` value won't be the same.

On running the preceding code, you will see the following output:

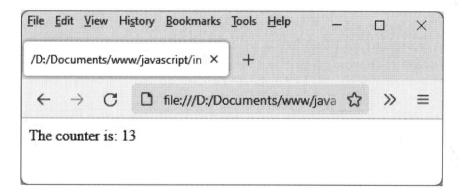

Figure 3.6 – Incrementing the counter in the component

Inserting a component from an external file

Rather than defining the component directly in the HTML page, it is preferable to define it in an external file. The component can be used in the HTML page thanks to the inclusion of the external file in the HTML page. For this, we use the concept of modules provided by JavaScript.

> **The Advantage of Components Defined in an External File**
> The advantage of defining the component in an external file is to be able to include this file in several different HTML pages, and therefore to use the component in several different applications.

The `<counter>` component is defined in an external `counter.js` file as follows:

`<counter>` component definition (counter.js file)

```
const Counter = {
  data() {
    return {
      count: 0
    }
  },
  template : "The counter is: {{count}}",
  created() {
    setInterval(() => {
      this.count += 1;
    }, 1000)
  }
}

export default Counter;
```

The `<counter>` component is defined as an object, having `template`, `data`, and `created` properties. Its definition is similar to the one shown previously in the `app.component()` method.

The `export default Counter` instruction makes the component accessible in the other files where this module is imported.

The `<counter>` component can now be integrated into the main file of our application. We use the JavaScript `import` statement for this. The code will look as follows:

Importing the component into the program (index.html file)

```
<html>
  <head>
    <meta charset="utf-8" />
    <script src="https://unpkg.com/vue@next"></script>
  </head>

  <body>
```

```
        <div id="app"></div>
    </body>

    <script type="module">

        import Counter from "./counter.js";

        var app = Vue.createApp({
            components : {
                Counter:Counter
            },
            template : "<counter />"    // or "<Counter />"
        });

        var vm = app.mount("div#app");

    </script>

</html>
```

In the preceding code, to import the `counter.js` file and use the corresponding component, the following takes place:

- The `type="module"` attribute is indicated in the `<script>` tag. This allows the use of the `import` statement in the JavaScript statements of the `<script>` tag.
- We use the `import` statement to import the corresponding module.
- We declare the imported components in the new `components` section. Components are declared as an object. The names of the properties in this object correspond to the name used by the component in the templates (`<counter>` or `<Counter>`), while the values correspond to the name of the imported component (`Counter`).

> **Using HTTP Instead of the FILE Protocol**
>
> However, as we use the import of JavaScript modules, it is necessary to run our application on an HTTP server, and no longer with a simple drag and drop as before. Hence the use of the URL that begins with `http://localhost`. If you need to know how to install an HTTP server, you can, for example, use the documentation here: `https://developer.mozilla.org/en-US/docs/Learn/Common_questions/set_up_a_local_testing_server`.

In the following figure, we can see that creating a component directly in the HTML page or in an external file produces the same result:

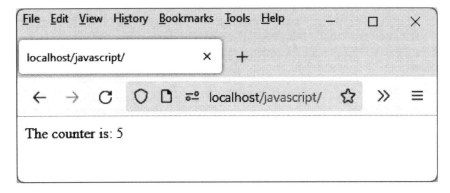

Figure 3.7 – Execution of the HTML file on an HTTP server (here, localhost)

The current component only has a simple reactive variable. It is possible, in a component, to add methods to it that will be used in the component. Now let's take a look at how to do it.

Adding methods in components

We have seen how to create reactive variables in a component, using the `data` section of the component. It is also possible to create methods in a component that can be used in the component template.

There are two ways to add methods to a component:

- The first is to define the method in the `methods` section of the component.
- The second is to create a so-called computed property that will be defined in the `computed` section of the component.

Let's look at these two ways to do it.

Defining methods in the methods section

For each incrementation of the counter, it should be necessary to display the time at which it occurs. A `time()` function would be very useful in the component, allowing us to display the time in the form HH:MM:SS. This `time()` function will be defined in the `methods` section of the component.

The `<counter>` component is modified to integrate the display of the time at the beginning of the line. We can achieve all this using the following code:

`<counter>` component displaying time (counter.js file)

```
const Counter = {
  data() {
    return {
      count: 0
    }
  },
  template : `{{time()}}    The counter is: {{count}}`,
  created() {
    setInterval(() => {
      this.count += 1;
    }, 1000)
  },
  methods : {
    time() {
      // return time as HH:MM:SS
      var date = new Date();
      var hour = date.getHours();
      var min = date.getMinutes();
      var sec = date.getSeconds();
      if (hour < 10) hour = "0" + hour;
      if (min < 10) min = "0" + min;
      if (sec < 10) sec = "0" + sec;
      return "" + hour + ":" + min + ":" + sec + " ";
    }
  }
}
```

```
}

export default Counter;
```

In the preceding code, the `time()` method is defined in the `methods` section and is then directly used in the component template within the double braces `{{ and }}`.

A method defined in the `methods` section can use the other methods of this section or the reactive variables of the `data` section by prefixing them with the `this` keyword.

The result is displayed in the following figure:

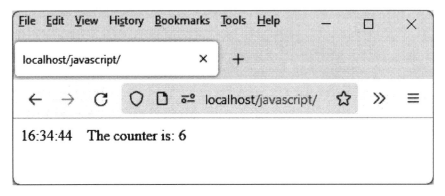

Figure 3.8 – Time display in the component

Vue.js allows you to define, in the form of methods, new variables that will be reactive. They are called computed properties. Let's see how to create and use them.

Defining computed properties in the computed section

A computed property is similar to a reactive variable. It is the result of the calculation performed on one or more reactive variables, and it will also be reactive. Any modification to one of the reactive variables associated with this computed property will cause it to be modified immediately.

Let's create a `countX2` property that calculates double the `count` variable as follows:

Defining a computed property countX2 in the component (counter.js file)

```
const Counter = {
  data() {
    return {
      count: 0
```

Adding methods in components 113

```
    }
  },
  template : `{{time()}}    The counter is:
  {{count}}, double is: {{countX2}}`,
  created() {
    setInterval(() => {
      this.count += 1;
    }, 1000)
  },
  methods : {
    time() {
      // return time as HH:MM:SS
      var date = new Date();
      var hour = date.getHours();
      var min = date.getMinutes();
      var sec = date.getSeconds();
      if (hour < 10) hour = "0" + hour;
      if (min < 10) min = "0" + min;
      if (sec < 10) sec = "0" + sec;
      return "" + hour + ":" + min + ":" + sec + " ";
    }
  },
  computed : {
    countX2() {
      return 2 * this.count;
    }
  }
}

export default Counter;
```

The output of the preceding code will look as follows:

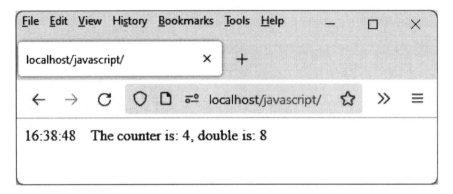

Figure 3.9 – Using a computed property

In the preceding figure, we can see the modification of the count variable. Every second leads to the automatic modification of the countX2 variable thanks to its definition in the computed section.

We have seen how to define methods and reactive variables in a component. Now let's see how to pass parameters to a component, using the component's attributes for this.

Using attributes in components

Attributes in a component allow it to pass parameters for its use. For example, we could use in the <counter> component a start attribute indicating at what value we start counting. If this attribute is not indicated, it is considered to be 0 (that is, counting starts at 0 as in the preceding code example).

For a component to be able to employ attributes during its use, it suffices to indicate the name of the attributes in the props section of the component. The component can access the attribute value using the this keyword (for example, this.start to access the start attribute in the component). We can see this in action in the following code:

Using the start attribute in the component (index.html file)

```
<html>
  <head>
    <meta charset="utf-8" />
    <script src="https://unpkg.com/vue@next"></script>
  </head>
```

```
<body>
  <div id="app"></div>
</body>

<script type="module">

  import Counter from "./counter.js";

  var app = Vue.createApp({
    components : {
      Counter:Counter
    },
    template : "<counter start='10' />"
  });

  var vm = app.mount("div#app");

</script>
</html>
```

In the following code, the attribute is passed when using the component, as is traditionally done in HTML. The value of the attribute here will be a character string `"10"` and not the value `10`:

Setting the start attribute in the <counter> component (counter.js file)

```
const Counter = {
  data() {
    return {
      count : parseInt(this.start),   // we initialize the
                                      // count to the value
                                      // of start
    }
  },
  template : `{{time()}}    The counter is:
{{count}}, double is: {{countX2}}`,
```

```
  created() {
    var timer = setInterval(() => {
      this.count += 1;
    }, 1000)
  },
  methods : {
    time() {
      // return time as HH:MM:SS
      var date = new Date();
      var hour = date.getHours();
      var min = date.getMinutes();
      var sec = date.getSeconds();
      if (hour < 10) hour = "0" + hour;
      if (min < 10) min = "0" + min;
      if (sec < 10) sec = "0" + sec;
      return "" + hour + ":" + min + ":" + sec + " ";
    }
  },
  computed : {
    countX2() {
      return 2 * this.count;
    }
  },
  props : [
    "start"
  ]
}

export default Counter;
```

In the preceding code, notice the use of the `parseInt()` function (defined as standard in JavaScript) to retrieve the value of `this.start` in integer form. Indeed, the attributes are transmitted in the form of character strings, hence the need to transform `this.start` into an integer value.

It is possible to avoid transforming the attribute value into an integer value. All you have to do is indicate when using the attribute that you want to keep the JavaScript value and not the character string. We prefix the name of the attribute with the character `:`, for example, `:start='10'`. In this case, the value `10` will be transmitted and not the string `"10"`.

This makes it possible to be able to transmit in the attributes any types of values: numeric values, character strings, arrays, or objects.

In the following figure we can see the counter has started from the value indicated in the `start` attribute:

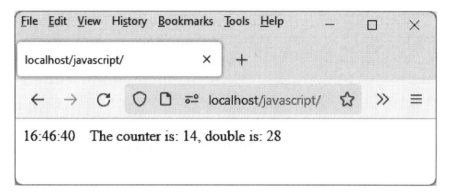

Figure 3.10 – Using the start attribute in the component

We have therefore seen how to create new attributes in a component. Vue.js has specific attributes as standard, which can be used in all components. These specific attributes, created by Vue.js, are called directives. We will study them now.

Using directives

Vue.js improves the writing of HTML code by offering to write its own components, as we have seen in the preceding section. The framework also makes it easier to write basic HTML code by adding new attributes to the HTML elements or to the components created. These new attributes are called directives.

> **Note**
> Directives are used exclusively in HTML elements or created components, that is, in the `template` section of components.

Their name begins with v-, so as not to be confused with other existing HTML attributes. The main directives are `v-if`, `v-else`, `v-show`, `v-for`, and `v-model`. They will be explained now.

The v-if and v-else directives

The `v-if` directive is used to specify a condition. If true, the HTML element (or component) will be inserted into the HTML page. Otherwise, it will not be present.

Let's use the `v-if` directive to indicate that we want to display the value of the counter only for values less than or equal to 20. As soon as the value 20 is exceeded, the counter is no longer displayed.

In the following snippet, we have only indicated the code of the `template` section of the component, knowing that the rest is not modified:

Using the v-if directive

```
template : `
  {{time()}}   
  <span v-if='count<=20'>The counter is: {{count}}</span>
`,
```

Using backticks ` and ` to define the template avoids having to manage the concatenation of character strings on several lines.

The `<span>` element on which the `v-if` directive is applied will be included in the HTML page only if the following condition is true: if `count<=20`. Beyond 20, only the time will be displayed without the counter value.

As long as the counter is less than or equal to 20, it is displayed as follows:

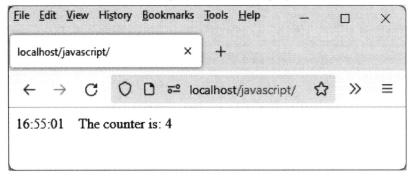

Figure 3.11 – Display of the counter whose value is less than 20

When the counter exceeds the value 20, it is no longer displayed:

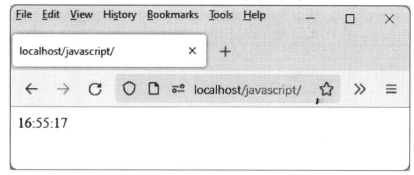

Figure 3.12 – Display as soon as the counter exceeds the value 20

The v-else directive is used to indicate an alternative when the condition expressed in v-if is false. The element on which the v-else directive is used will be inserted into the HTML page if the condition expressed in v-if is false.

Let's use the v-else directive to display another message when the counter exceeds the value 20:

Using the v-else directive

```
template : `
  {{time()}}   
  <span v-if='count<=20'>The counter is: {{count}}</span>
  <span v-else>The counter has exceeded 20, it is:
  {{count}}</span>
`,
```

When the counter exceeds the value 20, we now get the following:

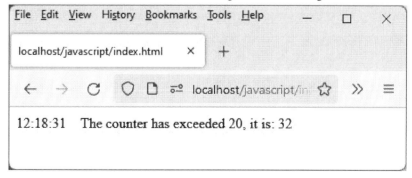

Figure 3.13 – Counter having exceeded the value 20

The v-show directive

The `v-show` directive is similar to the `v-if` directive. A condition is given next. If the condition is `true`, the element that uses the directive is displayed; otherwise, it is not.

The difference from the `v-if` directive is that the element, if not displayed, is only hidden, but it is still inserted into the page. Whereas with the `v-if` directive, the element is not inserted (if the condition is `false`).

The v-for directive

The `v-for` directive allows you to loop over a set of elements or over the properties of an object. For each iteration of the loop, it inserts the HTML element on which the directive is positioned.

Let us assume the `<counter>` component is a set of counters associated with the variable `counts`, which is a JavaScript array. Each counter is, in our example, a character string (for example, `"Counter 1"`), and we want to display the whole in the form of a list (see the following code snippets).

Let's look at the two possible forms of the `v-for` directive.

Using the directive v-for="count in counts"

Let's use the first form of the `v-for` directive. It allows access to each element of the array indicated in the directive (in our example, the JavaScript `counts` array):

Displaying counters as a list (counter.js file)

```js
const Counter = {
  data() {
    return {
      counts : ["Counter 1", "Counter 2", "Counter 3",
        "Counter 4", "Counter 5"]
    }
  },

  template : `
    <ul>
      <li v-for="count in counts">
        <span>{{count}}</span>
      </li>
```

```
    </ul>
  `,
}

export default Counter;
```

In the preceding code, we have positioned the `v-for` directive on the element that we want to repeat (in this case, the `<li>` element). The value associated with the `v-for` directive is a character string of the form `"count in counts"`, knowing that `counts` is the variable on which we are iterating. The `count` variable thus corresponds to each of the elements of the `counts` array:

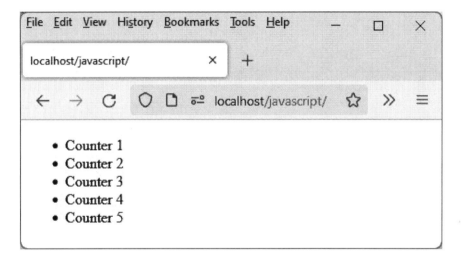

Figure 3.14 – Using the v-for directive

Using the directive v-for="(count, index) in counts"

A second form of the `v-for` directive gives access to each element of the array as before, but also to its index (starting from 0):

Displaying counters and their index (counter.js file)

```
const Counter = {
  data() {
    return {
      counts : ["Counter 1", "Counter 2", "Counter 3",
        "Counter 4", "Counter 5"]
```

```
        }
      },
      template : `
        <ul>
          <li v-for="(count, index) in counts">
            <span>Index {{index}} : {{count}}</span>
          </li>
        </ul>
        `,
}

export default Counter;
```

On running the preceding code, the following is displayed:

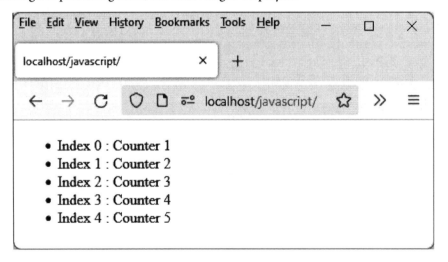

Figure 3.15 – Using index in the v-for directive

Using the key attribute with the v-for directive

The v-for directive can also be used to display large lists, for which reactivity must be maintained. That is, changing the reactive variable specified in the v-for directive should update the corresponding displayed list.

To perform the update as quickly as possible, Vue.js uses a special attribute (to be used only for this specific case) named key. This attribute can be positioned after the v-for directive. Its value must be unique for each item in the list. For example, the value of the index being unique for each list element can be used as a value in the key attribute:

Using the key attribute with the v-for directive

```
<li v-for="(count, index) in counts" :key="index">
```

In the preceding code, the value of the attribute is a JavaScript expression (the variable `index`). We use `:key` and not just `key`; otherwise, the attribute would constantly have the string `"index"` as its value (instead of the value of the variable `index`).

Of course, adding the `key` attribute does not produce any display changes, but the performance will be visible on subsequent changes to the displayed list (it helps Vue.js to keep track of the element and prevent unnecessary re-rendering).

The v-model directive

The `v-model` directive is used to manage form elements during an interaction (input in a field, a click on a checkbox or radio button, the choice of an element in a list).

The `v-model` directive is used to immediately retrieve the result of input or selection in a reactive variable without having to perform any particular processing. It's the `v-model` directive that performs this update (of the reactive variable) for us.

We use the `v-model` directive in the form `v-model="varname"`, where `varname` is the name of a reactive variable that will be updated on input or selection.

Let's use the `v-model` directive in a form input field. To clearly see what happens with or without its use, we display two input fields: one managed without `v-model`, the other with:

Using the v-model directive in an input field (counter.js file)

```
const Counter = {
  data() {
    return {
      count : 10
    }
  },
  template : `
    Without v-model:
      <input type="text" :value="count" />   
      count = {{count}} <br><br>
    With v-model:
```

```
            <input type="text" v-model="count" />   
            count = {{count}}
        ,
}

export default Counter;
```

Here are some notes on the preceding program:

- The first <input> field does not use v-model, but only uses the value attribute, which will be updated based on the count variable.
- The second <input> field uses the v-model directive associated with the same count variable.
- The value of the count variable is displayed after the two input fields.

When the program is launched, the value of the reactive variable count is transferred to the value attribute of the first input field, as well as to the second. This produces the initialization of the contents of the two input fields as seen here:

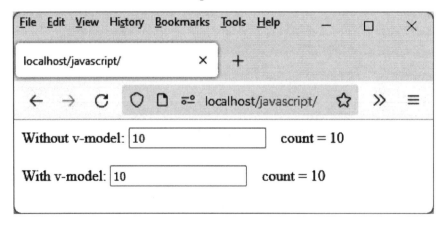

Figure 3.16 – Display when starting the program

If we change the contents of the first input field (which is not used with v-model), we will see something like this:

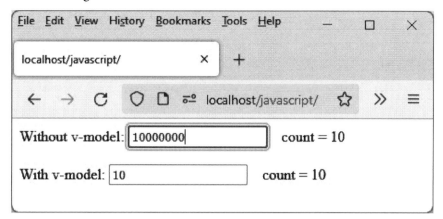

Figure 3.17 – Editing an input field without v-model

Note that modifying the input field (without v-model) has no effect on the reactive variable associated with it.

Now let's modify the contents of the second input field, managed by v-model:

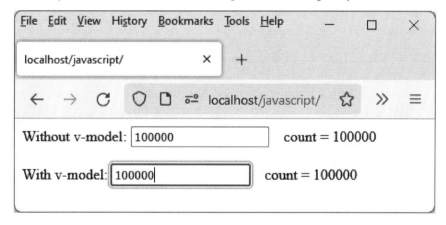

Figure 3.18 – Editing an input field with v-model

We now see that the use of v-model causes the immediate modification of the reactive variable to which it is associated, which then causes the modification of the value attribute of the first input field (because it is linked to the reactive variable).

Summary

In this chapter, we have mainly studied how to create a component and methods or attributes associated with it.

It is now necessary to study how to manage the actions of the user in a component, then how to assemble the components to form an application.

4
Advanced Concepts of Vue.js

In this chapter, we look at advanced uses of Vue.js. We will study the handling of events in components, then the assembly of the various components in order to form a whole Vue.js application.

Why is it important to know how to handle events in components?

A Vue.js component is often a set of HTML elements, like building blocks, such as buttons, lists, and input fields. It is therefore essential to know how to manage the interaction of these elements with the possible actions of the user, such as clicking on a button, entering a value in an input field, or selecting an element from a list.

Similarly, why is it important to know how to assemble the components?

A web application brings together many elements, which in the end, will represent the application as a whole. The principle of Vue.js is to break down an application into components, then assemble them to form the complete application. We will have to learn how to divide an application into components, then assemble them by allowing them, for example, to share data.

We end this chapter by showing how we can easily produce visual effects on your pages thanks to Vue.js.

Here are the main topics we explain in the following pages:

- Managing events
- Assembling components
- Using visual effects

Technical requirements

You can find the code files for this chapter on GitHub at: `https://github.com/PacktPublishing/JavaScript-from-Frontend-to-Backend/blob/main/Chapter%204.zip`.

Managing events

Now let's see how to handle events with Vue.js. To do this, use the `v-on` directive, followed by the character `:` and the name of the event to be handled. For example, if you want to perform a particular process when a button is clicked, we will use the `click` event on the button and we will write `v-on:click` to handle the `click` event. The value of the directive (which follows the = sign) corresponds to the JavaScript expression to be executed (either a statement or a function call).

> **Tip**
> Vue.js makes it easier to write `v-on:click` by writing `@click` more simply. This rule is valid for all events.

In this example, we will implement a button that increments a reactive variable `count` on each click. We will also define an `incr()` method in the `methods` section of the component that increments the `count` variable:

Increment counter count (counter.js file)

```
const Counter = {
  data() {
    return {
      count : 0
    }
  },
  template : `
```

Managing events

```
    <button @click="count++">Increment counter by
count++</button>
         count = {{count}} <br><br>
    <button @click="incr()">Increment counter by
incr()</button>
         count = {{count}}
`,
  methods : {
    incr() {
      this.count++;
    }
  }
}

export default Counter;
```

We have defined two buttons for which the value of @click is as follows:

- @click="count++" (first button)
- @click="incr()" (second button)

We thus show the equivalence of these forms of writing.

The counter is incremented by 1 with each click of the buttons.

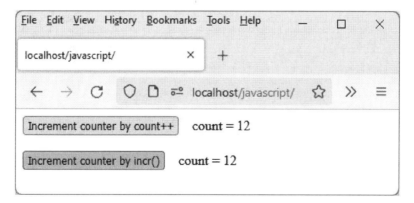

Figure 4.1 – Button click management

It is possible to write several method calls in a row during the processing to be performed (separated by a comma or a semicolon). It is enough that these methods are defined in the `methods` section of the component.

For example, `@click="incr();incr()"` allows the `incr()` method to be executed twice each time the button is clicked.

We have explained here how to catch an event and handle it in a method defined in the `methods` section of the component. Let's go further by using the parameters transmitted in the received event, for example, knowing which key on the keyboard was pressed.

Using the $event parameter

Vue.js provides access to the `Event` object associated with the event. This object can then be used to get additional information about the event. The information is different depending on the type of event:

- Mouse coordinates or buttons clicked on the mouse for a mouse-related event
- Keyboard key used, or the combination of keys pressed (*Ctrl*, *Shift*, *Esc*, and so on) for a keyboard-related event

The `Event` object can be accessed from the `$event` variable. It can be passed as a parameter to a processing method. This parameter will then be retrieved in the event processing function.

Let's see two examples of how to use this parameter when entering characters in an edit control:

- By displaying an error message as soon as the numerical value entered equals or exceeds the value 100
- By prohibiting the entry of characters other than numeric characters if the edit control can only contain numbers (this is an improvement of the previous example)

Checking that the entered value is less than 100

Let's use the `$event` parameter to check that the content of the `counter` input field is less than 100. If so, the `count` variable is updated with the entered value; otherwise, an error message is displayed.

To achieve this, we use the `blur` event on the input field, and in the processing of the event, we retrieve the value of the input field. A reactive `message` variable is used to display an error message, if necessary:

> **Note**
> The `blur` event is triggered when leaving the input field, for example, by clicking outside the input field.

Display an error message if the counter is greater than 100 (counter.js file)

```
const Counter = {
  data() {
    return {
      count : 0,
      message : ""
    }
  },
  template : `
    count (less than 100): <input type="text"
    :value="count" @blur="valid($event)" />
       count = {{count}}
    <br><br>
    <span>{{message}}</span>
  `,
  methods : {
    valid(event) {
      this.message = "";   // reset of the error message
                           // before each check
      if (event.target.value < 100) this.count =
      event.target.value;
      else this.message = "Error: count must be less than 100";
    }
  }
}

export default Counter;
```

The $event parameter is passed to the `valid(event)` processing function. The `event.target` property provides direct access to the HTML element. Its `value` property contains the value of the field.

If you type a value less than 100 (here, 45), the counter is updated:

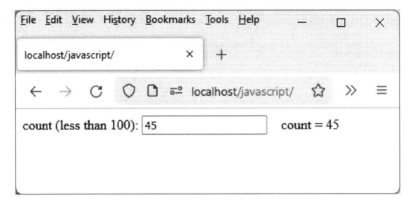

Figure 4.2 – Entering an authorized value

If you type a value greater than 100 (for example, `150`), an error is displayed and the old value of the counter (`45`) is restored.

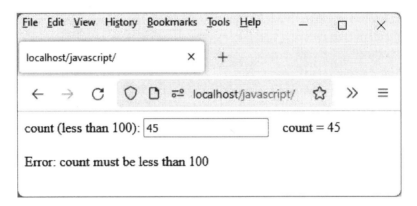

Figure 4.3 – Entering a prohibited value

Then, we'll look at another use of `$event` parameter-allowing only digits to be entered.

Allowing only digits to be entered

Another use of the `$event` parameter can be to only allow numbers to be entered into the field. Other keyboard keys are prohibited (except the *Backspace* and *Delete* keys, the right and left arrow keys, and the *Tab* key).

For this, we use the `keydown` event, which is triggered each time a key on the keyboard is pressed:

Disallow input of non-numeric characters (counter.js file)

```
const Counter = {
  data() {
    return {
      count : 0,
      message : ""
    }
  },
  template : `
    count (less than 100):
    <input type="text" :value="count" @blur="valid($event)"
    @keydown="verif($event)"/>
         count = {{count}}
    <br><br>
    <span>{{message}}</span>
  `,
  methods : {
    valid(event) {
      this.message = "";  // reset of the error message
                          // before each check
      if (event.target.value < 100) this.count = event.target.value;
      else this.message = "Error: count must be less than 100";
    },
    verif(event) {
      console.log(event.key);   // display in the console
                                // the value of the key
                                // pressed
      if (event.key != "Backspace" && event.key != "Delete"
      &&
          event.key != "ArrowLeft" && event.key !=
          "ArrowRight" &&
          event.key != "Tab") {
```

```
                // forbid the key if it is not numeric
                if (event.key < "0" || event.key > "9")
                event.preventDefault();   // forbidden key
            }
        }
    }
}

export default Counter;
```

The event used to filter the keys corresponds to `keydown` and gets activated when pressing a key on the keyboard. We therefore indicate to process each key press using the `verif()` method defined in the `methods` section.

> **Using event.key and event.preventDefault()**
>
> The `event.key` parameter contains the code of the key pressed. The key code is between "0" and "9" for a numeric value. To prohibit the other keys, we use the `event.preventDefault()` method (defined in JavaScript), which indicates not to take into account the event, therefore the pressing of the prohibited key.

We learned how to create a component in *Chapter 3, Getting Started with Vue.js*, and how to manage events in it (at the beginning of this chapter). A full application is composed of several components. Let's now explain how to proceed to assemble several components to form a complete application.

Assembling components

Vue.js divides an application into a set of components. These components are then assembled to form the final application.

Let's study an example of how to create components and then assemble the created components. The goal is to use three counters (associated with three input fields) like the one in the previous example, then display the total of these counters. The total updates, as numbers are typed into each of the input fields.

We will create two components for this:

- The `<counter>` component is used to manage a counter.
- The `<counters>` component allows you to manage the three counters together and display the total.

The `index.html` file will display the `<counters>` component in its `template` section:

index.html file

```
<html>
  <head>
    <meta charset="utf-8" />
    <script src="https://unpkg.com/vue@next"></script>
  </head>

  <body>
    <div id="app"></div>
  </body>

  <script type="module">

    import Counters from "./counters.js";

    var app = Vue.createApp({
      components : {
        Counters:Counters
      },
      template : `
        <counters />
      `,
    });

    var vm = app.mount("div#app");
```

```
        </script>

</html>
```

The included `counters.js` file describes the `<counters>` component. It partly repeats what has been explained in the previous sections, adding new concepts that we'll now describe.

These new concepts will explain how a parent component communicates with its child components (thanks to attributes, called `props`) and how a child component communicates with its parent component (thanks to events and the `$emit()` method).

These two concepts make it possible to assemble the components between them by allowing them to communicate between a child component and a parent component.

Using $emit() to communicate with a parent component

Let's first look at the `<counter>` component file, which describes a counter associated with an input field:

`<counter>` component (counter.js file)

```
const Counter = {
  data() {
    return {
      count : 0,
      old_value : 0
    }
  },
  template : `
    <input type="text" v-model="count"
      @keydown="verif($event)"
      @input="calcul()"
      @focus="focus()"
      @blur="blur()" />
  `,
  methods : {
    verif(event) {
```

```
      if (event.key != "Backspace" && event.key != "Delete" &&
          event.key != "ArrowLeft" && event.key !=
          "ArrowRight" &&
          event.key != "Tab") {
        // forbid the key if it is not numeric
        if (event.key < "0" || event.key > "9")
        event.preventDefault();   // key forbidden
      }
      this.old_value = event.target.value;
    },
    calcul() {
      this.$emit("sub", this.old_value || 0);   // subtract
                                                // old value
      this.$emit("add", this.count || 0);       // add new value
    },
    focus() {
      if (this.old_value == "0") this.count = "";
    },
    blur() {
      if (!parseInt(this.count)) {
        this.old_value = 0;
        this.count = 0;
      }
    }
  },
  emits : ["sub", "add"]     // declare events emitted to
                             // the parent
}

export default Counter;
```

138   Advanced Concepts of Vue.js

The `<counter>` component has been enriched with new methods, linked to new events to be taken into account during input. Also, a new reactive variable, `old_value`, has been created:

- The `old_value` variable contains the value that was entered in the field before pressing the key on the keyboard.
- The `count` variable contains the value that was entered in the field after pressing the key on the keyboard.

Why make this distinction? Because to calculate the total of all the counters, it will be necessary, with each typed key, to remove the previous value from the field (before pressing the key) and add the new value (after pressing the key).

Each keypress is handled by the `input` event, which here calls the `calcul()` method. As the calculation associated with the total of the three counters is performed at the higher level (in the `<counters>` component, which is the parent component), you must indicate to this parent component the sum to subtract (`old_value`) and the sum to add (`count`). This is done by sending `"sub"` and `"add"` events, using the `$emit(eventName, value)` method.

> **About the $emit(eventName, value) Method**
>
> The `$emit(eventName, value)` method, executed from a component, sends the `eventName` event to the parent component, which can process it using the `@eventName` directive. The `value` parameter corresponds to the value to be transmitted if necessary.

In addition, we indicate in the `emits` section of the component the list of events that this component can emit to its parent.

This way of communicating between a child component (here, the `<counter>` component) and its parent (here, the `<counters>` component), using events, is the one recommended by Vue.js.

Now let's see the description of the `<counters>` component, which encompasses the three counters and the calculation of the total counters as you type in each one:

`<counters>` component (counters.js file)

```
import Counter from "./counter.js";
const Counters = {
  data() {
```

```
      return {
        total : 0
      }
    },
    components : {
      Counter:Counter
    },
    template : `
        Counter 1 : <counter @add="add($event)"
        @sub="sub($event)" /> <br>
        Counter 2 : <counter @add="add($event)"
        @sub="sub($event)" /> <br>
        Counter 3 : <counter @add="add($event)"
        @sub="sub($event)" /> <br><br>
        Total : {{total}} <br>
    `,
    methods : {
      add(value) {
        this.total += parseInt(value);
      },
      sub(value) {
        this.total -= parseInt(value);
      }
    },
}

export default Counters;
```

The "add" and "sub" events emitted in the <counter> child component are processed in the attributes of the <counter> component when used. The add(value) and sub(value) processing methods are registered in the parent component, which allows the value of the total to be changed each time a numeric key is pressed on the keyboard.

As you type in the fields, **Total** updates:

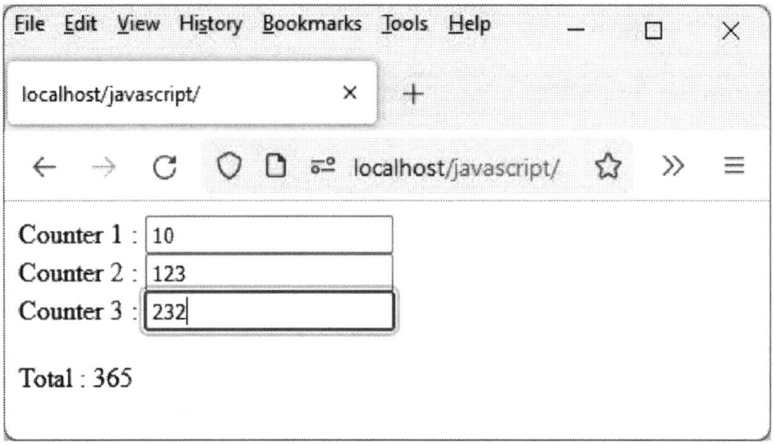

Figure 4.4 – Calculation of the sum of the three counters

We have seen how to communicate from a component to its parent using events. Now let's look at how to communicate in the other direction, from a component to its child. For this, we use attributes called props here.

Using props to communicate with children

We have seen that the communication of information from a child component to its parent is done with events. Communication in the reverse direction, from parent to child, is done through attributes called props. We have already seen the use of these attributes in the previous chapter, in the *Using attributes in components* section.

In this example, we will improve the `<counters>` component so that we tell it the number of counters we want to display. For this, we use the nb attribute in the component. For example, we will write `<counters nb="5" />` to display 5 counters on the page. Each counter is displayed as in the previous form, namely `Counter` followed by its index starting from 1 (see *Figure 4.5*).

First, we will modify the `index.html` file to write the `<counters>` component using the nb attribute. Let's modify the `index.html` file previously used:

Using <counters nb="5" /> (index.html file)

```
<html>
  <head>
    <meta charset="utf-8" />
    <script src="https://unpkg.com/vue@next"></script>
```

```html
  </head>

  <body>
    <div id="app"></div>
  </body>

  <script type="module">

    import Counters from "./counters.js";

    var app = Vue.createApp({
      components : {
        Counters:Counters
      },
      template : `
        <counters nb="5" />
      `,
    });

    var vm = app.mount("div#app");

  </script>
</html>
```

Now, we will modify the `counters.js` file to integrate the new "nb" props into the component:

Integration of the nb props in the <counters> component (counters.js file)

```js
import Counter from "./counter.js";

const Counters = {
  data() {
    return {
      total : 0
    }
```

```
  },
  components : {
    Counter:Counter
  },
  props : ["nb"],
  computed : {
    NB() {
      var tab = [];
      for(var i = 0; i < this.nb; i++) tab.push(i+1);
      return tab;
    }
  },
  template : `
    <div v-for="i in NB">
      Counter {{i}} : <counter @add="add($event)"
      @sub="sub($event)" />
    </div>
    <br>
    Total : {{total}} <br>
  `,
  methods : {
    add(value) {
      this.total += parseInt(value);
    },
    sub(value) {
      this.total -= parseInt(value);
    }
  },
}
export default Counters;
```

The "nb" props are listed in the component's props section. To display a list of counters, use the v-for directive on a <div> element.

> **How to Use the v-for Directive**
>
> For the value of the v-for directive, you must specify an array to browse. To do this, we transform the value of the "nb" props into an array [1, 2, 3, ..., nb]. This is done using a computed property named NB, which returns the desired array.

The number of counters indicated when using the <counters nb="5"> component is now displayed.

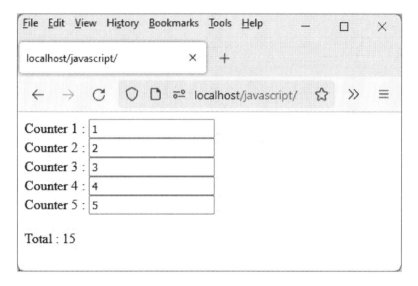

Figure 4.5 – Displaying five counters

We end the study of the Vue.js components here, which come together to form a full application.

Now, let's examine an aspect of Vue.js that helps you produce visual effects, allowing, for example, making HTML elements displayed on the HTML page appear or disappear using a visual effect.

Using visual effects

Visual effects make it possible to make HTML pages more dynamic by bringing visual animations to them. For example, to delete an item in a list, you can make it gradually disappear using an opacity effect rather than deleting it directly without using a visual effect.

It is possible to use visual effects with Vue.js, in particular, to make elements appear or disappear from the page. Visual effects that do not make HTML elements appear or disappear from the page (for example, making an element move by clicking on it) are also possible with Vue.js. You can refer to `https://vuejs.org/guide/extras/animation.html` for more details on these types of animations. We do not explain these effects here because the available documentation is clear enough to use them.

Going forward in this chapter, we will learn about the visual effects that are related to the appearance or disappearance of one or more elements on the page.

The element we want to help appear or disappear (using the visual effect) must be inserted in a component named `<transition>`. This component is used by Vue.js to produce the effect.

Moreover, Vue.js uses the definition of CSS classes in which the CSS properties of the effect are described. Simply define the contents of the CSS classes (described in the following section), and Vue.js uses them at the appropriate times to achieve the effect.

The CSS classes used by Vue.js on an element depend on the state of the element: should it appear or disappear? Depending on its state (visible or not), the CSS classes differ.

When the element appears

When the HTML element should appear, the names of the CSS classes used by Vue.js begin with the character string `"v-enter"`. The class name then contains the suffix `"-from"` or `"-to"`, which will be used to describe the CSS properties of the element at the start of the effect (with `"-from"`) or at the end of the effect (with `"-to"`).

CSS classes used by Vue.js

So, we will have the following two CSS classes:

- `v-enter-from`: This CSS class describes the CSS properties at the start of the element's appear effect.

- `v-enter-to`: This CSS class describes the CSS properties at the end of the element's appear effect.

> **Note**
>
> Note that at the start of the appear effect, the element is not visible, but the CSS properties described in the `v-enter-from` class are applied to it immediately. If, for example, we enter the CSS `opacity` property equal to 1 in the CSS properties of the `v-enter-from` class, the element becomes immediately visible as soon as the appearance effect starts.

Since the `v-enter-to` class describes the CSS properties of the element at the end of the effect, when the effect completes, Vue.js removes that CSS class from the element.

We thus see that the CSS classes `v-enter-from` and `v-enter-to` are used to describe the CSS properties of an element during the effect but are no longer used afterward on the element (i.e., outside the duration of the effect).

The appearance effect progresses the CSS properties described in `v-enter-from` to those described in `v-enter-to`. For this, Vue.js uses the `v-enter-active` class, which describes how each of the CSS properties evolves.

Example content of CSS classes

Let's look at some sample content from each of the three CSS classes mentioned above, `v-enter-from`, `v-enter-to`, and `v-enter-active`:

v-enter-from class example

```
.v-enter-from {
  opacity: 0;
  background-color:#FFCCCC;
}
```

Here, we indicate that the element will be invisible at the start of the effect (`opacity:0`) and will have a background color (`background-color:#FFCCCC`):

v-enter-to class example

```
.v-enter-to {
  opacity: 0.5;
  background-color:black;
}
```

Here, we indicate that the element will be half visible at the end of the effect (`opacity:0.5`) and will have a black background (`background-color:black`):

v-enter-active class example

```
.v-enter-active {
  transition: opacity 2s, background-color 2s;
}
```

Here, we indicate that the CSS `opacity` and `background-color` properties must evolve, each for two seconds. As all the specified CSS properties evolve for the same amount of time, we can simplify the code by writing it in shortened form. Here's how:

v-enter-active class example (simplified form)

```css
.v-enter-active {
  transition: all 2s;
}
```

The `all` keyword overrides all specified CSS properties.

Using CSS classes

Now let's show how to use these CSS classes in a program using a button that displays a paragraph with effect. The role of the button will be to hide or display, alternatively, a paragraph on which the effect will occur when the paragraph appears.

This shows how the `v-enter-from`, `v-enter-to`, and `v-enter-active` CSS classes are used by Vue.js to produce an effect when an element appears on the page:

Use a button to produce the appearance effect (index.html file)

```html
<html>
  <head>
    <meta charset="utf-8" />
    <script src="https://unpkg.com/vue@next"></script>

    <style type="text/css">
      .v-enter-from {
        opacity: 0;
        background-color:#FFCCCC;
      }
      .v-enter-to {
        opacity: 0.5;
        background-color:black;
      }
      .v-enter-active {
        transition: opacity 2s, background-color 2s;
      }
```

```
      </style>
   </head>

   <body>
      <div id="app"></div>
   </body>

   <script>

      var app = Vue.createApp({
         data() {
            return {
               show: false    // initially hidden
            }
         },
         template : `
            <button @click="show=!show">Produce the
            effect</button>
            <transition>
              <p v-if="show">
                 Paragraph 1
              </p>
            </transition>
         `,
      });

      var vm = app.mount("div#app");

   </script>
</html>
```

We have described the contents of the v-enter-from, v-enter-to, and v-enter-active CSS classes, which will be used by Vue.js to produce the effect. Then we inserted the **Produce an effect** button in the page so that when the button is clicked, the paragraph on which the effect is set to occur will alternately be hidden or displayed. To do this, the paragraph was inserted in an HTML <transition> element, thus allowing Vue.js to know the element on which to apply the effect.

The paragraph is hidden at startup (because the reactive variable show is set to false). Clicking the **Produce the effect** button changes the value of the show variable to true, which starts the effect.

> **Note**
>
> The effect is started on the paragraph thanks to the <transition> component, which includes the paragraph to be displayed. It is thanks to this <transition> component that Vue.js knows the element on which to produce the effect.

Notice that the effect lasts two seconds as indicated in the CSS transition property, and when the effect is finished, the CSS classes are removed from the <p> element, which then becomes a normal paragraph (without background color and with an opacity of 1). So, you see that the paragraph has an opacity of 0.5 at the end of the effect (the one indicated in v-enter-to), then suddenly changes to an opacity of 1 when the v-enter-to class is removed by Vue.js at the end of the effect.

> **Note**
>
> It is therefore preferable to indicate in the v-enter-to class the CSS values of the element when it no longer produces an effect, in order to make the effect more harmonious.

Let's run the previous program. When the program is launched, the paragraph is hidden:

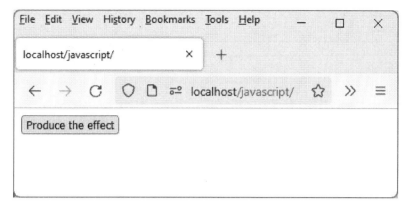

Figure 4.6 – The paragraph is hidden when the program is launched

After clicking the **Produce the effect** button, the paragraph begins to appear, according to the CSS properties indicated in the v-enter-from, v-enter-to, and v-enter-active classes.

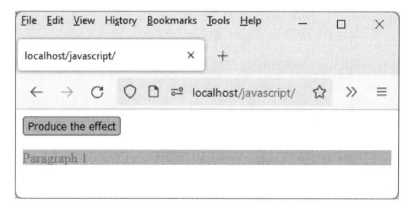

Figure 4.7 – After clicking on the Produce the effect button, the paragraph appears progressively

Just before the effect ends, the paragraph has the CSS properties set in the `v-enter-to` class, so its background color is black, but with an opacity of 0.5, the background color remains gray, and the paragraph text is not visible.

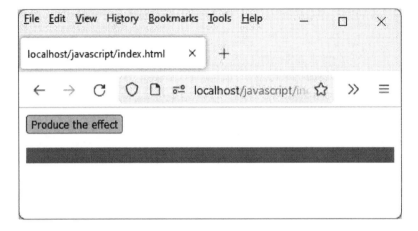

Figure 4.8 – Paragraph just before the end of the effect

At the end of the effect, the CSS classes are removed so that the paragraph appears in a normal way, in black and without a background color.

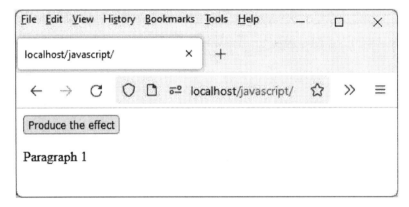

Figure 4.9 – Paragraph at the end of the appear effect

Once the paragraph has appeared, clicking on the **Produce the effect** button makes it disappear immediately (without producing any effect). This is due to the reactive variable `show` being set to `false` when the button is clicked.

We have seen the different classes and stages when an element appears on the page. Now let's see what happens when an element disappears from the page. We will see that there are many similarities between the appearance and disappearance of the element.

When the element disappears

When the element should disappear, Vue.js uses CSS classes similar to the previous ones, replacing the string `"enter"` with the string `"leave"`.

CSS classes used by Vue.js

So, we will have the following two CSS classes:

- `v-leave-from`: This CSS class describes the CSS properties at the start of the element's disappearing effect.
- `v-leave-to`: This CSS class describes the CSS properties at the end of the element's disappearing effect.

The disappearing effect is going to be to progress the CSS properties described in `v-leave-from` to those described in `v-leave-to`. After the effect is complete, the `v-leave-to` class is removed from the element's CSS classes.

To progress CSS properties between the values shown in these two classes, Vue.js uses the `v-leave-active` CSS class, which describes the progression of CSS properties.

Example content of CSS classes

Let's look at some example content from each of the three CSS classes mentioned above: `v-leave-from`, `v-leave-to`, and `v-leave-active`:

v-leave-from class example

```
.v-leave-from {
  opacity: 1;
  background-color:#FFCCCC;
}
```

Here, we indicate that the element will be fully visible at the start of the effect (`opacity:1`) and will have a background color (`background-color:#FFCCCC`):

v-leave-to class example

```
.v-leave-to {
  opacity: 0;
  background-color:black;
}
```

Here, we indicate that the element will be invisible at the end of the effect (`opacity:0`) and will have a black background color (`background-color:black`):

v-leave-active class example

```
.v-leave-active {
  transition: opacity 2s, background-color 2s;
}
```

Here, we indicate that the CSS `opacity` and `background-color` properties must evolve, each for two seconds. As all the specified CSS properties evolve for the same amount of time, you can simplify the code by writing it in shortened form:

v-leave-active class example

```
.v-leave-active {
  transition: all 2s;
}
```

The `all` keyword overrides all specified CSS properties.

Using CSS classes

Now let's show how to use these CSS classes in a program, using a button that hides a paragraph with an effect. It's almost the same program as before, but here we produce an effect when the paragraph disappears:

Using a button to produce the disappearing effect (index.html file)

```
<html>
  <head>
    <meta charset="utf-8" />
    <script src="https://unpkg.com/vue@next"></script>

    <style type="text/css">
      .v-leave-from {
        opacity: 1;
        background-color:#FFCCCC;
      }
      .v-leave-to {
```

```
      opacity: 0;
      background-color:black;
    }
    .v-leave-active {
      transition: all 2s;
    }
  </style>
</head>

<body>
  <div id="app"></div>
</body>

<script>

  var app = Vue.createApp({
    data() {
      return {
        show: true    // visible at start
      }
    },
    template : `
      <button @click="show=!show">Produce the effect</button>
      <transition>
        <p v-if="show">
          Paragraph 1
        </p>
      </transition>
    `,
  });

  var vm = app.mount("div#app");

</script>

</html>
```

The `v-leave-from` class is applied at the beginning of the effect. It indicates that the element is visible (`opacity` at 1) and has a background color #FFCCCC (salmon).

The `v-leave-to` class indicates the values of CSS properties when the effect ends. The paragraph becomes invisible (`opacity` at 0) and has a black background color. But as the element becomes more and more invisible (`opacity` tends toward 0), the black background color also becomes less and less visible.

If we write the `enter` and `leave` classes in the CSS part in the same program, with each click on the button, we obtain an effect of appearing or disappearing for the paragraph concerned.

The CSS classes used here have fixed names, regardless of the effect used. This does not allow using multiple effects, as the visual effects would all use the same CSS class names.

For this, Vue.js allows you to give a name to each effect, and thus be able to use different CSS class names.

Using a name for the effect

Classes of type `"v-enter-xxx"` or `"v-leave-xxx"` can be renamed to symbolize the effect with which they are associated. We just need to replace the character string `"v-"` with the name of the effect followed by `"-"`.

For example, `"v-enter-from"` will be replaced by `"fade-enter-from"` to give the name `"fade"` to the effect. We then add the `name="fade"` attribute to the `<transition>` component, indicating `<transition name="fade">`.

This allows us to integrate several effects into our application, by defining the CSS classes corresponding to each effect.

The previous program, integrating the effect named `"fade"` in the paragraph, is then written as follows:

Fade effect (index.html file)

```
<html>
  <head>
    <meta charset="utf-8" />
    <script src="https://unpkg.com/vue@next"></script>

    <style type="text/css">
      .fade-leave-from {
```

```
      opacity: 1;
      background-color:#FFCCCC;
    }
    .fade-leave-to {
      opacity: 0;
      background-color:black;
    }
    .fade-leave-active {
      transition: all 2s;
    }

    .fade-enter-from {
      opacity: 0;
      background-color:#FFCCCC;
    }
    .fade-enter-to {
      opacity: 1;
      background-color:black;
    }
    .fade-enter-active {
      transition: opacity 2s, background-color 2s;
    }
  </style>
</head>

<body>
  <div id="app"></div>
</body>

<script>

  var app = Vue.createApp({
    data() {
      return {
        show: true
      }
```

```
    },
    template : `
      <button @click="show=!show">Produce the
      effect</button>
      <transition name="fade">
        <p v-if="show">
          Paragraph 1
        </p>
      </transition>
      `,
  });

  var vm = app.mount("div#app");

</script>

</html>
```

The `<transition>` component can only have one element, which will be the one on which the effect will occur. To include multiple elements, you must use the `<transition-group>` component, which we explain below.

Producing an effect on several elements

The `<transition>` component can contain only one element. When the effect must be applied to several elements, it is necessary to create several `<transition>` components or group the elements in a `<transition-group>` component. In this example, let's look at using the `<transition-group>` component:

Using the <transition-group> component

```
<transition-group name="fade">
  <p v-if="show">
    Paragraph 1
  </p>
  <p v-if="show">
    Paragraph 2
```

```
    </p>
</transition-group>
```

The elements on which the effect occurs (here, the two paragraphs) are grouped in a `<transition-group>` element instead of the `<transition>` element that was used previously when there was a single paragraph on which the effect was produced.

Now, we will take a look at how to write the CSS classes associated with some classic effects.

Examples of commonly used effects

Below are some descriptions of effects. With a few lines of CSS code, you can easily produce classic effects such as the shrinking/enlargement of a paragraph (shrink effect), its gradual disappearance/appearance (opacity effect), and its vertical displacement (ymove effect). You are free to choose the names given to these effects and symbolize the effect produced.

The shrink effect

To use the shrink effect (here called `"shrink"`), we use the CSS `font-size` property.

At the beginning of the effect, the paragraph is of normal size:

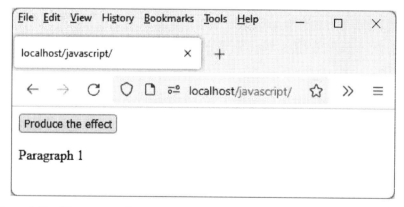

Figure 4.10 – The paragraph is normal size at the beginning of the disappearing effect

Once the effect has started following a click on the button, the paragraph decreases in size until it disappears.

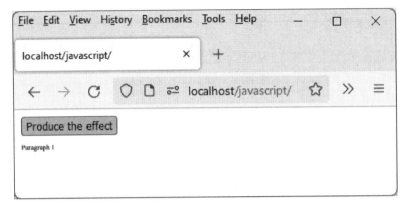

Figure 4.11 – The paragraph decreases in size until it disappears

Once the paragraph has disappeared, it can reappear after another click on the button. The paragraph size will increase until it reaches its normal size:

CSS classes to handle shrink effect

```
.shrink-leave-from {
}
.shrink-leave-to {
  font-size: 0px;
}
.shrink-leave-active {
  transition: all 2s;
}

.shrink-enter-from {
  font-size: 0px;
}
.shrink-enter-to {
}
.shrink-enter-active {
  transition: all 2s;
}
```

The CSS class `shrink-leave-to` indicates, for the disappearance effect, to go to a font size of 0px, that is, a reduction to 0 of the font size for the paragraph, which makes the paragraph invisible.

The `shrink-enter-from` CSS class tells the effect to start with a font size of 0px, gradually growing to the normal paragraph size when visible.

If CSS properties are not indicated in a starting class (for example, the `shrink-leave-from` class does not contain the `font-size` property), this means that the current value of this CSS property is used in the element.

Similarly, if CSS properties are not indicated in an arrival class (for example, the `shrink-enter-to` class does not contain the `font-size` property), this means that we are progressing toward the value of this CSS property of the element when it will be visible at the end of the effect.

The opacity effect

The effect named `"fade"` uses the CSS `opacity` property. This effect consists of varying the CSS `opacity` property from 0 to 1 (to gradually make an element appear) or from 1 to 0 (to make it disappear).

Here is, for example, the effect of disappearance. The paragraph is disappearing with an opacity that tends toward 0. When the opacity is at 0, the element will be completely invisible on the screen.

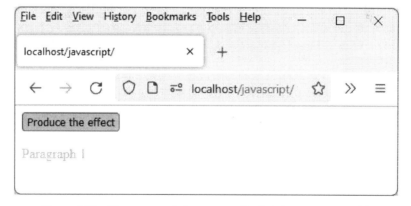

Figure 4.12 – The paragraph has an opacity that decreases toward 0

Once the paragraph is invisible, just click again on the **Produce the effect** button to make it reappear gradually:

CSS classes to manage opacity

```css
.fade-leave-from {
}
.fade-leave-to {
  opacity : 0;
}
.fade-leave-active {
  transition: all 0.5s;
}

.fade-enter-from {
  opacity : 0;
}
.fade-enter-to {
}
.fade-enter-active {
  transition: all 1s;
}
```

The `fade-leave-to` CSS class indicates to go to an opacity of 0. The current opacity (of value 1) is the starting one. Since the initial value of the opacity is not defined in `fade-leave-from`, it will use the value defined by the CSS of the element (i.e., 1).

Similarly, the `fade-enter-from` class indicates the current opacity at the start of the element's appearance effect. The destination value of the opacity does not need to be specified as it will use the default value from the element CSS, that is, 1.

The move-down effect

To manage this effect (here, called `"ymove"`), we use the CSS properties `transform` (set to `translateY(100px)`) and `opacity` (set to 0). This gradually moves the element 100px horizontally downward, gradually decreasing its opacity to 0. The element disappears as it moves down the page.

For example, here is what is displayed when the element has started to slide down by decreasing its opacity, which makes it less visible:

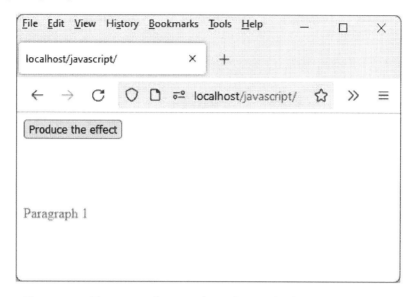

Figure 4.13 – The paragraph moves down the page by decreasing its opacity

As the effect continues, the paragraph moves down the page, until it reaches the distance of 100 pixels specified in the effect. The closer you get to this distance, the more the paragraph decreases in opacity, until it becomes invisible (opacity of 0).

Figure 4.14 – The paragraph becomes almost invisible toward the end of the effect

Once the paragraph has disappeared, clicking on the **Produce the effect** button makes it reappear gradually from the bottom of the screen:

CSS classes to handle moving down

```css
.ymove-leave-from {
}
.ymove-leave-to {
  transform: translateY(100px);
  opacity : 0;
}
.ymove-leave-active {
  transition: all 0.5s;
}

.ymove-enter-from {
  transform: translateY(100px);
  opacity : 0;
}
.ymove-enter-to {
}
.ymove-enter-active {
  transition: all 0.5s;
}
```

The `ymove-leave-to` CSS class indicates the values of the CSS properties toward which we want to vary the indicated CSS properties. The `transform` property can contain the `translateY(100px)` value, indicating to perform a vertical translation (Y) of 100 pixels. Adding an opacity of 0 makes the element disappear by moving it vertically.

The `ymove-enter-from` CSS class allows you to indicate the values of CSS properties at the beginning of the appearance effect. The element is located at 100 pixels vertical distance, with an opacity of 0. The CSS properties will evolve to those specified in the `ymove-enter-to` class, and if nothing is specified in this class, the CSS properties usually used for an element (opacity of 1 and vertical distance of 0, i.e., the normal location) are those toward which we will evolve during the appearance effect.

The CSS `transform` property is very useful for producing visual effects, for example, rotation, enlargement, and displacement.

This brings us to the end of the chapter.

Summary

After learning how to handle events and act when an external event (e.g., a click) occurs, we saw in this chapter how components created with Vue.js can be assembled to form complete applications. We learned the following:

- To communicate from a component to its parent, we use events.
- To communicate from a component to its child, we use the attributes in the component's `props` section.

Finally, to produce visual effects, all you have to do is write the CSS classes managed by Vue.js.

In the next chapter, we will see an example of an application that allows us to put into practice the elements studied in the previous chapters.

5
Managing a List with Vue.js

After going through the basic and advanced concepts of Vue.js, with this chapter, let's finish our study of the Vue.js library by building an application to manage a list of elements.

Why make this type of application? Quite simply because it allows you to perform fairly standard operations on the HTML elements of a page, such as inserting an element, modifying it, and deleting it.

These are the basic operations that you need to know how to perform, for example, to manage the elements in a database. In this chapter, we will learn how to perform these operations on the elements displayed on the screen, and in the next part (where we study Node.js and MongoDB), we will see how to simultaneously update a database.

Here are the topics covered in this chapter:

- Splitting the application into components
- Adding an element to the list
- Removing an element from the list
- Modifying an element in the list

166 Managing a List with Vue.js

But let's start by discovering the screens of the application that we want to create with Vue.js.

Technical requirements

You can find the code files for this chapter on GitHub at: `https://github.com/PacktPublishing/JavaScript-from-Frontend-to-Backend/blob/main/Chapter%205.zip`.

Displaying application screens

As mentioned earlier, we'll be building an application to manage a list of elements. Before writing the source code of our application, let's show the different screens of the application by explaining their sequence.

Initially, the list is empty. The **Add Element** button allows, on each click, to insert a new element in the list.

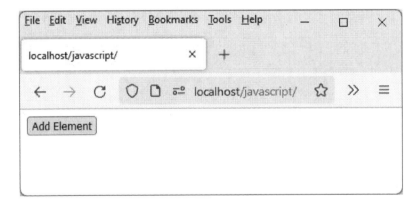

Figure 5.1 – Screen when launching the application

Let's click the **Add Element** button several times (here, three times):

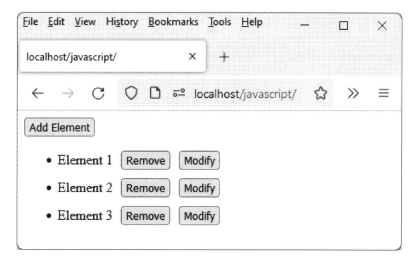

Figure 5.2 – After three clicks on the Add Element button

Each element inserted has the index (starting from 1) of the element in the list. A **Remove** button and a **Modify** button are inserted after the item in the list.

Let's click on the **Modify** button on the second line. The item text is replaced by an input field, in which the cursor flashes to allow editing.

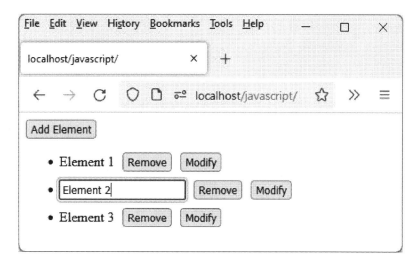

Figure 5.3 – The second item in the list can be changed

Let's modify the text in the input field, by typing `New Element 2`.

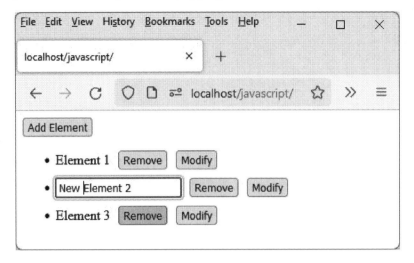

Figure 5.4 – Editing a list item

For the modification of the element to be reflected, you must leave the input field, by clicking elsewhere on the page.

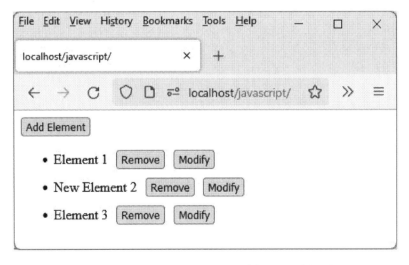

Figure 5.5 – Taking into account the modification of the element

Finally, to remove the first and third elements, click on their corresponding **Remove** buttons.

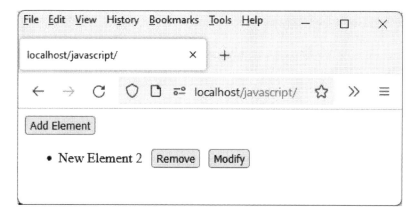

Figure 5.6 – After deleting the first and last element

We have administered here a list of elements on which we have performed basic operations, namely, inserting a new element, modifying the element, and deleting it.

> **Using HTTP Protocol**
>
> This application uses a PHP server to work because the import of JavaScript modules with the JavaScript `import` statement only works under the HTTP protocol. We will see in the next part (*Chapter 9, Integrating Vue.js with Node.js*) how to use a Node.js server to also make it work, by coupling it in addition with a MongoDB database.

We have described the operation of the application, and the sequence of the various windows. Now let's see how to build this application with Vue.js. We first explain how the application can be broken down into different components.

Splitting the application into components

When you create an application with Vue.js, you have to start by asking yourself what components you will need to build it.

In our case, it would be the following:

- A `<GlobalApp>` component that groups the whole application. It is this `<GlobalApp>` component that will be integrated into our `index.html` page. It will display the **Add Element** button as well as the list of elements below.
- An `<Element>` component that displays a list element line, which will include the element's text, the **Remove** button, and the **Modify** button.

The list of elements will be associated with a reactive variable named `elements`, which will be an array containing, for each element, the displayed text. This reactive variable will be registered in the `<GlobalApp>` component. It will be modified when adding a new element to the list or when deleting or modifying an element in the list.

So, the core files of our app are as follows:

- The `index.html` file, which is the main file
- The `global-app.js` file, which contains the `<GlobalApp>` component, and is imported into the `index.html` file
- The `element.js` file, which describes an element of the displayed list (the `<Element>` component), namely the text of the element, as well as the **Remove** and **Modify** buttons

Here is the content of these files:

index.html file

```
<html>
  <head>
    <meta charset="utf-8" />
    <script src="https://unpkg.com/vue@next"></script>
  </head>

  <body>
    <div id="app"></div>
  </body>

  <script type="module">

    import GlobalApp from "./global-app.js";

    var app = Vue.createApp({
      components : {
        GlobalApp:GlobalApp
      },
```

```
        template : "<GlobalApp />"
    });

    var vm = app.mount("div#app");

    </script>

</html>
```

The `index.html` file displays the `<GlobalApp>` component, which corresponds to the main component of the application, which we'll now describe:

`<GlobalApp>` component (global-app.js file)

```
import Element from "./element.js";
const GlobalApp = {
  data() {
    return {
      elements : []
    }
  },
  components : {
    Element:Element
  },
  template : `
    <button>Add Element</button>
    <ul></ul>
  `,
}

export default GlobalApp;
```

We find the reactive variable `elements`, as well as the **Add Element** button and the `<ul>` list of elements, empty for the moment.

The `<Element>` component is described below. It is empty for the moment and will be enriched in the following sections:

`<Element>` component (element.js file)

```
const Element = {
  data() {
    return {
    }
  },
  template : `
  `,
}

export default Element;
```

> **Using HTTP Protocol**
>
> As the JavaScript code comprises module `import` instructions, it is necessary to use a web server accessible by HTTP to display the HTML page corresponding to `index.html`. The `file` protocol would not work here.

Let's display the result of this temporary code on the screen:

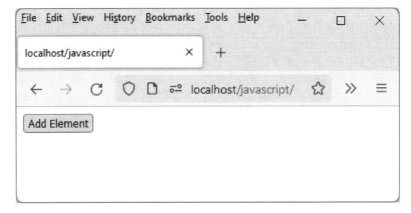

Figure 5.7 – Result displayed with our startup code

In *Figure 5.7*, we see the rendering of the `<GlobalApp>` component, which currently only displays the **Add Element** button. Let's see how to process a click on this button in order to insert a new element in the list.

Adding an element to the list

We will start with the functionality to add an item to the list. The `global-app.js` file is modified to process a click on the **Add Element** button (this button is included in the `global-app.js` file).

Let's add the code that should be run when the **Add Element** button is clicked:

Taking into account the click on the Add Element button (global-app.js file)

```
import Element from "./element.js";
const GlobalApp = {
  data() {
    return {
      elements : []
    }
  },
  components : {
    Element:Element
  },
  template : `
    <button @click="add()">Add Element</button>
    <ul>
      <li v-for="(element, index) in elements"
      :key="index">{{element}}</li>
    </ul>
  `,
  methods : {
    add() {
      var element = "Element " + (this.elements.length +
      1);   // "Element X"
      this.elements.push(element);
    }
  }
}

export default GlobalApp;
```

A click on the **Add Element** button is handled by the `click` event, which calls the `add()` method defined in the `methods` section. The `add()` method adds a new element to the reactive variable `elements`.

The list of elements is updated in the component template. For the moment, we'll use the `<li>` tag to define the list element to insert, but below, we will use the `<Element>` component, which will integrate the **Remove** and **Modify** buttons.

Now let's verify that our modification of the `<GlobalApp>` component works. To do this, click several times on the **Add Element** button. List items are inserted with each click, as seen in the following figure.

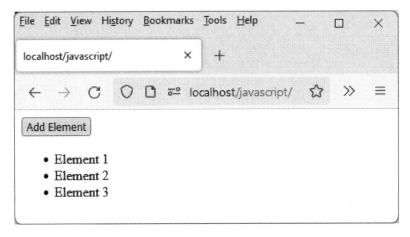

Figure 5.8 – Add Element button clicks

The element inserted here is an HTML `<li>` element. But it is interesting to replace the element `<li>` with a Vue.js component because it allows using the philosophy of Vue.js, which is the maximum use of components. Let's name this new component `<Element>`, which will replace the `<li>` element..

Using the \<Element\> component

Next, let's use the `<Element>` component, instead of the previous `<li>` element.

The `<GlobalApp>` component is modified to integrate the `<Element>` component:

Using \<Element\> component in list (global-app.js file)

```
import Element from "./element.js";
const GlobalApp = {
  data() {
```

```
      return {
        elements : []
      }
    },
    components : {
      Element:Element
    },
    template : `
      <button @click="add()">Add Element</button>
      <ul>
        <Element v-for="(element, index) in elements"
        :key="index" :text="element" />
      </ul>
    `,
    methods : {
      add() {
        var element = "Element " + (this.elements.length +
        1);
        this.elements.push(element);
      }
    }
}

export default GlobalApp;
```

The text to display in the list item is passed as an attribute (via `props`) to the `<Element>` component, which will display it in its template. We use the `text` attribute (or any other attribute name) for this.

The `<Element>` component is modified to consider the `text` attribute passed and display the list element. The two buttons **Remove** and **Modify** are inserted after the text:

Using the text attribute and buttons (element.js file)

```
const Element = {
  data() {
    return {
    }
```

```
  },
  template : `
    <li>
      <span> {{text}} </span>
      <button> Remove </button>
      <button> Modify </button>
    </li>
  `,
  props : ["text"],
}

export default Element;
```

Let's check that the result is equivalent to the previous one (with the addition of the **Remove** and **Modify** buttons).

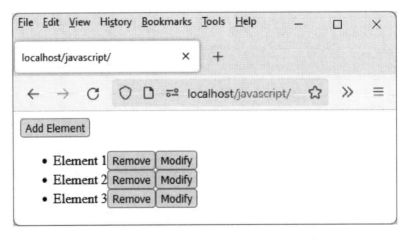

Figure 5.9 – Using the <Element> component in the list

Clicking on the **Remove** and **Modify** buttons in the list does not work yet but will soon, in the following sections.

The **Remove** and **Modify** buttons are placed side by side, with no spacing. Let's add some CSS code to better lay them out on the screen.

Changing the appearance of the list using CSS code

Before handling button clicks in the list, let's use some CSS to display the list items in a nicer way.

The CSS code is indicated directly in the `index.html` file:

Using CSS code to display the list (index.html file)

```html
<html>
  <head>
    <meta charset="utf-8" />
    <script src="https://unpkg.com/vue@next"></script>

    <style type="text/css">
      li {
        margin-top:10px;
      }
      ul button {
        margin-left:10px;
      }
    </style>
  </head>

  <body>
    <div id="app"></div>
  </body>

  <script type="module">

    import GlobalApp from "./global-app.js";

    var app = Vue.createApp({
      components : {
        GlobalApp:GlobalApp
      },
      template : "<GlobalApp />"
```

```
    });

    var vm = app.mount("div#app");

  </script>

</html>
```

We can see that the appearance of the list is now more pleasant.

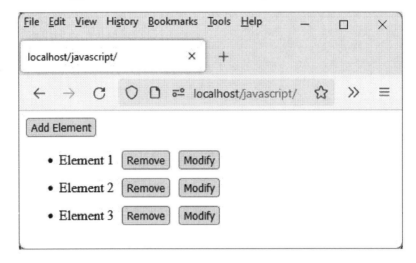

Figure 5.10 – List of elements improved with CSS code

The displayed list now has a look that suits us! We must now manage clicks on the **Remove** and **Modify** buttons. Let's start with the **Remove** button.

Removing an element from the list

Now let's deal with a click on the **Remove** button for a list item. Removing an item from the list will be done by removing the element from the reactive variable `elements`.

> **Note**
> Indeed, the variable `elements` being reactive, any modification of this variable will lead to the re-display of the list.

To do this, a click on the **Remove** button is managed by associating it with a process during the click. We therefore call the `remove()` method defined in the `<Element>` component on each click:

Taking into account the click on the Remove button (element.js file)

```
const Element = {
  data() {
    return {
    }
  },
  template : `
    <li>
      <span> {{text}} </span>
      <button @click="remove()"> Remove </button>
      <button> Modify </button>
    </li>
  `,
  props : ["text"],
  methods : {
    remove() {
      // process the click on the Remove button
    },
  },
}

export default Element;.
```

The process involved in clicking on the **Remove** button is discussed later in the chapter.

> **Note**
> To process the click on the **Remove** button, we must update the reactive variable `elements`, but since this is located in the parent component `<GlobalApp>`, we must send an event to this parent component to ask it to remove the element in the variable `elements`.

To indicate the element to be deleted, it must be referenced by its index. For this, we need to indicate the index of the element when creating the `<Element>` component. We, therefore, create a new attribute (named `"index"`) in this component. Thus the `remove()` method sends a `"remove"` event to the `<GlobalApp>` parent component, indicating in the parameters the index of the element to be removed from the list.

The `<Element>` component becomes as follows:

Handling the click on the Remove button (element.js file)

```js
const Element = {
  data() {
    return {
    }
  },
  template : `
    <li>
      <span> {{text}} </span>
      <button @click="remove()"> Remove </button>
      <button> Modify </button>
    </li>
  `,
  props : ["text", "index"],
  methods : {
    remove() {
      // process the click on the Remove button
      this.$emit("remove", { index : this.index });
    },
  },
  emits : ["remove"]
}

export default Element;
```

The `<GlobalApp>` component is modified to process the reception of the `"remove"` event sent when clicking on the **Remove** button:

Handling the reception of the "remove" event (global-app.js file)

```
import Element from "./element.js";
const GlobalApp = {
  data() {
    return {
      elements : []
    }
  },
  components : {
    Element:Element
  },
  template : `
    <button @click="add()">Add Element</button>
    <ul>
      <Element v-for="(element, index) in elements"
      :key="index" :text="element"
          :index="index"
             @remove="remove($event)"
      />
    </ul>
  `,
  methods : {
    add() {
      var element = "Element " + (this.elements.length +
      1);
      this.elements.push(element);
    },
    remove(params) {
      var index = params.index;
      this.elements.splice(index, 1);   // delete element in
                                        // array
    }
  }
}
```

```
}

export default GlobalApp;
```

We have indicated in the `<Element>` component the new attribute `index`, which will allow knowing the index of the element in the list.

Let's add three items to the list (see *Figure 5.11*), then click the **Remove** button for the item on the second line (see *Figure 5.12*):

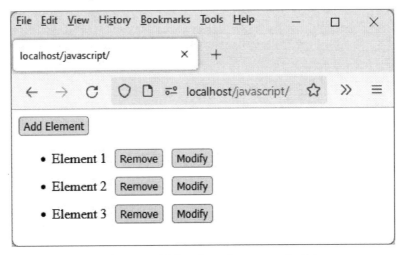

Figure 5.11 – Adding three elements to the list

Here's what we will see after clicking the **Remove** button:

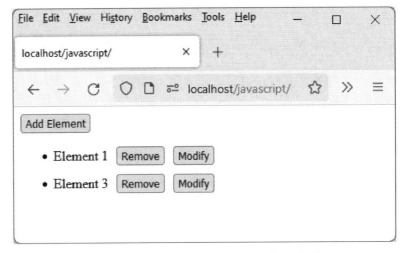

Figure 5.12 – Deleting item Element 2 from the list

By clicking on the **Remove** button, **Element 2** has been removed from the list. Let's now see how to manage the modification of an element, following a click on the **Modify** button.

Modifying an element in the list

Modifying a list element is done in several steps:

1. Following a click on the **Modify** button, we transform the text of the list element (currently a `<span>` element) into an HTML `<input>` element initialized with the text of the element.
2. Then we manage the exit of the input field, by retrieving the value entered in the field, then by replacing the input field with a `<span>` element with the new content.
3. Finally, we improve the input by allowing the input control to automatically have the focus after clicking on the **Modify** button.

Let's see these different steps in depth.

Transforming the <span> element into an <input> element

The first step is to transform the `<span>` element into an `<input>` element, which will allow the text of the element to be modified. To do this, we will add a new reactive variable (named `"input"`) in the `<Element>` component. It indicates whether to display a text as a `<span>` element (if `input` is `false`) or whether to display an `<input>` input field (if `input` is `true`). By default, the `input` variable is set to `false` (the text is displayed). It will change to `true` when clicking on the **Modify** button:

Turning a <span> element into an <input> element (element.js file)

```
const Element = {
  data() {
    return {
      input : false    // display element text by default
    }
  },
  template : `
    <li>
      <span v-if="!input"> {{text}} </span>
```

```
    <input v-else type="text" :value="text" />
    <button @click="remove()"> Remove </button>
    <button @click="input=true"> Modify </button>
  </li>
`,
props : ["text", "index"],
methods : {
  remove() {
    // process the click on the Remove button
    this.$emit("remove", { index : this.index });
  },
},
emits : ["remove"]
}

export default Element;
```

> **Note**
> The `v-if` and `v-else` directives are used to display the text of the element as a `<span>` element or as an `<input>` element.

After inserting three items into the list, let's edit the second item:

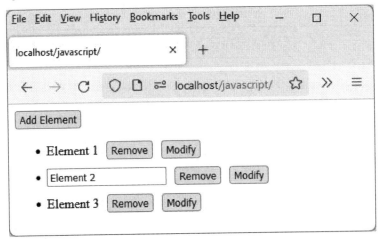

Figure 5.13 – Editing the second item in the list

We now need to show how to leave the input field and redisplay the text as a list element.

Exiting from the input field

Once the edit control has been modified, you must retrieve the value entered to display it instead of the edit control. To do this, in the <Element> component, we use the blur event, which indicates that we have left the input field.

During the processing of this event, the value of the input field is retrieved, which is transmitted to the parent <GlobalApp> component by means of an event named "modify", for example. The <GlobalApp> component modifies the element value in the elements variable when processing the received modify event.

> **Note**
> The modification of a reactive variable located in a parent component must be done by sending an event to the parent component, which will have to process it.

Finally, the transformation of the input field into text is done by modifying the reactive variable input defined in the <Element> component by positioning it again to false.

The <Element> component is modified as shown here:

Taking into account the output of the input field (element.js file)

```
const Element = {
  data() {
    return {
      input : false
    }
  },
  template : `
    <li>
      <span v-if="!input"> {{text}} </span>
      <input v-else type="text" :value="text"
        @blur="modify($event)" />
      <button @click="remove()"> Remove </button>
      <button @click="input=true"> Modify </button>
    </li>
  `,
  props : ["text", "index"],
  methods : {
```

```
    remove() {
      // process the click on the Remove button
      this.$emit("remove", { index : this.index });
    },
    modify(event) {
      var value = event.target.value;     // value entered
                                          // in the field
      this.input = false;                 // delete input field
      this.$emit("modify", { index : this.index, value :
      value });     // update element in list
    }
  },
  emits : ["remove", "modify"]
}

export default Element;
```

The `<GlobalApp>` component is also modified to process the reception of the `"modify"` event and thus modify the list displayed:

Processing the modify event (global-app.js file)

```
import Element from "./element.js";
const GlobalApp = {
  data() {
    return {
      elements : []
    }
  },
  components : {
    Element:Element
  },
  template : `
```

```
      <button @click="add()">Add Element</button>
      <ul>
        <Element v-for="(element, index) in elements"
        :key="index" :text="element"
          :index="index"
          @remove="remove($event)" @modify="modify($event)"
        />
      </ul>
`,
    methods : {
      add() {
        var element = "Element " + (this.elements.length +
        1);
        this.elements.push(element);
      },
      remove(params) {
        var index = params.index;
        this.elements.splice(index, 1);
      },
      modify(params) {
        var index = params.index;
        var value = params.value;
        this.elements[index] = value;   // new element value
      }
    }
  }

export default GlobalApp;
```

The following figure shows the result after editing the second list item.

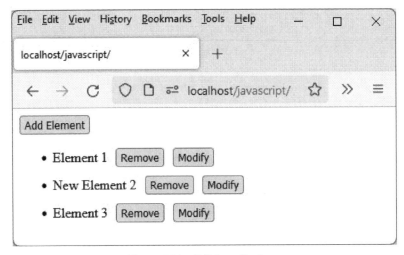

Figure 5.14 – Editing a list item

A final improvement that we can make to our program is to give focus to the input field directly after clicking on the **Modify** button. Let's see how to proceed.

Giving focus to the input field

Giving focus to the input field requires using the `focus()` method, which is defined in the **Document Object Model** (**DOM**). The DOM is an internal API (in the JavaScript language) implemented in browsers.

Vue.js makes it possible to make a relationship between the components defined in Vue.js and the HTML elements used by the DOM. For this, we use the `ref` attribute, which makes it possible to make a correspondence between the two systems.

> **Note**
>
> This `ref` attribute can be used for each HTML element defined in our component templates. But it should be used only for necessary cases, such as here, to use the `focus()` method defined in the DOM, which otherwise would be inaccessible.

Once the `ref` attribute has been positioned (here, on the `<input>` element allowing input), all that remains is to use it to give focus to the input field. The question then is: in which method of our component should we call the `focus()` method?

We must use a method in which we are sure that the input field is created. The template written in the component must be transformed into HTML code and integrated into the memory of the browser (in the DOM), which can then display it. So, we see that a transformation process takes place, which takes some time to execute.

Vue.js has defined a number of methods that are called automatically when using components. In the previous chapter, we saw a method called `created()`. There are other methods, in particular, the `mounted()` and `updated()` methods.

Here are the specifics of these three methods:

- The `created()` method is called when creating the component. This is the first method called.

- The `mounted()` method is called when the component is transformed into HTML elements and integrated into the DOM. We can therefore have access, in this method, to HTML elements with the DOM API.

- The `updated()` method is called when a modification is made in the component. For example, when a `<span>` element is replaced by an `<input>` element following a click on the **Modify** button. Or when, conversely, the `<input>` element turns back into a `<span>` element (when leaving the input field).

We see that the `updated()` method is the method in which we can do the processing giving focus to the input field. But as this method is called both when transforming into an input field or simple text, it will be necessary to check that the `<input>` element associated with the reference indicated in the `ref` attribute exists. Otherwise, an error visible in the console will occur:

Giving focus to the input field as soon as it appears (element.js file)

```
const Element = {
  data() {
    return {
      input : false
    }
  },
  template : `
    <li>
      <span v-if="!input"> {{text}} </span>
      <input v-else type="text" :value="text"
        @blur="modify($event)" ref="refInput" />
```

```
      <button @click="remove()"> Remove </button>
      <button @click="input=true"> Modify </button>
    </li>
`,
  props : ["text", "index"],
  methods : {
    remove() {
      // process the click on the Remove button
      this.$emit("remove", { index : this.index });
    },
    modify(event) {
      var value = event.target.value;
      this.input = false;
      this.$emit("modify", { index : this.index, value :
      value });
    }
  },
  emits : ["remove", "modify"],
  updated() {
    // check that the ref="refInput" attribute exists, and
    // if so, give focus to the input field
    if (this.$refs.refInput) this.$refs.refInput.focus();
  }
}

export default Element;
```

When using the ref attribute in a template, Vue.js stores it in the component's internal $refs variable. We can therefore access the corresponding HTML element using this.$refs.refInput if we wrote ref="refInput" in the component template.

Let's check (see the following figure) that the edit control gets the focus directly when clicking on the **Modify** button.

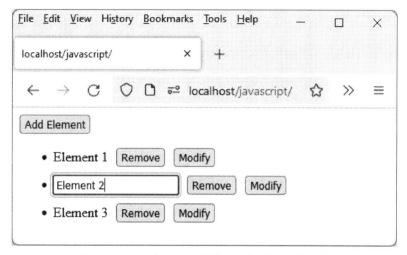

Figure 5.15 – The input field gets the focus directly

This brings us to the end of the chapter.

Summary

This chapter and the example discussed in it shows that it is very easy to manage the elements of an HTML page interactively without leaving the page.

Here, we first decomposed the application into different components, then we assembled them, making them communicate through events and `props` attributes. We have learned, thanks to this complete example, how to manage a list of elements to carry out the main operations, which are the insertion, the modification, and the deletion of an element.

In the next few chapters, we will see how to use Node.js to connect our application to a MongoDB database and thus be able to store the elements of the list in a database. We will begin by learning how to work with node.js modules in the next chapter.

Part 3: JavaScript on the Server-Side

This part is about using JavaScript in a Node.js server. It explains the use of modules such as Express (to quickly create a Node. js-based web application using the MVC pattern) and the MongoDB database.

We end our study by building an application on a single page (this principle is called Single Page Application) which is written with Vue.js on the client-side, and with Node.js, Express and MongoDB on the server-side. The purpose of this book is to enable you to know how to make this type of application.

This section comprises the following chapters:

- *Chapter 6, Creating and Using Node.js Modules*
- *Chapter 7, Using Express with Node.js*
- *Chapter 8, Using MongoDB with Node.js*
- *Chapter 9, Integrating Vue.js with Node.js*

6
Creating and Using Node.js Modules

Modules are at the heart of Node.js. They correspond to JavaScript files and can be used in our applications. A program for the Node.js server will consist of a set of modules, that is, JavaScript files.

There are three kinds of modules:

- Modules that we write ourselves for our applications.
- Modules internal to Node.js and usable directly.
- Modules that can be downloaded from the internet using a utility called npm (npm stands for Node.js package manager). This npm utility is installed with Node.js itself.

In this chapter, we will learn how to create and use these different types of modules.

Regardless of the type of modules used, the `require(moduleName)` instruction (see below) allows the module called `moduleName` to be included in the current file. The functionalities of the module will then be accessible.

Here are the topics covered in this chapter:

- Using our own modules
- Using internal Node.js modules
- Using downloaded modules with npm

Let's first see how to create and use our own modules with Node.js.

Technical requirements

You can find the code files for this chapter on GitHub at: `https://github.com/PacktPublishing/JavaScript-from-Frontend-to-Backend/blob/main/Chapter%206.zip`.

Creating and using our own modules

In this example, we use two modules, each corresponding to a JavaScript file:

- The first module (here named `test.js`) will be the main file of our application, the one we execute using the `node test.js` command in a command window.
- The second module (here named `module1.js`) will be the one we want to use in our main `test.js` module. The `module1.js` module will then be enriched to show how its functionalities are accessible outside the module (and will therefore be used in the main `test.js` module).

Let's go ahead and create these two modules.

Creating a module

Here is the content of the two files, `module1.js` and `test.js`:

module1.js file

```
console.log("module1.js is loaded");
```

The module currently has a simple `console.log()` statement. The module will then be enriched. The main module test.js is the following:

test.js file

```
var mod1 = require("./module1.js");
// or require("./module1") without specifying the .js extension
console.log("mod1 =", mod1);
```

Here, we use the `require(moduleName)` instruction, which allows us to load in memory the `moduleName` module. Any use of the functionalities of the `moduleName` module requires the `require(moduleName)` instruction beforehand.

The `require(moduleName)` instruction returns a reference to the module loaded in memory. This reference is stored in a variable (here, `mod1`), which will then allow access to the functionalities described in the module (here, none for the moment).

The `test.js` file is the main file that loads the other modules. It is therefore this `test.js` file that is executed using the `node test.js` instruction in a command window.

```
D:\Documents\Node.js>node test.js
module1.js is loaded
mod1 = {}

D:\Documents\Node.js>
```

Figure 6.1 – Using a module with require(module)

We can see here that the execution of the main `test.js` module invokes the call of the `require("./module1.js")` instruction, which executes the content of the `module1.js` file, hence the display text specified in the `console.log()` statement in the `module1.js` module.

After loading `module1.js`, the `mod1` variable is initialized and we will be able to access functionalities that the module exports later on.

Before adding functionalities to the `module1.js` module, let's see how to manage the location of modules using the `node_modules` directory. The `node_modules` directory is used by Node.js to locate modules for which it does not have a path. Using this directory simplifies the writing of module names when loading them into memory with the `require(moduleName)` instruction.

Using the node_modules directory

Note that the previous `require(moduleName)` statement requires indicating the access path to the module, for example, `"./"` to indicate the current directory.

However, if the module is in the `node_modules` directory, it is not necessary to indicate the path because we are sure that the module is inside the `node_modules` directory (and moreover, it should *not* be specified). The `node_modules` directory can be in the main application directory (called the *local* `node_modules` directory) or in a dedicated directory created by Node.js (called the *global* `node_modules` directory: in this case, it is automatically created during the installation of Node.js).

> **Note**
>
> If the module is not found in the `node_modules` directory (local or global) and if the access path to the module is not indicated, an error occurs when loading the module with the `require(moduleName)` instruction.

Now, we will create a `node_modules` directory in the current directory where the main file, `test.js`, is located. Let's transfer the `module1.js` file to this directory and use the `require("module1.js")` statement without specifying the path to the module. You can also write `require("module1")` without indicating the extension of the JavaScript file:

Include module1 located in node_modules directory (test.js file)

```
var mod1 = require("module1.js");   // or require("module1")
console.log("mod1 =", mod1);
```

The `module1.js` file must be in the locally created `node_modules` directory, while the `test.js` file remains in the current directory, as described here:

```
root/
|- node_modules/
|          |- module1.js
|- test.js
```

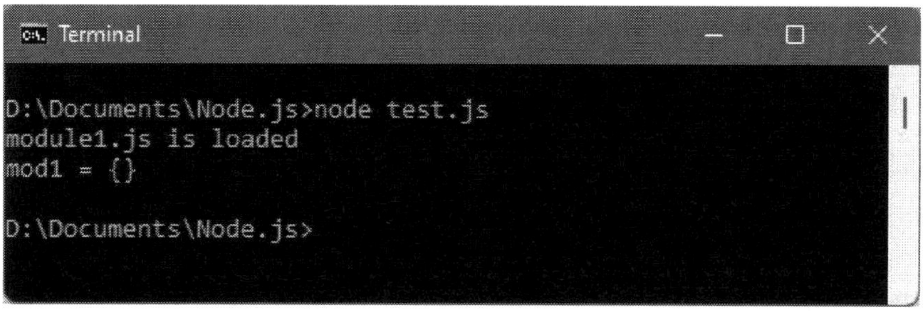

Figure 6.2 – The module is loaded from the node_modules directory

We can see that the module is indeed found by Node.js, because Node.js looks for it in the node_modules directory, which was created in the current directory.

Now let's see how to allow a module's files to be grouped in a directory, using the package.json file associated with the module.

Using the package.json file

The node_modules directory (whether located in the application directory or the Node.js installation directory) can contain a lot of files and sometimes a module can consist of many files and directories. It would be easier to associate a module with a directory in the node_modules directory.

Let's create the module1 directory inside the node_modules directory. The module1 directory contains the module1.js file but may also contain other files and directories related to this module.

The file system is displayed here:

root/

|- node_modules/

| |- module1/

| |- module1.js

|- test.js

> **Note**
>
> The moduleName indicated in the require(moduleName) statement represents, in this case, the name of the *directory* that contains the module files.

But as it is necessary to know which file of the directory we must use first when loading the module (as there can be many files in this directory), we indicate this correspondence in the package.json file in the "main" key.

The package.json file is a text file in JSON format, located in the directory of each Node.js module.

Now, we will create the package.json file in the module1 module directory and indicate in this file the "main" key with the value "module1.js".

The file system is as follows:

```
root/
|- node_modules/
|          |- module1/
|                  |- module1.js
|                  |- package.json
|- test.js
```

package.json file in the node_modules/module1 directory (package.json file)

```
{
   "main" : "module1.js"
}
```

We indicate in the "main" key that we must load the module1.js file during the require("module1") instruction:

Including module1 located in node_modules/module1 directory (test.js file)

```
var mod1 = require("module1"); //"module1" is the directory name
console.log("mod1 =", mod1);
```

> **Note**
>
> Please note that the module name in the require("module1") statement in this case is the name of the directory that contains the module in the node_modules directory. So, we cannot write the instruction here in the form require("module1.js"), which would cause an error.

We now visualize the execution of the `test.js` file:

```
D:\Documents\Node.js>node test.js
module1.js is loaded
mod1 = {}

D:\Documents\Node.js>
```

Figure 6.3 – Module loaded with the package.json file

The `"main"` key in the `package.json` file is optional if the main module file is named `index.js`. In all other cases, the `"main"` key must be indicated in `package.json`.

We know how to run a module, but for now, the module contains a simple `console.log()` statement. Let's see how to add features to the module and then use them.

Adding functionalities to the module

The newly created `module1.js` module is accessible but does not currently offer any functionality. Let's see how to add some.

Exporting multiple functions in the module

For example, let's create the function `add(a, b)`, which returns the sum of a and b:

---

add(a, b) function defined in module1.js (module1.js file)

```
console.log("module1 is loaded");

function add(a, b) {
   return a+b;
}
module.exports = {
   add : add       // make the add() function accessible
                   // outside the module
};
```

To export a function outside of a module (and make it accessible to users of the module), you can just embed it in the `module.exports` object defined by Node.js in each module. Each key defined in the `module.exports` object will be a function accessible outside the module.

We can thus define several functions in the module that will be accessible thanks to the `module.exports` object.

The usage of the `add(a, b)` function in the `test.js` file is as follows:

Using add() function in test.js file (test.js file)

```
var mod1 = require("module1");
console.log("mod1 =", mod1);

var total = mod1.add(2, 3);        // call of the add() function
                                    // defined in module1
console.log("mod1.add(2, 3) = ", total);   // displays 5
```

The following display is obtained:

Figure 6.4 – The add() function added to the module

Let's add a second function in the module. For example, the function `mult(a, b)`, which returns a*b.

If we add the `mult(a, b)` function in the module, it is written as follows:

Adding the mult(a, b) function to the module (module1.js file)

```
console.log("module1 is loaded");

function add(a, b) {
```

```
    return a+b;
}

function mult(a, b) {
    return a*b;
}

module.exports = {
    add : add,
    mult : mult
}
```

Now, we will use the two functions add() and mult() in the test.js file. This verifies that a module can provide several functionalities to other modules that use it:

Using the module's add() and mult() functions (test.js file)

```
var mod1 = require("module1");
console.log("mod1 =", mod1);


var total = mod1.add(2, 3);
console.log("mod1.add(2, 3) = ", total);          // 2 + 3 = 5
var total = mod1.mult(2, 3);
console.log("mod1.mult(2, 3) = ", total);         // 2 * 3 = 6
```

The following display is obtained:

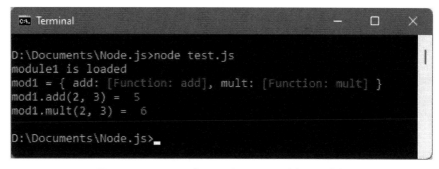

Figure 6.5 – Using the two functions of the module

Now let's see how to improve the module concept by using a so-called main function in the module.

Allowing a function to be the main function of the module

Often, the module wishes to make a function its main function (the other functions defined in the module are secondary functions). This allows access to this main function in a simplified form.

Suppose (as before) that `module1` makes available the `add(a, b)` function and the `mult(a, b)` function. We want the `add()` function to be the main function of the module, which means that we can use it outside the module as `mod1(2, 3)` instead of `mod1.add(2, 3)`. The `mult(a, b)` function will remain accessible in the form `mod1.mult(2, 3)`.

> **Note**
> Note that only one function can be defined as the main function in a module.

In this case, just specify it in the `module.exports` object like so:

Making the add() function accessible as a main module function (module1.js file)

```
console.log("module1 is loaded");

function add(a, b) {
   return a+b;
}

function mult(a, b) {
   return a*b;
}

// first define the main function
module.exports = add;    // the add() function defined outside
                         // the module, is made main

// then define the secondary functions
module.exports.mult = mult;    // and the mult() function
                               // becomes usable as well
```

> **Note**
>
> It is important to assign the values in this order in the module.exports object (define the main function first, then the secondary functions). If you make the assignment in the other direction (module.exports.mult first, then module.exports), the assignment of module.exports last will erase the value already positioned in module.exports.mult.

Also, we can no longer assign module.exports as an object, because that would remove the previously assigned value if we wrote module.exports = { mult : mult }.

We now use the module as follows:

Using the module1.js module that has a main function (test.js file)

```
var mod1 = require("module1");
console.log("mod1 =", mod1);


var total = mod1(2, 3);              // instead of mod1.add(2, 3)
console.log("mod1(2, 3) = ", total);
var total = mod1.mult(2, 3);
console.log("mod1.mult(2, 3) = ", total);
```

The following display is obtained:

```
D:\Documents\Node.js>node test.js
module1 is loaded
mod1 = [Function: add] { mult: [Function: mult] }
mod1(2, 3) = 5
mod1.mult(2, 3) = 6

D:\Documents\Node.js>
```

Figure 6.6 – Using the module with the main function

> **Note**
>
> Notice that instead of using the `mod1` variable as an object, we now use it as a function. In the call to `mod1(a, b)` causes the addition of a and b, so it is preferable that the variable be named `"add"` rather than `"mod1"` in the instruction `require(moduleName)`.

We saw how to create and use our own module. Now let's take a look at how to use internal Node.js modules.

Using internal Node.js modules

Node.js already has internal modules. They can also be used with the `require(moduleName)` instruction seen previously.

Let's look at an example of an internal module. There is, for example, the `"fs"` module in the Node.js system. The name `"fs"` is short for file system. This module allows you to interact with the internal file system of Node.js.

Now, we will use the `"fs"` module to read the contents of a file.

Reading the contents of a file

Let's use the `"fs"` module to read the file named `file1.txt` located in the current directory (where the `test.js` file is located). Here are the contents of this file:

file1.txt file (in the directory where test.js is located)

```
This is the content
of the file file1.txt
located in
the current directory.
```

The program that uses the `"fs"` module and displays the contents of the file is as follows:

Reading and displaying the contents of the file (test.js file)

```javascript
var fs = require("fs");

var data = fs.readFileSync("file1.txt");
console.log("File content:");
console.log(data);
```

We use the `readFileSync()` method defined in the `"fs"` module. It returns the contents of the file in the corresponding variable, which is then displayed.

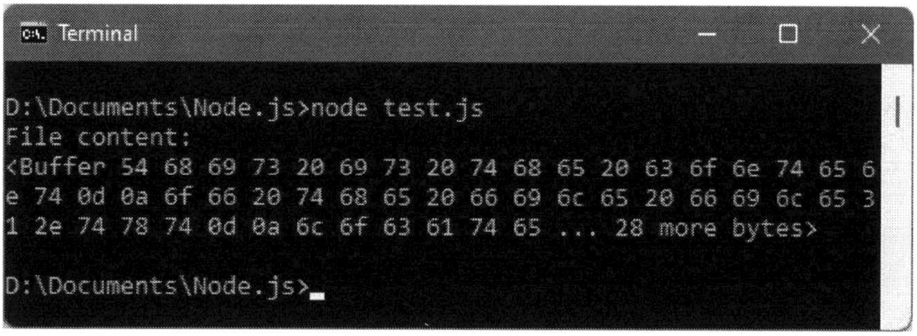

Figure 6.7 – Displaying file contents using the "fs" module

The contents of the file are displayed but as hexadecimal characters. Next, let's display the contents of the file as strings.

Displaying file contents as strings

The contents of the file are displayed in the form of a buffer of bytes (see *Figure 6.7*). Node.js makes it easy to manipulate byte streams. It is also possible to view the contents of the file directly as strings by specifying the `{encoding: "utf-8"}` option in the second parameter (`options`) of the `readFileSync(name, options)` method:

Displaying file contents as strings (test.js file)

```
var fs = require("fs");

var data = fs.readFileSync("file1.txt", { encoding : "utf-8"
});
console.log("File content:");
console.log(data);
```

The result is now displayed as strings (see the following figure):

```
D:\Documents\Node.js>node test.js
File content:
This is the content
of the file file1.txt
located in
the current directory.

D:\Documents\Node.js>
```

Figure 6.8 – Displaying file contents as strings

The contents of the file are displayed. However, the program waits for the contents of the file to be retrieved in order to display them. By using the `readFile()` method instead of the `readFileSync()` method, it is possible to not block the program while waiting for the file.

Using non-blocking file reading

If you observe the previous `readFileSync()` method, you will see that the contents of the file are rendered in return for the method call. This means that the Node.js program is blocked while the file is being read (even if only for a few milliseconds). Within our small program, this is not noticeable, but in a case where the reading of the file is carried out by thousands of simultaneous users (for example, on a server), this will slow down access to the server.

For this, Node.js has provided, for all blocking features such as this one, a non-blocking version of the method. Rather than returning the return result of the method (as before), we use a callback function indicated as a parameter of the method. In the case of reading the file, we will therefore use the `readFile(name, options, callback)` method, also defined in the `"fs"` module. The result of reading the file will be passed as a parameter in the callback function.

Let's use the non-blocking form of reading the file, using the `readFile()` method instead of the `readFileSync()` method:

Using readFile() method to read the file (test.js file)

```
var fs = require("fs");
console.log("File content:");
```

```
fs.readFile("file1.txt", { encoding : "utf-8" },
function(error, data) {
  console.log(data);
});
console.log("The readFile() method was called");
```

> **Note**
> The callback function uses the `error` and `data` parameters (in that order), which respectively correspond to a possible error message (`null` if none), and to the contents of the file if the latter has been read. The `options` parameter indicated as the second parameter of `readFile()` is similar to that of the `readFileSync(name, options)` method.

The result is displayed here:

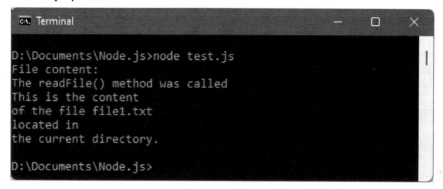

Figure 6.9 – Displaying file contents using the non-blocking readFile() method

We can check in the result displayed above that the `readFile()` method is really non-blocking. Indeed, the text indicated following the call to the `readFile()` method is displayed in the console even though the file has not yet been read and displayed, which would have been impossible using the blocking method `readFileSync()`.

> **Note**
> We can therefore see that the use of modules internal to Node.js is done very simply by using the `require(moduleName)` instruction, and then by calling methods on the object returned by this instruction.

We have seen how to create and use your own modules, and how to use internal Node.js modules.

Now let's see how to use modules available on the internet using the npm command.

Using downloaded modules with npm

In addition to the modules internal to Node.js, it is possible to import modules from the internet using the `npm` utility provided with Node.js.

For this, the `npm` command is used (in a command interpreter) by indicating arguments that allow you to perform the corresponding actions on the imported modules.

Using the npm command

Here are some common uses of the `npm` command:

- `npm install moduleName`: Installs the indicated module in the *local* `node_modules` directory. The module will only be accessible for the current application and not for other applications (unless it is installed again).
- `npm install moduleName -g`: Installs the specified module in the *global* `node_modules` directory. The `-g` option allows you to indicate that this module can be accessed by other applications because it is installed in the `node_modules` directory of Node.js (globally).
- `npm link moduleName`: It is possible that a module installed globally (with the `-g` option) is inaccessible (you get a module loading error during the `require(moduleName)` statement). In this case, it is necessary to run the `npm link moduleName` command.
- `npm ll`: Lists modules already present in the *local* `node_modules` directory.
- `npm ll -g`: Lists modules already present in the *global* `node_modules` directory.
- `npm start`: Starts the Node.js application according to the command indicated in the `"scripts"` key, then the `"start"` key of the `package.json` file. For example, if you specify `"scripts": { "start": "node test.js" }` in the `package.json` file, you can type `npm start` instead of `node test.js` to run the `test.js` file. It is common to use `npm start` to start a Node.js application. This will be used to start an application under **Express** (see the next chapter).

> **Note**
>
> If you want to remove an npm-installed module, use the same commands as before, specifying `uninstall` instead of `install`.

As an example, let's create the following package.json file in the directory of the test.js file:

package.json file (in the same directory as test.js)

```
{
  "scripts" : {
    "start" : "node test.js"
  }
}
```

Then use the npm start command to start the program:

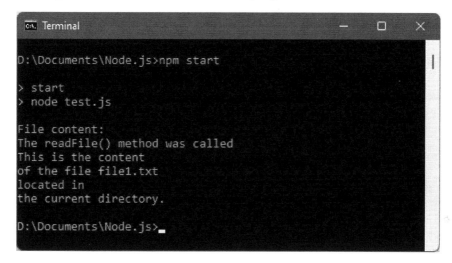

Figure 6.10 – Starting the Node.js application with npm start

We can see that the npm start command thus makes it possible to execute the test.js program. The npm start command is often used to start a Node.js program, thanks to the mechanism explained above.

Now let's see how to use modules written by other developers by downloading them using npm.

Using a downloaded module with npm

Let's look at an example of using npm. Here, we will use npm to install the module named colors. It allows you to display colored text in the console.

Installing the colors module in the node_modules local directory

We use the command `npm install colors`. The result of the installation of the `"colors"` module is displayed in the following figure.

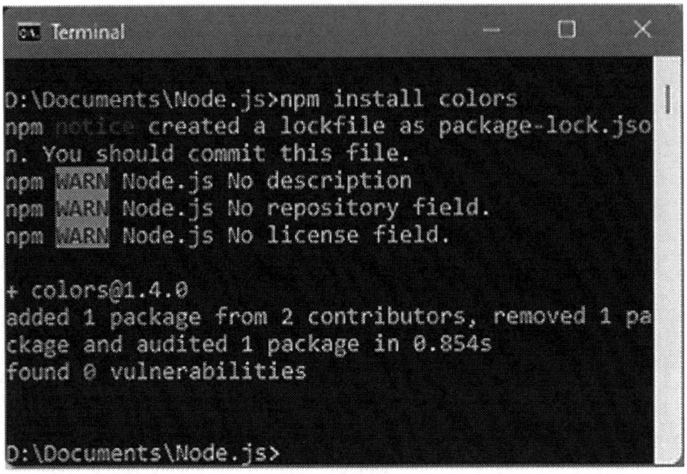

Figure 6.11 – Installing the colors module with npm

Once the module has been installed by npm, you can see that the `colors` directory of the module has inserted itself into the `node_modules` local directory of the application.

Using the features of the colors module

One of the ways to have an overview of the functionalities offered by a module is to display the content of the object returned by the `require(moduleName)` instruction:

Displaying contents of colors object returned by require("colors") (test.js file)

```
var colors = require("colors");
console.log("colors = ", colors);
```

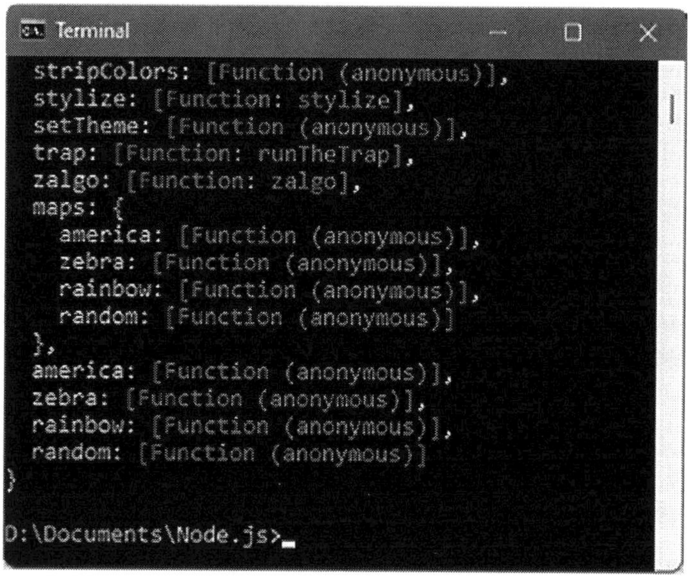

Figure 6.12 – Displaying contents of the colors module

For example, let's use the last method listed in the module, namely the `random()` method. It allows you to transform a character string into a string with random colors for each character:

Using the random() method of the colors module (test.js file)

```
var colors = require("colors");
console.log(colors.random("First text in random colors"));
console.log(colors.random("Second text in random colors"));
```

> **Note**
>
> The `random()` method is used by prefixing its name with the name of the variable returned by `require("colors")`, that is, with the name of the module.

The display of the following figure is obtained, in which each character displayed is a random color:

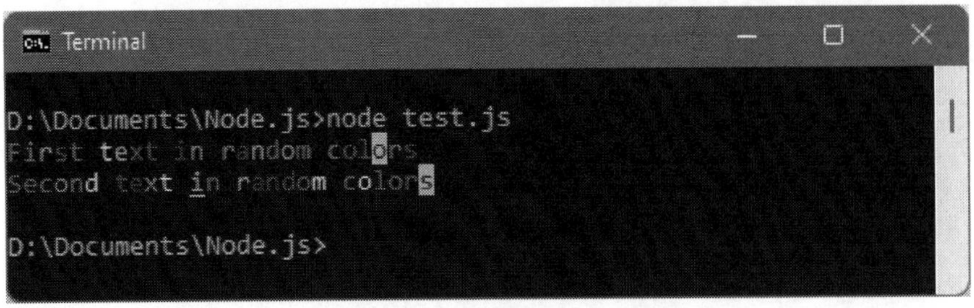

Figure 6.13 – Using the colors module

We have seen here the three types of modules used with Node.js:

- Modules written by ourselves, for our own needs
- Existing internal modules in Node.js, such as the `fs` module allowing access to the internal file system of Node.js
- Modules downloadable using the `npm` command, such as the colors module used above

All that remains is to use these different types of modules in our programs. We will discuss that later on.

This brings us to the end of the chapter.

Summary

We have seen in this chapter how to create and use modules with Node.js, which are the essential components of programs created with Node.js.

Whether the module is created by us, is an internal Node.js module, or is a module downloaded with npm, its use is the same in all cases. We use the `require(moduleName)` instruction and with the value returned in a variable, we access the functionality of the module.

Next, we are going to study the Express module, which is one of the main modules used with Node.js, allowing us to easily structure our applications according to the rules of the MVC model, currently widely used.

7
Using Express with Node.js

We saw in the previous chapter that a program for the Node.js server is an assembly of different modules. Many modules have been created by Node.js developers, which can be inserted into our programs using the npm utility (see *Chapter 6, Creating and Using Node.js Modules*). One of these modules is called **Express**. It is one of the most used modules with Node.js because it allows you to structure server programs according to the **Model View Controller** (**MVC**) model.

In this chapter, we'll study how to create a Node.js application while respecting the characteristics of the MVC model by using the Express module.

Here are the topics we will cover:

- Using the Node.js `http` module
- Installing the Express module
- The MVC pattern used by Express
- Using routes with Express
- Displaying views with Express

Node.js integrates into its internal modules the possibility to create a web server using the `http` module internal to Node.js. We first explain how to use this `http` module, and then we will see the contribution that the external Express module makes to more easily create a web application built according to the MVC model.

Technical requirements

You can find the code files for this chapter on GitHub at: `https://github.com/PacktPublishing/JavaScript-from-Frontend-to-Backend/blob/main/Chapter%207.zip`.

Using the Node.js http module

The `http` module is an internal Node.js module. It is, therefore, directly accessible in our programs using the `require("http")` instruction. With this module you can create a web server based on the HTTP protocol and thus display web pages in an internet browser.

For creating a web server based on HTTP, we use the `http.createServer(callback)` method of the `http` module. The callback function indicated as a parameter is of the form `callback(req, res)`, in which `req` corresponds to the request received, and `res` corresponds to the response to be sent to the browser. Depending on the request received, the corresponding response will be sent.

> **Note**
>
> In the `req` parameter, there is, among other things, the URL of the request received, thus making it possible to return, via the `res` parameter, the correct response to the browser according to this request.

Let's see in the following program how to use the `createServer()` method:

Creating a web server using the http module (test.js file)

```
var http = require("http");

var server = http.createServer(function(req, res) {
  // display the received request in the console
  console.log("Request received:", req.url);
```

```
    // indicate that the response is HTML in utf-8
    res.setHeader("Content-type", "text/html; charset=utf-8");

    // we always send the same response, regardless of the
    // request received
    res.write("<h1>")
    res.write("Good morning all");
    res.write("</h1>");
    res.end();
});
// make the server listen on port 3000 (for example)
server.listen(3000);

console.log("\nThe server was started on port 3000\n");
console.log("You can make a request on:");
console.log("http://localhost:3000");
```

The createServer() method returns an object, here used through the variable named server, on which we indicate to wait for requests coming from port 3000 (the one indicated in the server.listen(port) method). This means that each time URLs of the form http://localhost:3000 are accessed via the browser, the program previously launched (with the node test.js command) will be activated and will display the result in the browser.

> **Note**
>
> The use of the server.listen(port) method is mandatory because it is not enough to create a server with the http.createServer() method. This server must also be listening (with server.listen(port)) to HTTP requests addressed to it by browsers connecting to this server (here using a URL such as http://localhost:3000). Port 3000 is used here, but another port number could be used (provided that this port is not already used by another server, which would cause an access conflict to know to which server the request on the port is addressed).

We send the response to the browser using res.write(string) instructions. You must finish sending the response with the res.end() instruction, which means that the browser has received all the elements to display (the server waits to receive the res.end() instruction to display all the elements sent).

> **Note**
>
> The `res.setHeader()` method is used to set HTTP header fields. Here, `"Content-type"` is set to the value `"text/html; charset=utf-8"`.

Let's launch the previous program by typing the command `node test.js`. The program displays a message, then waits for HTTP requests on port 3000:

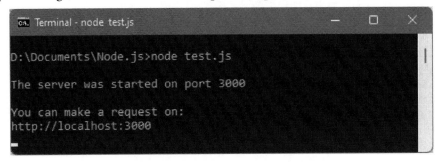

Figure 7.1 – HTTP server waiting on port 3000

To test the program, display the URL beginning with `http://localhost:3000` in a browser. When an HTTP request uses port 3000 (the port on which the server is listening), the callback function indicated in the `createServer(callback)` method is activated and then the response is sent to the browser.

Let's type the URL `http://localhost:3000` in the browser (see the following figure):

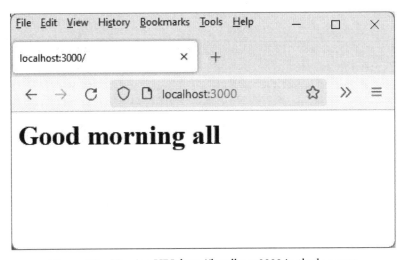

Figure 7.2 – Viewing URL http://localhost:3000 in the browser

Regardless of the URL specified in the browser (which uses port 3000), the display in the browser remains the same. For the display to be different for different URLs, it must be considered in the callback function by using the value of req.url, which contains the URL typed and returns different strings according to the request received.

Using the Express module makes it easy to manage the different requests received and display different results depending on the URL entered.

Installing the Express module

Since the Express module is installed using npm, we type the npm install express command to install it.

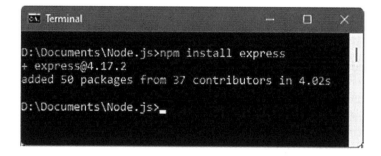

Figure 7.3 – Installing the Express module with npm

The Express module is now installed.

> **Note**
> A utility related to Express is also useful for creating the architecture of our web applications. This is the "express-generator" module (this module was previously included with Express but is now separate from it, hence it's uploaded here).

Let's also install the "express-generator" module using the npm install express-generator -g command. We use the -g option so that the express command defined in this module is accessible from any directory.

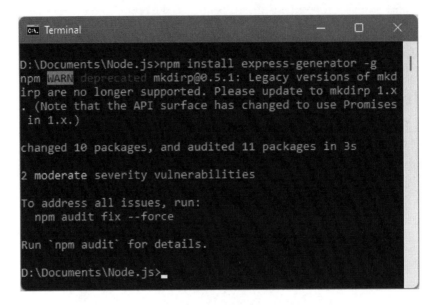

Figure 7.4 – Installing the "express-generator" module with npm

> **Note**
> You can verify that the installation is correct by typing the command express -h. If the installation of the module is correct, help for the express command is displayed in the window (otherwise an error is displayed).

Once these two modules are installed, you can create a first web application based on Express.

To do this, type the `express apptest` command to create the application named `apptest`. You should see the following result:

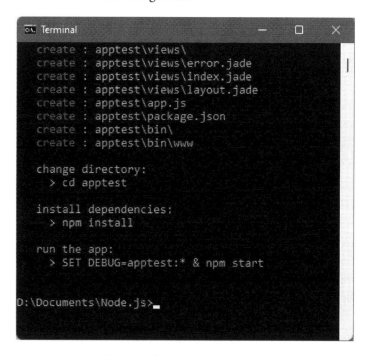

Figure 7.5 – Creating the apptest application with Express

This command creates an `apptest` directory containing the basic files to run the application. You must then type the three commands indicated at the end of the display: `cd apptest`, `npm install`, and `npm start`.

Once these commands are typed, open a browser and display the URL `http://localhost:3000`.

This is what you will see:

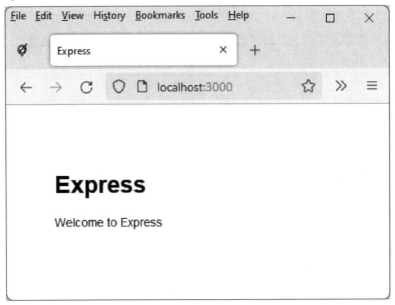

Figure 7.6 – Default app home page created with Express

If we look at the source files of the application created in the `apptest` directory, we see the `app.js` and `package.json` files, as well as the `bin`, `node_modules`, `public`, `routes`, and `views` directories. These directories are those that describe the MVC architecture used by Express, which we explain below.

The MVC pattern used by Express

The MVC model is an application architecture model allowing an application to be broken down into different parts: models, views, and the controller:

- Models correspond to the data manipulated by the application. In general, this is data from databases. Node.js is closely tied to the MongoDB database, which is explored in the next chapter.

- Views correspond to the visualization of data, for example, input forms and displayed lists. Each display corresponds to a view that will be in the `views` directory of the application.

- The controller allows navigation between the different views, depending on the data. For this, we use routes (in fact, URLs) that indicate the processing to be performed. The `routes` directory describes the routes used by the application (and the processing performed for each of them).

We can therefore see that the MVC model makes it possible to separate the processing, the display, and the data. This split is widely used in web projects and is the one proposed by Express.

Let's first look at how routing works in Express. This corresponds to the controller part of the MVC model.

Using routes with Express

Routes indicate the processing to be performed based on the requested URL. Compared to what we wrote when using the `http` module of Node.js with the `createServer(callback)` method, this consists of writing the content of the `callback(req, res)` function according to the `req` request received.

The routes are described in the `app.js` file, which is the main file created by Express. Let's examine its content.

The initial content of the app.js file

To understand how routes work in Express, open the `app.js` file located in the main application directory, and you will see the content of this file, like this:

app.js file

```
var createError = require('http-errors');
var express = require('express');
var path = require('path');
var cookieParser = require('cookie-parser');
var logger = require('morgan');

var indexRouter = require('./routes/index');
var usersRouter = require('./routes/users');

var app = express();

// view engine setup
app.set('views', path.join(__dirname, 'views'));
app.set('view engine', 'jade');

app.use(logger('dev'));
```

```
app.use(express.json());
app.use(express.urlencoded({ extended: false }));
app.use(cookieParser());
app.use(express.static(path.join(__dirname, 'public')));

app.use('/', indexRouter);
app.use('/users', usersRouter);

// catch 404 and forward to error handler
app.use(function(req, res, next) {
  next(createError(404));
});

// error handler
app.use(function(err, req, res, next) {
  // set locals, only providing error in development
  res.locals.message = err.message;
  res.locals.error = req.app.get('env') === 'development' ?
  err : {};

  // render the error page
  res.status(err.status || 500);
  res.render('error');
});

module.exports = app;
```

This file describes how the application built with Express works. It uses the `app` variable, which is the return from the `express()` function call and symbolizes the application. On this `app` object, the `use()` method is used many times, which makes it possible to add processing to be performed for each request received on the server.

For example, `app.use(logger("dev"))` triggers the `logger()` function for each request received on the server. This is why the server console displays the URL that was requested in the browser during each request to the server.

By having displayed in the browser the URLs `http://localhost:3000` and `http://localhost:3000/users`, we obtain the following in the server console.

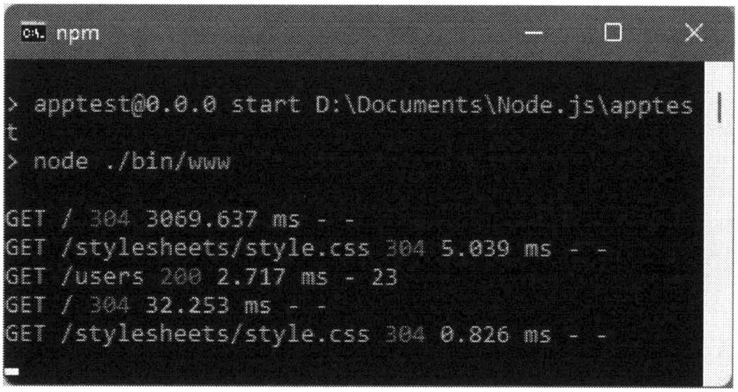

Figure 7.7 – Display of URLs in the server console

Now, let's look at the meaning of the lines displayed in the server console.

Different types of routes possible

In the previous figure, you'll notice that the word GET is displayed in front of each URL: `GET /`, `GET /users`.

The word GET means that the URL / or /users is accessed by an HTTP request of the GET type. The GET type is the one used when the accessed URL is displayed in the address bar of the browser, for example, when you type it directly or when you click on a link on a page.

> **Note**
>
> Other types of HTTP requests exist. They make it possible not to display the corresponding URL in the address bar of the browser, and thus to hide it from users. For example, if the URL for deleting records from the database was visible in the browser's address bar, it would suffice to refresh the page to continue deleting records from the database. Hence the interest in other types of HTTP requests that allow the current URL to be hidden.

The other types of HTTP requests (in addition to GET) are mainly PUT, POST, and DELETE type requests. These types of requests are used in programs to signify an action to be performed on one or more pieces of data (called resources):

- GET means reading a resource.
- POST means creating a resource.
- PUT means updating a resource.
- DELETE means deleting a resource.

Although multiple types of HTTP requests exist, these are the main ones. They are used to manipulate resources, allowing them to be created (POST), updated (PUT), deleted (DELETE), and read (GET).

> **Note**
> A route is the association of an HTTP request with a URL. For example, the GET /users route associates the /users URL with the HTTP GET request, while the DELETE /users route associates the same /users URL with the HTTP DELETE request. Although these routes use the same URL, they are different routes because the HTTP requests are different.

Now that we've seen the different types of HTTP requests used, let's look at how Express uses them internally.

Analyzing routes defined in the app.js file

The app.use() method is also used to define new routes, that is, to define the processing that will be performed for each new URL used (with the associated request type).

The app.use(url, callback) method is used to define the processing to be performed when the specified URL is activated. As the type of request is not indicated here, all types of requests will activate the treatment indicated in the callback function. To indicate the type of request, you must use methods similar to app.use(). These are the app.get(), app.put(), app.post(), and app.delete() methods.

> **Note**
>
> The callback function of the form `callback(req, res, next)` returns the response to the browser. The `next()` parameter corresponds to a function to be called at the end of the callback if the processing must continue in the next callback function (if the processing to be performed is handled by multiple callback functions).

The routes already defined in `app.js` are `/` and `/users`, thus making it possible to run the processes associated with these routes. These routes are examples to show how to implement routes in the `app.js` file. The processing instructions are defined in the `indexRouter` and `usersRouter` functions. These functions are the variables used in return for the instructions `require('./routes/index')` and `require('./routes/users')`. The processing of routes is therefore done here in the `index.js` and `users.js` files defined in the `routes` directory.

Let's open these two files and analyze their contents:

index.js file (routes directory)

```
var express = require('express');
var router = express.Router();

/* GET home page. */
router.get('/', function(req, res, next) {
  res.render('index', { title: 'Express' });
});

module.exports = router;
```

users.js file (routes directory)

```
var express = require('express');
var router = express.Router();

/* GET users listing. */
router.get('/', function(req, res, next) {
  res.send('respond with a resource');
```

```
});

module.exports = router;
```

Each of these files uses the `router.get(url, callback)` method, meaning that the route is associated with the **GET** type request. The URL given is / (it will be concatenated with the URL given in the `app.js` file), followed by the callback function of the form `callback(req, res, next)`. The `next` parameter corresponds to a function to call if the processing must continue in the callback function that follows (if such a function exists, which is not the case here).

The processing performed in each of the callback functions consists of sending the response, which will be displayed in the browser. Here, we use the `res.send()` and `res.render()` methods, which allow the response to be sent:

- The `res.send()` method is similar to `res.end()` (defined in the "http" module of Node.js), but also allows you to indicate that you are using HTML and **utf-8** characters. Only one call to the `res.send()` method must be made in the processing, otherwise, an error occurs.

- The `res.render()` method allows an external file (called a view) to be displayed. Views are written in a special language that depends on the format of the view. By default, the views used by Express are JADE files, but it is possible to use other formats.

Here, the view displayed by the `res.render()` method corresponds to the `index.jade` file located in the `views` directory. Its contents are as follows:

index.jade file (views directory)

```
extends layout

block content
  h1= title
  p Welcome to #{title}
```

This file is written using a particular syntax, called JADE. The file will be transformed into HTML code by Express before being sent to the browser (which can only interpret HTML).

> **Note**
> Express allows files associated with views to be written using a variety of syntaxes. The most common are **JADE** and **EJS**.
>
> We will explore the JADE syntax in the *Displaying views with Express* section in this chapter.

Note that the `app.js` file allows you to configure the directory associated with the views and the syntax used in the views. Here are the corresponding instructions from the `app.js` file:

Configuring views (app.js file)

```
app.set('views', path.join(__dirname, 'views'));
app.set('view engine', 'jade');
```

We have described the routes already listed in the `app.js` file. Let's see how to create new routes in this file.

Adding a new route in the app.js file

Adding a new route in the `app.js` file can be done either by writing the processing directly in the `app.js` file or by creating an external file that will be in the `routes` directory.

> **Warning**
> Any modification of the `app.js` file requires restarting the server by performing the `npm start` command; otherwise, the modifications are not taken into account.

Let's look at these two ways to create a new route.

Adding route processing directly in the app.js file

Let's add the `/clients` route activated following a **GET** type request. It displays the list of clients. We use the `app.get()` method to define the route:

Add the GET /clients route

```
app.use('/', indexRouter);
app.use('/users', usersRouter);
```

```
app.get("/clients", function(req, res, next) {
  res.send("<h1>Client list</h1>");
});
```

The result is displayed in the following figure (*Figure 7.8*).

Creating an external file to define route processing

We use the same principle as that used for the GET / and GET /users routes defined in the app.js file. We create the clients.js file in the routes directory, which will be included in the app.js file by means of the statement clientsRouter = require("./routes/clients). The route is defined in app.js with the statement app.use("/clients", clientsRouter).

The clients.js file describing the processing performed on the route is as follows:

clients.js file (routes directory)

```
var express = require('express');
var router = express.Router();

router.get('/', function(req, res, next) {
  res.send("<h1>Client list</h1>");
});

module.exports = router;
```

In both cases, the result is the same, as seen in the following figure.

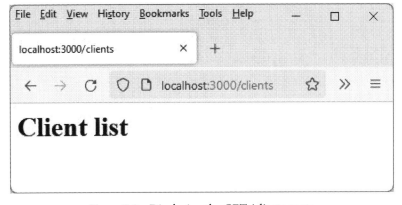

Figure 7.8 – Displaying the GET /clients route

We studied the controller part of the MVC model using the route system defined in Express. Now let's see how Express allows us to manage the view part of the MVC model.

Displaying views with Express

A view is an external file used to describe the display that you want to view. Specific syntaxes have been created to program the view, for example, JADE or EJS syntaxes.

The `res.render(name, obj)` method is used to display the `name` view using any properties provided in the `obj` object. The view is a file defined in the `views` directory using JADE syntax or another.

One of the features of Express is to allow you to create views using the desired syntax. The JADE syntax is offered as standard by Express, but other syntax support libraries can be added with npm.

The JADE syntax is, therefore, the one used by default in Express. It makes it possible to replace HTML tags with their tag (for example `<h1>` simply becomes `h1`), and the indentation of tags in the code makes it possible to specify their nesting. It is also no longer necessary to close the tag previously opened because the indentation allows you to see the nesting of the tags.

> **Note**
> Full JADE documentation can be found at `https://jade-lang.com/`.

Let's use JADE to display the previous client list. We create the `clients.jade` view in the `views` directory, and we indicate in `clients.js` that we display this view when accessing the `GET /clients` route:

clients.js file (routes directory)

```
var express = require('express');
var router = express.Router();

router.get('/', function(req, res, next) {
  res.render("clients");      // display clients.jade view
                              // (.jade extension is enabled by
                              // default)
});

module.exports = router;
```

Note that if you do not indicate the file extension of the view (for example, by writing `res.render("clients")`), the extension used will be the one indicated in the instruction `app.set('view engine', 'jade')` from `app.js`.

If, on the other hand, you specify an extension to the view file, it will be the one used to display the view even if it is different from the one configured in `app.js`. The view `clients.jade` is as follows:

clients.jade file (views directory)

```
h1 Client list
ul
   li Bill Clinton
   li Barack Obama
   li Joe Biden
```

Notice the indentation of the tags. The `ul` tag is at the same level as the `h1` tag, otherwise, it would be seen as included in the `h1` tag. The `li` tags are shifted to the right to show their inclusion in the preceding `ul` tag. The offset must be at least one character. Because of the offsets, we do not use a closing tag as in HTML.

Let's restart the server with `npm start` because one of the routing files has been modified.

> **Note**
> Editing files associated with views does not require a server restart, unlike the `app.js` file and files associated with routes (in the `routes` directory).

Once the server restarts, let's display the URL `http://localhost:3000` again:

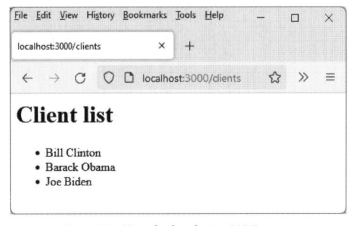

Figure 7.9 – View displayed using JADE syntax

The list of clients is, in this example, entered directly into the JADE view. It is better to pass it as parameters using the second parameter of the `res.render(name, obj)` method. The `clients.js` file then becomes the following:

clients.js file (routes directory)

```
var express = require('express');
var router = express.Router();

router.get('/', function(req, res, next) {
  res.render("clients", {
    clients : [
      { firstname : "Bill", lastname : "Clinton" },
      { firstname : "Barack", lastname : "Obama" },
      { firstname : "Joe", lastname : "Biden" },
    ]
  });
});

module.exports = router;
```

The `obj` parameter of the `res.render("clients", obj)` method is an object containing the list of clients.

The `clients.jade` view uses this passed object as follows:

clients.jade file (views directory)

```
h1 Client list
ul
  li #{clients[0].lastname + " " + clients[0].firstname}
  li #{clients[1].lastname + " " + clients[1].firstname}
  li #{clients[2].lastname + " " + clients[2].firstname}
```

The `obj` object passed in parameters is used in the JADE view, by using its `clients` property here.

> **JADE Syntax**
>
> JavaScript statements can be used in the JADE view by surrounding them with #{ and }. Anything between these two markers will be considered JavaScript code.

You can also use a syntax simplification allowed by JADE, by writing the = sign directly after each `li` tag. This means that everything following on the line must be interpreted in JavaScript. We can use this simplification of writing here.

Let's write the `clients.jade` view as follows:

clients.jade file (views directory)

```
h1 Client list
ul
   li= clients[0].lastname + " " + clients[0].firstname
   li= clients[1].lastname + " " + clients[1].firstname
   li= clients[2].lastname + " " + clients[2].firstname
```

Rather than listing each element of the `clients` array in the view, you can also perform a loop using the `each` statement of the JADE syntax to iterate over a JavaScript array.

The `clients.jade` view therefore becomes the following:

clients.jade file (views directory)

```
h1 Client list
ul
   each client in clients
      li= client.lastname + " " + client.firstname
```

The writing of the view is simplified, but you really have to take into account the indentations of the lines otherwise the view will not be displayed.

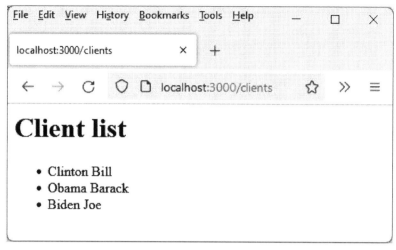

Figure 7.10 – List of clients displayed by the each statement

We see in this example that the JADE syntax makes it easy to display lists of data in the views of the application.

With this, we come to the end of this chapter.

Summary

The Express module makes it possible to structure your application efficiently by allowing (thanks to the MVC model it uses) you to separate the management of routes, the views displayed, and the management of data.

We have explained how to write the views of the application using the JADE syntax provided by default by Express. Other syntaxes, for example, the EJS syntax, are also available by downloading them via npm.

We have also seen the importance of the app.js file created by Express, and the use of HTTP requests such as **GET**, **POST**, **PUT**, and **DELETE**. We will see in *Chapter 9, Integrating Vue.js with Node.js*, the importance of these HTTP requests to build a MEVN application (short for MongoDB, Express, Vue.js, Node.js) that manipulates the MongoDB database.

Indeed, data management is often done using the **MongoDB** database, the use of which we will explore in the next chapter.

8
Using MongoDB with Node.js

MongoDB is the database traditionally associated with Node.js. It is a NoSQL type database, which means that SQL will not be used to access the information it contains.

MongoDB is a document-oriented database in which we store so-called *documents*; that is, a data structure of any type, such as information written on a sheet of paper (which is then equivalent to a document). Several sheets of paper, thus corresponding to several documents, form what is called a *collection*.

An example of a document is, for example, the first name, the last name, and the address of a customer. Aggregated information from multiple customers would be called a collection.

In this chapter, we'll study how to use MongoDB in conjunction with Node.js in order to store, read, delete, or update information in the database.

Inserting, searching, updating, or deleting data are the main actions that can be performed in a database. Therefore, in this chapter, we'll see how to perform these operations with the MongoDB database.

Here are the topics covered in this chapter:

- Installing MongoDB and the mongoose module
- Connecting to the MongoDB database
- Creating documents
- Searching documents
- Updating documents
- Deleting documents

Let's start by installing MongoDB and the **mongoose** module, which will allow MongoDB to be used in Node.js programs.

Technical requirements

You can find the code files for this chapter on GitHub at: `https://github.com/PacktPublishing/JavaScript-from-Frontend-to-Backend/blob/main/Chapter%208.zip`.

Installing MongoDB

The MongoDB database is independent of Node.js, which requires installing it separately. To do this, go to the site `https://www.mongodb.com/docs/manual/administration/install-community/`. Download the version suitable for your system.

Once MongoDB is installed, verify that the installation is correct by typing the `mongo -h` command in a command interpreter. The `mongo` command is located in the `Server/x.x/bin` directory of MongoDB, where `x.x` is the version number of MongoDB installed.

> **Note**
>
> At the time of writing, the `mongo` utility is available directly when installing MongoDB. However, it is possible that this utility will soon be available separately and called `mongosh`. In this case, download this utility from `https://www.mongodb.com/docs/mongodb-shell/install/`.
>
> The `mongo` command will simply be replaced by the equivalent `mongosh` command. Both commands work identically.

Installing MongoDB 239

After installing MongoDB, we will look into the mongo (or mongosh) utility. The mongo utility makes it easy to see the contents of database collections, without having to write program lines. It is therefore useful for checking, for example, whether a document has been correctly inserted into a collection, or that its deletion has been successful. Let's see how to use the mongo utility.

Using the mongo utility

The mongo utility enables you to easily view databases and the collections they contain. The mongo utility is launched by simply typing the mongo command in a command interpreter. The program then waits for database access commands, or the exit command to exit.

Here is the list of the main commands available in the mongo utility:

- show dbs: This shows a list of existing databases. A database will be visible here only if it contains at least one collection.

- db=connect("mydb_test"): This is to connect to the database mydb_test. The db variable will then be used to access the database collections.

- show collections: This shows the collections of the connected database. A collection will be present if it contains at least one document.

- db.clients.find(): This shows all documents in the clients collection.

- db.clients.find({name:"Clinton"}): This lists documents in the clients collection whose name is Clinton.

- db.clients.find().sort({name:1}): This sorts documents in ascending order of the name field. Use {name:-1} for descending sort.

- db.clients.count(): This counts the number of documents found in the clients collection.

- db.clients.renameCollection("clients2"): This renames the clients collection to clients2.

- db.clients.drop(): This drops the clients collection (all documents are dropped).

- db.dropDatabase(): This drops the connected database (all collections are removed).

Other commands exist, in particular, for inserting, updating, or deleting documents in a collection. But since these actions are performed through the mongoose module instead, we will describe them using the mongoose module.

Installing the mongoose module

To establish the relationship between MongoDB and Node.js, several npm modules have been created. The most widely used one currently is the `mongoose` module. It is installed in the `node_modules` directory of the current directory by typing the `npm install mongoose` command.

Figure 8.1 – Installing the mongoose module

Once mongoose has been downloaded by npm, we check whether it is accessible for our programs. Let's display the mongoose version for our programs. We write this snippet in the file `test.js`:

Displaying mongoose version (test.js file)

```
var mongoose = require("mongoose");
console.log("mongoose version =", mongoose.version);
```

Let's use the `node test.js` command to run the previous program:

Figure 8.2 – Checking that mongoose is accessible

> **Warning**
>
> If you get an error loading the mongoose module, it's probably because you installed it globally (with the `-g` option). In this case, just type the `npm link mongoose` command in the terminal to get rid of the error.

The mongoose module will allow us to use the MongoDB database to create documents, search them, update them, or destroy them. These are the classic operations that can be performed on a database.

But to be able to perform these operations, it is necessary to first connect to the database.

Connecting to the MongoDB database

All operations to access MongoDB require establishing a connection with it. Now let's see how to establish a connection with MongoDB.

The `mongoose.connect(url)` instruction connects the mongoose module to the database specified in the `url` parameter. The `url` parameter is of the form `"mongodb://localhost/mydb_test"` to connect to the `mydb_test` database on the localhost server.

The database will actually be created (and visible with the execution of the `show dbs` command of the mongo utility) when the first document is inserted into it:

Connecting to the mydb_test database (test.js file)

```
var mongoose = require("mongoose");
mongoose.connect("mongodb://localhost/mydb_test");

console.log("Connecting to mydb_test database in progress...");
```

Let's run the previous program:

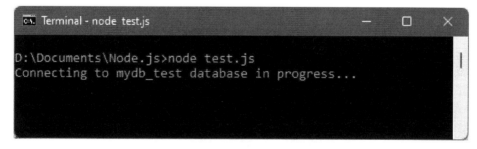

Figure 8.3 – Database connection

To know whether the connection to the database has actually been made, mongoose sends the `open` event (if the connection was successful) or the `error` event (if the connection fails) on the `mongoose.connection` object.

Next, we will take these two events into account and integrate them into the previous program. This is done using the on(event, callback) method defined on the mongoose.connection object:

> **Note**
> The on(event, callback) method is used to process the reception of the event and to associate it with the processing described in the callback function.

Using open and error events on database connection (test.js file)

```
var mongoose = require("mongoose");
mongoose.connect("mongodb://localhost/mydb_test");

mongoose.connection.on("error", function() {
 console.log("mydb_test database connection error")
});
mongoose.connection.on("open", function() {
 console.log("Successful connection to mydb_test
 database");
});

console.log("Connecting to mydb_test database in progress...");
```

Let's run the previous program:

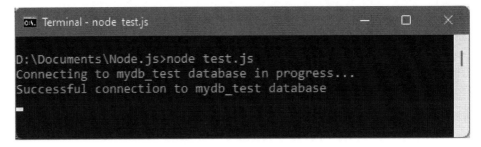

Figure 8.4 – Successful connection to the database

We have seen how to connect to the database. We will therefore be able to create documents in a collection of the database.

Creating documents in MongoDB

Once the database has been accessed, you can create documents in it.

A document will be inserted into a *collection*. A collection will therefore group together a set of documents. The database will therefore be a set of collections, each containing documents.

In order to be able to insert documents, mongoose asks us to describe the structure of these documents. For this, we will use schemas and models.

Describing document structure using schemas and models

To access the documents in the database, the documents must be described by means of schemas and models.

> **Definitions**
>
> A *schema* allows you to define the structure of a document that is stored in a collection. The structure is defined according to MongoDB data types.
>
> A *model* is the representation of a schema as a JavaScript class. It links a schema to a MongoDB collection.

Let's look at how to create a schema and then a model.

Creating a schema

A schema defines the fields of a document using Node.js internal object classes. These are the following classes:

- `String`: This defines a string of characters.
- `Number`: This defines a numeric field.
- `Boolean`: This defines a Boolean.
- `Array`: This defines an array.
- `Buffer`: This defines a buffer of bytes.
- `Date`: This defines a date.
- `Object`: This defines a JavaScript object.

The `mongoose.Schema(format)` method is used to define the schema associated with the document. The `format` parameter is a JavaScript object that associates each field in the document with the type (in the above list) that represents it.

Let's create the schema defining a client. A client is characterized by its `lastname`, `firstname`, and `address`. All these fields are of type `String`:

Defining the schema associated with a client (test.js file)

```
var mongoose = require("mongoose");
mongoose.connect("mongodb://localhost/mydb_test");

var clientSchema = mongoose.Schema({
 lastname : String,
 firstname : String,
 address : String
});
```

Now let's explain how to create a model from the schema.

Creating a model

The schema is then used to define the model associated with the document. The model corresponds to a JavaScript class that will be used to create the documents in a collection.

The `mongoose.model(collection, schema)` method returns a JavaScript class associated with the schema. This class is called a model.

Documents created with this class will be inserted into the specified `collection`. The collection may not exist before inserting a document. A collection requires at least one document within it.

> **Summary**
> A schema specifies the format of a document stored in a collection,
> while a model is a JavaScript class used to create each such document.
> We associate a document schema with a collection using the `mongoose.model(collection, schema)` method call. This returns a JavaScript class that can then be used to generate individual document instances.

Let's create the `Client` class, which will create the clients that will be stored in the `clients` collection. It is traditional to name the collection based on the name of the model, in lowercase and in plural:

Creating the Client model from the schema (test.js file)

```
var mongoose = require("mongoose");
mongoose.connect("mongodb://localhost/mydb_test");

var clientSchema = mongoose.Schema({
  lastname : String,
  firstname : String,
  address : String
});

// creation of the Client class associated with the clients
// collection
var Client = mongoose.model("clients", clientSchema);
```

The `Client` class is now available to create the documents that will be inserted into the `clients` collection.

Creating the document

There are two methods for creating the documents in a collection. These are the `doc.save(callback)` instance method and the `create(doc, callback)` class method. Let's look at these two ways to create documents in a collection.

Let's start by using the `doc.save(callback)` instance method.

Using the doc.save(callback) instance method

The client document is created in memory from the previously created class (by means of `var client = new Client()`), then saved in the `clients` collection by means of the `client.save()` method.

The callback function allows processing when the document has finished being inserted into the collection. This is especially useful if it is necessary to wait for the document to be inserted into the database before continuing processing:

Using the save() instance method to save document (test.js file)

```javascript
var mongoose = require("mongoose");
mongoose.connect("mongodb://localhost/mydb_test");

var clientSchema = mongoose.Schema({
 lastname : String,
 firstname : String,
 address : String
});

// creation of the Client class associated with the clients
// collection
var Client = mongoose.model("clients", clientSchema);

// create the document in memory
var c = new Client({lastname :"Clinton", firstname:"Bill",
address:"Washington"});

console.log("Before the save() statement");

// save the document in the database (clients collection)
c.save(function(err) {
  if (!err) console.log("The client is inserted into the
  collection");
});

console.log("After the save() statement");
```

The callback function takes the `err` parameter, which corresponds to a possible error message (otherwise, it is `null`).

We get the following result:

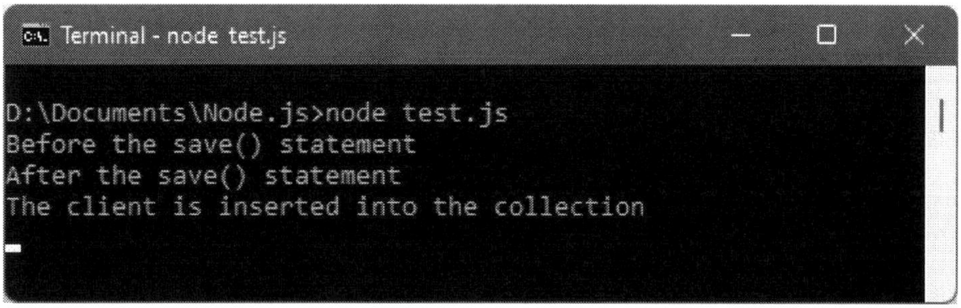

Figure 8.5 – Using the doc.save() instance method

Using the traces displayed in the console, we can see that the message `The client is inserted into the collection` is displayed after the other messages, which means that inserting a document is not blocking other tasks (i.e., other tasks can be done while waiting for insertion in the database).

The `save()` method can also be used as a `Promise` object (see *Chapter 2, Exploring the Advanced Concepts of JavaScript*). For this, we use the `then(callback)` method afterward, possibly followed by the `catch(callback)` method to process the cases of error when calling the `save()` method.

In this case, we write the following:

Using the save() method as a Promise objet

```
c.save().then(function(doc) {
  console.log(doc);
  console.log("The client is inserted into the collection");
}).catch(function(err) {
  console.log(err);   // display the error
});
```

Now let's see the other method of creating a document with the `create(doc, callback)` class method.

Using the create(doc, callback) class method

A class method means that we can use the method without having instantiated an object, unlike an instance method, which requires that the object of the class be created (with `c = new Client()`).

To create the document associated with the client identified by `{lastname:"Obama", firstname:"Barack", address:"Washington"}`, we would write the following:

Using the Client.create(doc, callback) class method to save document (test.js file)

```
var mongoose = require("mongoose");
mongoose.connect("mongodb://localhost/mydb_test");

var clientSchema = mongoose.Schema({
  lastname : String,
  firstname : String,
  address : String
});

// creation of the Client class associated with the clients
// collection
var Client = mongoose.model("clients", clientSchema);

console.log("Before the create() statement");

// save the document in the database (clients collection)
Client.create({lastname:"Obama", firstname:"Barack",
address:"Washington"}, function(err, doc) {
  console.log("The client is inserted into the collection",
    doc);
});

console.log("After the create() statement");
```

The `create(doc, callback)` class method is used by prefixing it with the name of the JavaScript class (here, the `Client` class).

The document to be saved is written in the form of a JavaScript object (JSON format) but can also be an object instantiated with `c = new Client()`.

The callback function of the form `callback(err, doc)` is executed at the end of saving the document in the database. This callback function is useful if you want to perform a process while being certain that the document has been saved in the collection.

> **Note**
>
> Note that the callback function `callback(err, doc)` of the `create(doc, callback)` method has the two parameters `err` and `doc`, which are the possible error and the document saved in the database, respectively.

Let's run the previous program:

```
D:\Documents\Node.js>node test.js
Before the create() statement
After the create() statement
The client is inserted into the collection {
  lastname: 'Obama',
  firstname: 'Barack',
  address: 'Washington',
  _id: new ObjectId("622cea6f296e71dfa619a7fa"),
  __v: 0
}
```

Figure 8.6 – Using the Client.create() class method

The saved document has the fields indicated in the format associated with the model (here, the lastname, firstname, and address fields), but also the _id and __v fields, added automatically by MongoDB:

- The _id field is a field used by MongoDB to give a unique identifier to each document in a collection. It plays the role of a primary key.
- The __v field is a field added by mongoose, associated with the document version number. We will not use it here.

As with the save() instance method, the create(doc) class method can be used as a Promise object. For this, we do not use the callback parameter in the create(doc) method and instead use the then(callback) and catch(callback) methods following the create(doc) method call.

For example, we could also write the following:

Using create() method as a Promise object

```
Client.create({lastname:"Obama", firstname:"Barack",
address:"Washington"}).then(function(doc) {
    console.log("The client is inserted into the collection",
    doc);
});
```

In the previous examples, we have inserted two documents into the clients collection. Let's use the mongo utility to display the inserted documents and verify the documents that are present in the collection.

Using the mongo utility to view inserted documents

To display the inserted documents, use the mongo utility and type the following commands:

1. db=connect("mydb_test") to connect to the database
2. show collections to show the collections already present

3. `db.clients.find()` to display documents from the `clients` collection

```
> 
> db=connect("mydb_test")
connecting to: mongodb://127.0.0.1:27017/mydb_test
Implicit session: session { "id" : UUID("5b1032bf-6cee-4ace-b407-d42a5bb6760e") }
MongoDB server version: 5.0.6
mydb_test
> 
> show collections
clients
> 
> db.clients.find()
{ "_id" : ObjectId("622cea56a5108be2d85e9e8b"), "lastname" : "Clinton", "firstname" : "Bill", "address" : "Washington", "__v" : 0 }
{ "_id" : ObjectId("622cea6f296e71dfa619a7fa"), "lastname" : "Obama", "firstname" : "Barack", "address" : "Washington", "__v" : 0 }
> 
> 
```

Figure 8.7 – Using the mongo utility to view documents

We thus check that the two documents of the `clients` collection are indeed present.

Let's see how to search for them with mongoose module methods.

Searching for documents in MongoDB

Once the documents have been inserted into the collection, they can be searched for using the `find()` class method.

> **Note**
>
> The `find()` method is a class method, which means that it is used by prefixing it with the class name associated with the model, for example, `Client.find()`.

The `find(conditions, callback)` method is used to perform a search in the collection associated with the model, then to retrieve the results of the search in the callback function indicated as a parameter.

Let's take an in-depth look at the parameters:

- The `conditions` parameter is a JavaScript object used to specify search conditions. If no condition is specified, do not indicate anything (or indicate an empty object { }).
- The callback function is of the form `callback(err, results)` where `err` is an error message (`null` otherwise) and `results` is an array containing the search results (empty `[]` if none).

There is also the `findOne(conditions, callback)` class method, which allows you, on the same principle, to find only the first document that satisfies the search. The callback function is of the form `callback(err, result)` where `result` is the first document found.

> **Note**
> The `findOne(conditions, callback)` method will be useful if you are looking for a single document, for example, from its identifier `_id`.

You can also use the `find(conditions)` and `findOne(conditions)` methods without specifying the callback function as a parameter. For this, we use the `then(callback)` and `catch(callback)` methods to perform the processing on the documents found or in the event of an error. We can also use the `exec(callback)` method, as explained in the following section.

Let us now examine how to write the `conditions` parameter used in the two methods `find()` and `findOne()`.

Writing search conditions

In the `conditions` parameter, we indicate an object whose properties are the fields of the documents in the collection, and the associated values are the values sought for the field, of the form `{field1:value1, field2:value2...}`, for example, `{lastname:"Clinton", firstname:"Bill"}`.

Other properties can be used as keywords to express conditions. They start with the $ sign, such as: `$or`, `$exists`, `$type`, `$where`, `$gt`, and `$lt`.

> **Note**
> A list of possible keywords can be found here: `https://docs.mongodb.com/manual/reference/operator/query/`.

Here are some examples of conditions:

- `{ }`: All documents in the collection. You can also write `find()`, which is equivalent to `find({})`.
- `{ lastname: "Clinton" }`: All documents whose lastname is `Clinton`.
- `{ lastname: "Clinton", firstname: "Bill" }`: All documents whose lastname is `Clinton` and first name is `Bill`.
- `{ $or: [{ lastname: "Clinton"}, { firstname: "Jimmy" }] }`: All documents whose lastname is `Clinton` or first name is `Jimmy`.
- `{ lastname: /obama/i }`: All documents whose lastname contains the string `obama` regardless of case (regular expression).
- `{ address: { $exists: true} }`: All documents whose `address` field exists, regardless of its type (String, Object, etc.).
- `{ address: { $exists: true, $type: 2 } }`: All documents whose `address` field exists, and which is of type 2 (String).
- `{"address.city": "Washington" }`: All documents containing the `address` field that itself has a city field whose value is `Washington`.
- `{lastname:{$type:2}, $where:"this.lastname.match(/^Clinton|carter$/i)"}`: All documents whose lastname is a string (type = 2) and whose lastname begins with `Clinton` or ends with `carter`, regardless of case. You must indicate that the lastname is a character string, otherwise you may have an error with names that are not in this form.
- `{lastname: { $gt: "J", $lt: "S" }}`: All documents whose lastname is greater than `"J"` and less than `"S"`.
- `{lastname: { $in:["Clinton", "Carter", "Obama"] }}`: All documents whose lastname is `Clinton`, `Carter`, or `Obama`.

Once the search conditions have been expressed, the results found must be retrieved and displayed. Let's see how to do it.

Retrieving and displaying the results

Whatever the condition expressed, the corresponding results can be retrieved in the callback function associated with the `find()` method, of the form `callback(err, results)`. We will also see that it is possible to use the `exec(callback)` method to retrieve the results.

Let's look at these two ways to retrieve search results.

Using the callback parameter of the find(conditions, callback) method

Let's find all clients whose lastname is `Clinton` or firstname is `Barack`. The result will be displayed in the callback function:

Displaying clients whose lastname is "Clinton" or firstname is "Barack" (test.js file)

```javascript
var mongoose = require("mongoose");
mongoose.connect("mongodb://localhost/mydb_test");

var clientSchema = mongoose.Schema({
  lastname : String,
  firstname : String,
  address : String
});

// creation of the Client class associated with the clients
// collection
var Client = mongoose.model("clients", clientSchema);

Client.find({ $or : [ { lastname : "Clinton" }, { firstname : "Barack"} ] }, function(err, clients) {
  console.log(clients);
});
```

We obtain the result shown in the following figure:

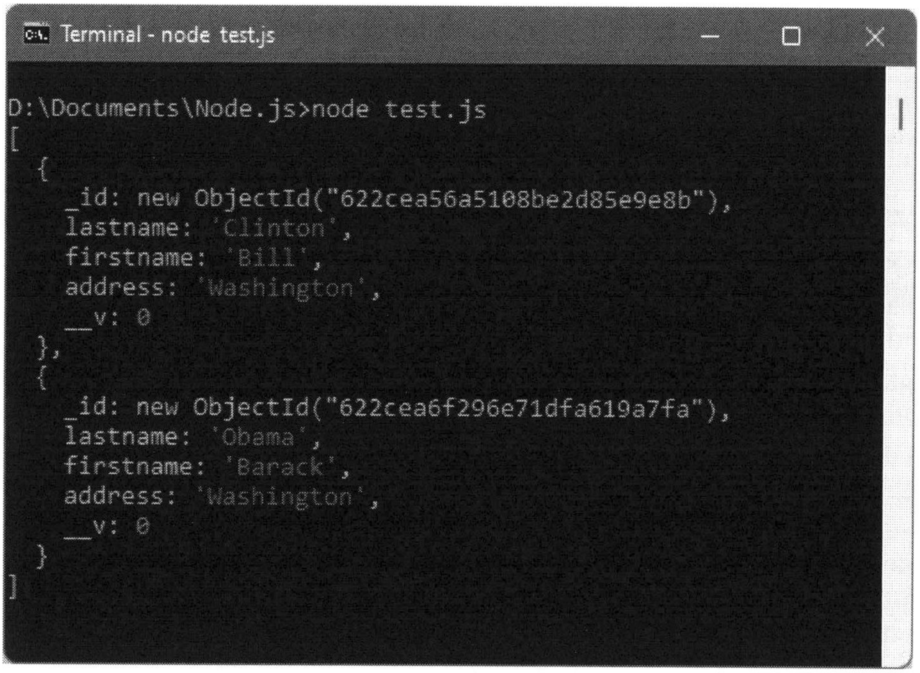
Terminal - node test.js
D:\Documents\Node.js>node test.js
[
{
_id: new ObjectId("622cea56a5108be2d85e9e8b"),
lastname: 'Clinton',
firstname: 'Bill',
address: 'Washington',
__v: 0
},
{
_id: new ObjectId("622cea6f296e71dfa619a7fa"),
lastname: 'Obama',
firstname: 'Barack',
address: 'Washington',
__v: 0
}
]

Figure 8.8 – Displaying search results with find(conditions, callback)

The callback function can be expressed in the `find()` method as before, or be specified in the `exec()` method used after the `find()` method. Let us now examine this second possibility.

Using the exec(callback) method

Another way to retrieve results is to use the `exec(callback)` method following the `find(conditions)` method. The `find(conditions)` method is used here without indicating a callback function in its parameters because the callback function is indicated in the `exec(callback)` method.

The advantage of this is that we can insert new methods between the `find()` method and the `exec()` method. For example, if we want to add as additional conditions that the `lastname` field must be equal to `Clinton`, we can write the following:

Adding as search conditions that lastname is "Clinton" (test.js file)

```
var mongoose = require("mongoose");
mongoose.connect("mongodb://localhost/mydb_test");

var clientSchema = mongoose.Schema({
  lastname : String,
  firstname : String,
  address : String
});

// creation of the Client class associated with the clients
// collection
var Client = mongoose.model("clients", clientSchema);

Client.find({ $or : [ { lastname : "Clinton" }, { firstname : "Barack"} ] })
.where("lastname")
.eq("Clinton")
.exec(function(err, clients) {
  console.log(clients);
});
```

> **Note**
> Methods such as `where(field)` and `eq(value)` can be chained after the `find()` method. The execution of the search will be effective when calling the `exec()` method. Other usage possibilities are described here: https://mongoosejs.com/docs/api/query.html#query_Query-where.

You can also use the `exec(callback)` method without specifying the callback function as a parameter. For this, we use the `then(callback)` and `catch(callback)` methods to perform the processing on the documents found or in the event of an error.

We write the following for this:

Using exec() method as a Promise object

```
Client.find({ $or : [ { lastname : "Clinton" }, { firstname :
"Barack"} ] })
.where("lastname")
.eq("Clinton")
.exec()
.then(function(clients) {
  console.log(clients);  // display the clients
})
.catch(function(err) {
  console.log(err);  // display the error
});
```

The result is displayed in the following figure.

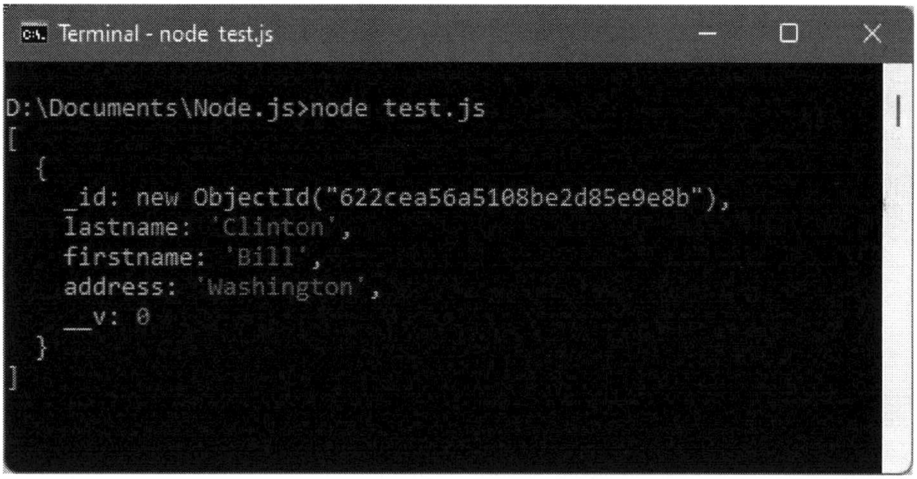
Terminal - node test.js
D:\Documents\Node.js>node test.js
[
{
_id: new ObjectId("622cea56a5108be2d85e9e8b"),
lastname: 'Clinton',
firstname: 'Bill',
address: 'Washington',
__v: 0
}
]

Figure 8.9 – Using the exec(callback) method

We've learned how to create documents, then search for them. Now let's look at how to update them.

Updating documents in MongoDB

It is possible to modify one or more documents of a collection. The `updateOne()` and `updateMany()` class methods are used respectively to modify the first document found or all of the documents found.

These two methods have similar parameters:

- `updateMany(conditions, update, callback)` indicates modifying the data indicated in the `update` object on the documents specified by the indicated `conditions`. The callback function of the form `callback(err, response)` is called after the update.

- `updateOne(conditions, update, callback)` indicates modifying the data indicated in the `update` object on the first document found by the indicated `conditions`. The callback function of the form `callback(err, response)` is called after the update.

- Only the `conditions` and `update` parameters are mandatory in the two methods.

> **Warning**
>
> If the callback is not present in the method, you must use the `then()` or `exec()` method afterward, otherwise the update is not done.

Let's modify the address of `Clinton`, which will now be `New York`:

Using updateOne() to modify the address of "Clinton" (test.js file)

```
var mongoose = require("mongoose");
mongoose.connect("mongodb://localhost/mydb_test");

var clientSchema = mongoose.Schema({
 lastname : String,
 firstname : String,
 address : String
});

// creation of the Client class associated with the clients
// collection
```

```
var Client = mongoose.model("clients", clientSchema);

Client.updateOne({ lastname : "Clinton" }, { address : "New 
York" }, function(err, response) {
  console.log("response =", response);
});
```

Here, we use the callback function to display the content of the `response` parameter returned by the function. We get the following result:

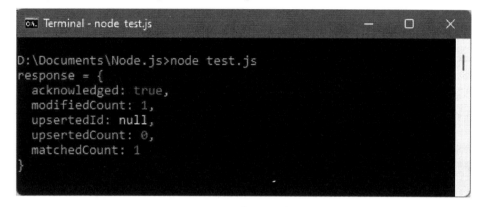

Figure 8.10 – Updating a document

> **Note**
> The `response.modifiedCount` field indicates the number of modified documents.

If you do not want to perform any processing at the end of the update, you can omit the callback function, but in this case, you must use the `then()` or `exec()` method afterward, otherwise, the update will not take place.

Let's use the `exec()` method to perform the update:

Performing update using exec() method (test.js file)

```
var mongoose = require("mongoose");
mongoose.connect("mongodb://localhost/mydb_test");

var clientSchema = mongoose.Schema({
  lastname : String,
```

```
  firstname : String,
  address : String
});

// creation of the Client class associated with the clients
// collection
var Client = mongoose.model("clients", clientSchema);

Client.updateOne({ lastname : "Clinton" },
                 { address : "New York" })
.exec();      // exec() mandatory!
```

Once you know how to create, search for, and then modify documents, you just have to know how to delete them. Let's look at how to do it.

Deleting documents in MongoDB

Similar to `updateOne()` and `updateMany()`, there are the two class methods, namely `deleteOne(conditions, callback)` and `deleteMany(conditions, callback)` that allow you to delete the first document (`deleteOne()`) or all the documents (`deleteMany()`) that satisfy the conditions expressed.

In addition, the instance method `doc.remove(callback)` also makes it possible to delete the `doc` document when it is in memory.

Let's remove `Clinton` from the collection by using the `deleteOne()` method, then display the new contents of the collection:

Using deleteOne() to delete client "Clinton" (test.js file)

```
var mongoose = require("mongoose");
mongoose.connect("mongodb://localhost/mydb_test");

var clientSchema = mongoose.Schema({
  lastname : String,
  firstname : String,
  address : String
```

```
});

// creation of the Client class associated with the clients
// collection
var Client = mongoose.model("clients", clientSchema);

Client.deleteOne({ lastname : "Clinton" }, function(err,
response) {
  console.log("After Clinton's removal");
  console.log("response = ", response);

  Client.find(function(err, clients) {
    console.log("clients = ", clients);
  });
});
```

In the same way as for the `updateOne()` and `updateMany()` methods, it is the presence of the callback function that triggers the update of the database. If you do not indicate a callback function, you must in this case use the `then()` or `exec()` method following the `deleteOne()` or `deleteMany()` method.

The result is displayed in the following figure:

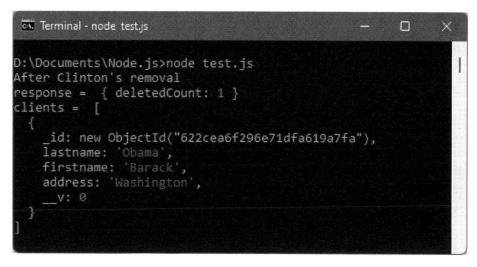

Figure 8.11 – Deleting the "Clinton" client with deleteOne()

The `response` object returned in the callback of the `deleteOne()` (or `deleteMany()`) method indicates the `deletedCount` field, which contains the number of documents deleted.

We have successively studied the four possible operations on documents in a MongoDB database, namely inserting, searching, modifying, and deleting documents. And with this, we come to the end of this chapter.

Summary

Data management with MongoDB is relatively easy, thanks to the use of external modules such as mongoose. All possible actions on a database are easily achievable.

The mongo utility, available when installing MongoDB, makes it easy to view collections and the documents they contain.

Using the MongoDB database is essential for building client-server applications and maintaining user information.

All that's left is to see how to interconnect a client side made with Vue.js and a server side made with Node.js. We will see this in the following chapter. We will build a 100% JavaScript application in order to show how simple and efficient it is.

9
Integrating Vue.js with Node.js

In this chapter, we will learn how to integrate a Vue.js application into a Node.js server, using Express to structure the server code (according to the MVC model) and MongoDB to store the information.

For this, we will use the example of the list management application built in *Chapter 5, Managing a List with Vue.js*. But here, the server used will be a Node.js server, and the list items will be stored in the MongoDB database. This will allow them to be redisplayed later, if necessary.

In the end, we will obtain a client-server application entirely made in JavaScript (both on the client side and on the server side).

Here are the topics covered in this chapter:

- Displaying application screens
- Building the app with Express
- MongoDB database structure
- Installing the Axios library
- Inserting a new element in the list

- Displaying list elements
- Modifying an element in the list
- Removing an element from the list

The application uses the same screens as those already used in *Chapter 5, Managing a List with Vue.js*. We repeat them below to make them easier for you to understand.

Technical requirements

You can find the code files for this chapter on GitHub at: `https://github.com/PacktPublishing/JavaScript-from-Frontend-to-Backend/blob/main/Chapter%209.zip`.

Displaying application screens

Here, we visualize the screens of the application, allowing the following:

- Displaying the already existing list (empty at first)
- Inserting a new element at the end of the list
- Modifying an element of the list
- Removing an item from the list

> **Note**
> The URL to access the list is `http://localhost:3000`. The server used here is a Node.js server running with the **Express** module. The database used is **MongoDB**.

Initially, the list is empty. Only the **Add Element** button is present on the page (see the following figure):

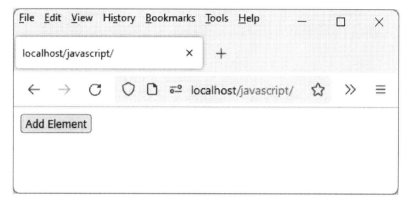

Figure 9.1 – Empty item list

Clicking the **Add Element** button multiple times creates multiple rows with the text **Element X** followed by **Remove** and **Modify** buttons (here, we clicked on the **Add Element** button three times):

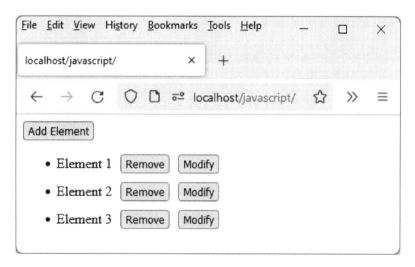

Figure 9.2 – Adding three items to the list

266   Integrating Vue.js with Node.js

Next, let's modify the second element. An input field appears in place of the item text. Let's type `New Element 2` in place of the text displayed in the input field:

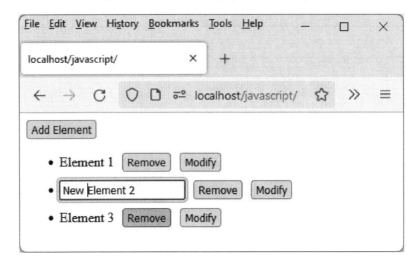

Figure 9.3 – Editing the second item in the list

By clicking outside the input field, the input field disappears, and the text of the element appears modified:

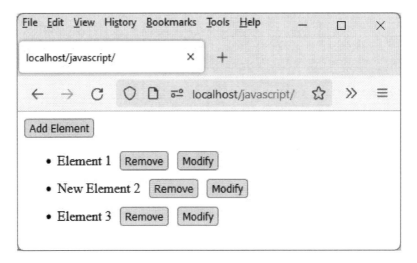

Figure 9.4 – Second list item changed

Finally, let's remove the first and third items from the list:

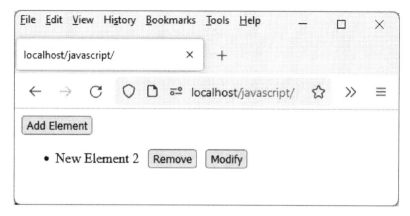

Figure 9.5 – First and third list items removed

Now, when we refresh the previous window, we see that the list is re-displayed with `New Element 2`, thus indicating that the modifications made are indeed stored in a database. This was not the case when we made this application in *Chapter 5, Managing a List with Vue.js*, with only Vue.js, because the elements of the list were not saved in a database:

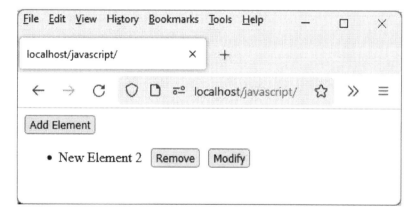

Figure 9.6 – New list display: the list is preserved

To create this application, we will, of course, use the Vue.js program that we have already written in *Chapter 5, Managing a List with Vue.js*. But it will have to be modified so that this application works on a Node.js server with the Express module and that the data displayed is stored in the MongoDB database.

We'll indicate here the files of the `<GlobalApp>` and `<Element>` components, written previously, in *Chapter 5, Managing a List with Vue.js*, to explain the modifications that will be made to them hereafter.

Here's the `<GlobalApp>` component:

`<GlobalApp>` component (global-app.js file)

```
import Element from "./element.js";
const GlobalApp = {
  data() {
    return {
      elements : []
    }
  },
  components : {
    Element:Element
  },
  template : `
    <button @click="add()">Add Element</button>
    <ul>
      <Element v-for="(element, index) in elements"
        :key="index"
          :text="element" :index="index"
          @remove="remove($event)" @modify="modify($event)"
      />
    </ul>
  `,
  methods : {
    add() {
      var element = "Element " + (this.elements.length + 1);
      this.elements.push(element);
    },
    remove(params) {
      var index = params.index;
      this.elements.splice(index, 1);
```

```
    },
    modify(params) {
      var index = params.index;
      var value = params.value;
      this.elements[index] = value;
    }
  }
}

export default GlobalApp;
```

Here's the `<Element>` component:

`<Element>` component (element.js file)

```
const Element = {
  data() {
    return {
      input : false
    }
  },
  template : `
    <li>
      <span v-if="!input"> {{text}} </span>
      <input v-else type="text" :value="text"
       @blur="modify($event)" ref="refInput" />
      <button @click="remove()"> Remove </button>
      <button @click="input=true"> Modify </button>
    </li>
  `,
  props : ["text", "index"],
  methods : {
    remove() {
      // process the click on the Remove button
      this.$emit("remove", { index : this.index });
    },
```

```
    modify(event) {
      var value = event.target.value;
      this.input = false;
      this.$emit("modify", { index : this.index, value :
      value });
    }
  },
  emits : ["remove", "modify"],
  updated() {
    // check that refInput exists, and if so, give focus to
    // the input field
    if (this.$refs.refInput) this.$refs.refInput.focus();
  }
}

export default Element;
```

The index.html file that allows you to include the `<GlobalApp>` component is the following:

index.html file

```
<html>
  <head>
    <meta charset="utf-8" />
    <script src="https://unpkg.com/vue@next"></script>

    <style type="text/css">
      li {
        margin-top:10px;
      }
      ul button {
        margin-left:10px;
```

```
    }
   </style>
 </head>

 <body>
   <div id="app"></div>
 </body>

 <script type="module">

   import GlobalApp from "./global-app.js";

   var app = Vue.createApp({
     components : {
       GlobalApp:GlobalApp
     },
     template : "<GlobalApp />"
   });

   var vm = app.mount("div#app");

 </script>

</html>
```

To create this application, we start by creating the Node.js application, which will host the JavaScript code written with Vue.js. To do this, the application is created using the `express` command. The application will be named *list* (for example), so we will have to type the `express list` command to create this application, as is explained in the following section.

Building the app with Express

Let's start by creating the application with Express. To do this, type the `express list` command, which creates the application named *list*. This application will be accessible using the URL http://localhost:3000, as seen in *Chapter 7, Using Express with Node.js*.

Let's type the `express list` command in the current directory:

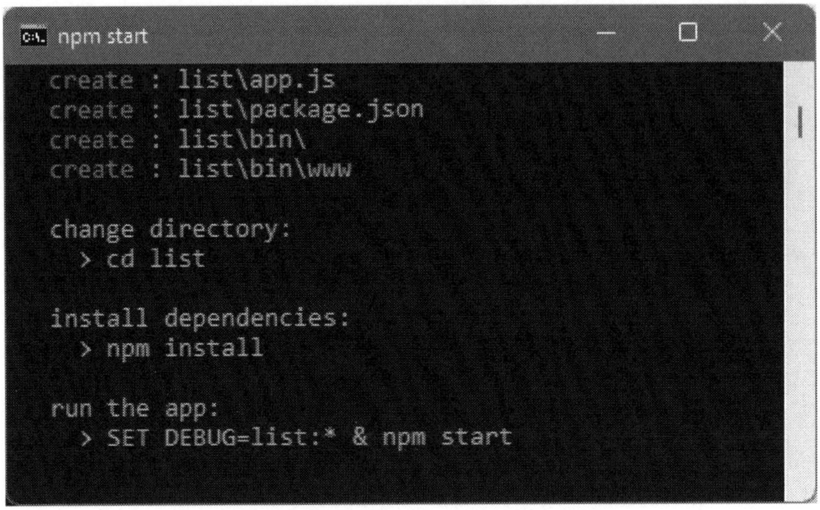

Figure 9.7 – Creating the application list with Express

The server is started by typing the indicated commands, namely: `cd list`, `npm install`, followed by `npm start`.

The application is started by typing the URL http://localhost:3000 in the browser.

We display the basic application created as standard by Express (see *Figure 9.8*).

If an error occurs while loading the Express modules, you can type the `npm link express` command in order to locate the Express module within the application. And if an error occurs while loading the mongoose module, you can type the `npm link mongoose` command.

If all is okay, you obtain the following:

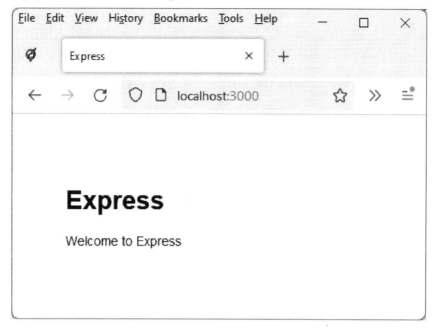

Figure 9.8 – Standard application created with Express

The goal now is to visualize our list management application, created with Vue.js. It consists of three files:

- The `index.html` file, which is the file to view at startup
- The `global-app.js` file, which describes the main `<GlobalApp>` component of the application
- The `element.js` file, which describes the `<Element>` component corresponding to a displayed element line

The main directory of the Express application (the `list` directory) includes a `public` subdirectory containing the `images`, `javascripts`, and `stylesheets` subdirectories.

Let's drop the three files `index.html`, `global-app.js`, and `element.js` in the `public` directory, directly under the root.

> **Note**
>
> Modifying files in the `public` directory does not require a server restart. On the other hand, modifying the `app.js` file of the Express application requires restarting the server with `npm start`.

Let's view the URL `http://localhost:3000` again in the browser. The Vue.js application we built in *Chapter 5*, *Managing a List with Vue.js*, will now appear. Button clicks will also start working.

The only difference is that our Vue.js application runs on a Node.js server instead of running on another application server like in *Chapter 5*, *Managing a List with Vue.js*.

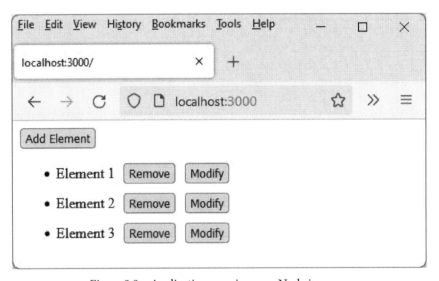

Figure 9.9 – Application running on a Node.js server

However, if the page displayed is refreshed, the list previously displayed is deleted because there is currently no persistence of the information displayed in the database.

We will now see how our application can interact with the Node.js server and the MongoDB database.

MongoDB database structure

To build our application, we will have to perform data reads and updates on the server in the database. For example, each click on the **Add Element** button should insert a new line into the displayed HTML page but should also insert a new document into MongoDB's `elements` collection. Indeed, each document of the `elements` collection will represent the text of the element displayed in the list on the screen.

> **Note**
>
> To access the MongoDB database, you start by installing the mongoose module (see the previous chapter), which allows you to manipulate database documents in JavaScript.
>
> To do this, type the `npm install mongoose` command (from the main directory, `list`, of the Express application).

The `elements` collection will be the one that will store the list items in MongoDB. A document in the `elements` collection will consist of its text associated with the `text` property. Each document will also have the `_id` property, whose unique value is assigned by MongoDB for each document inserted into the collection.

> **Note**
>
> The structure of the database is described using the `listSchema` schema, which will be associated with the `List` model used to create the documents of the `elements` collection.

Express's `app.js` file is modified to include these definitions:

Adding List model to use MongoDB's elements collection (app.js file)

```
var createError = require('http-errors');
var express = require('express');
var path = require('path');
var cookieParser = require('cookie-parser');
var logger = require('morgan');

var indexRouter = require('./routes/index');
var usersRouter = require('./routes/users');

var mongoose = require("mongoose");
mongoose.connect("mongodb://localhost/mydb_test"); // we
                                                   // connect
                                                   // to
                                                   // mydb_test

var listSchema = mongoose.Schema({
  text : String      // text associated with the list item
```

```javascript
});

// association of the List model with the elements collection
var List = mongoose.model("elements", listSchema);

var app = express();

// view engine setup
app.set('views', path.join(__dirname, 'views'));
app.set('view engine', 'jade');

app.use(logger('dev'));
app.use(express.json());
app.use(express.urlencoded({ extended: false }));
app.use(cookieParser());
app.use(express.static(path.join(__dirname, 'public')));

app.use('/', indexRouter);
app.use('/users', usersRouter);

// catch 404 and forward to error handler
app.use(function(req, res, next) {
  next(createError(404));
});

// error handler
app.use(function(err, req, res, next) {
  // set locals, only providing error in development
  res.locals.message = err.message;
  res.locals.error = req.app.get('env') === 'development' ?
  err : {};

  // render the error page
  res.status(err.status || 500);
  res.render('error');
```

```
});

module.exports = app;
```

The `app.js` file will then be enriched to define the new routes that will update the database. These routes will be created by using the `app.use()` method (as explained in *Chapter 7, Using Express with Node.js*). The creation of these routes will be described in the following sections.

> **Note**
> Thanks to the `List` model that we have created, we will have access to the methods `List.create()`, `List.find()`, and so on for manipulating documents in the `elements` collection of the MongoDB database.

To create interactions between the client (here, the browser) and the server (here, the Node.js server) in order to update the database containing the list of elements, we use the **Axios JavaScript library** here.

Installing the Axios library

We see that, for now, we can manipulate the list items displayed on the HTML page, but we cannot yet update them in the database on the server.

For this, the Vue.js program must be able to communicate with the Node.js server. This is possible using a JavaScript library such as Axios (see `https://github.com/axios/axios`). All you have to do is include the library in the HTML page (here, it will be in the `index.html` file) in order to be able to use its features.

> **Note**
> The Axios library is a library allowing communication between a browser and a server using **Ajax technology**. This technology allows a browser and a server to exchange information while remaining on the same HTML page, which is what we want here. This is called a **single-page application** (**SPA**) (when the application consists of a single HTML page).

Let's include the Axios library in the `index.html` file (using the `<script>` tag), and display the value of the `axios.VERSION` variable, which contains the version number of the library. This verifies that the Axios library is accessible:

Including Axios library and displaying version number (index.html file)

```html
<html>
  <head>
    <meta charset="utf-8" />
    <script src="https://unpkg.com/vue@next"></script>
    <script src="https://unpkg.com/axios/dist/
    axios.min.js"></script>

    <style type="text/css">
      li {
        margin-top:10px;
      }
      ul button {
        margin-left:10px;
      }
    </style>
  </head>

  <body>
    <div id="app"></div>
  </body>

  <script type="module">

    console.log("axios.VERSION = " + axios.VERSION);
    // display Axios version number

    import GlobalApp from "./global-app.js";

    var app = Vue.createApp({
      components : {
        GlobalApp:GlobalApp
      },
      template : "<GlobalApp />"
```

```
    });

    var vm = app.mount("div#app");

</script>

</html>
```

We simply added in the `index.html` file the Axios library (using the `<script>` tag) and the instruction to display the version number of the Axios library in the console, which allows us to check that the Axios library is accessible afterward.

Let's display the page again in the browser (with the URL `http://localhost:3000`).

We get a message in the console indicating the version number of Axios used (see the following figure), thus showing that we have access to the functionalities of the Axios library:

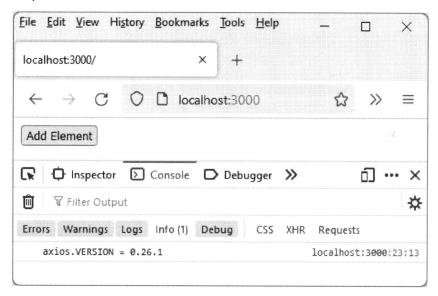

Figure 9.10 – Displaying the Axios version number

Now let's see how to use Axios to interact with the server and update the database documents.

The goal is, of course, to make maximum use of the Vue.js code that we have already written by modifying it to use the Axios library and thus perform communication with the Node.js server.

Subsequently, we will therefore modify the following files (in addition to the `index.html` file previously modified to include the Axios library):

- The `global-app.js` file, to make calls to the Axios library
- The `element.js` file, to adapt it to the structure of the database
- The `app.js` file (created by Express), to perform database queries

We have seen how to install and use Axios in our program. Now let's see how to use it to insert an element into the database.

Inserting a new element in the list

Let's see how to store a new element in the list, following a click on the **Add Element** button.

The text associated with this element must be transmitted to the server, which will be of the form **Element X**. We will see later how to modify this text after clicking on the **Modify** button.

The `add()` method defined in the `<GlobalApp>` component is used to insert a new element into the displayed list. It will be necessary to add instructions that use the Axios library in order to also insert this new element in the MongoDB `elements` collection.

Before starting to use Axios, it is useful to slightly modify the JavaScript program written with Vue.js. To do this, we will use a new attribute when creating the `<Element>` component, replacing the `text` and `index` attributes with the `element` attribute.

Replacing the text and index attributes with the element attribute

When creating an element, we currently use the element's text and index, which are then used in the `<Element>` component, to display it (with its text) or to modify or delete it (with its index).

The use of the index to identify the element in the list displayed on the screen was relevant before, but this is no longer the case if we want to modify or delete the element in the database. This is because the documents of a MongoDB collection are not identified by their index but rather by their identifier `_id`.

Rather than passing the text and index parameters in the <Element> component, we simplify by passing only the element parameter, which is a { text, _id } object. The element.text field allows you to retrieve the text to be displayed, while the element._id field allows you to access the unique identifier of the element (such as the index, which was unique for each element).

We modify the global-app.js and element.js files to take this into account.

These files are modified below but will be modified again to take into account the connection with the database:

global-app.js file

```
import Element from "./element.js";
const GlobalApp = {
  data() {
    return {
      elements : []   // array of object { text, _id }
                      // (_id = document id in MongoDB)
    }
  },
  components : {
    Element:Element
  },
  template : `
    <button @click="add()">Add Element</button>
    <ul>
      <Element v-for="(element, index) in elements"
        :key="index" :element="element"
         @remove="remove($event)" @modify="modify($event)"
      />
    </ul>
  `,
  methods : {
    add() {
      var text = "Element " + (this.elements.length + 1);
      this.elements.push({text:text,
       _id:this.elements.length});
```

```
                          // to modify to retrieve the real
                          // _id provided by MongoDB
    },
    remove(params) {
      var id = params.id;
      // remove the element with this id from the elements
      // array
      this.elements = this.elements.filter(
      function(element) {
        if (element._id == id) return false;
        else return true;
      });
    },
    modify(params) {
      var id = params.id;
      var value = params.value;
      // modify the text of the element with this id in the
      // elements array
      this.elements = this.elements.map(function(element) {
        if (element._id == id) {
          element.text = value;
          return element;
        }
        else return element;
      });
    }
  }
}

export default GlobalApp;
```

The following remarks can be made about the preceding code:

- The reactive `elements` variable now becomes an array of `{ text, _id }` objects. To do this, we write in the `add()` method the instruction `this.elements.push({text:text, _id:this.elements.length})` by inserting an object of the form `{text, _id}` into the `elements` array.

- The value of the `_id` property is temporary here: in fact, you must then retrieve the identifier provided by MongoDB when the document has been saved in the database.
- Each `<Element>` component is constructed (in the template) by passing it an `element` attribute that represents a `{ text, _id }` object.
- The `remove()` method must remove from the list the element having the passed identifier. To do this, we use the JavaScript `filter()` method to keep all the elements except the one with this identifier.
- Similarly, the `modify()` method must modify the value of the element of the list having this identifier. We use the JavaScript `map()` method to return a new array of elements, for which the element with this identifier has its value modified.

The `element.js` file becomes the following:

element.js file

```
const Element = {
  data() {
    return {
      input : false
    }
  },
  template : `
    <li>
      <span v-if="!input"> {{element.text}} </span>
      <input v-else type="text" :value="element.text"
        @blur="modify($event)"
                  ref="refInput" />
      <button @click="remove()"> Remove </button>
      <button @click="input=true"> Modify </button>
    </li>
  `,
  props : ["element"],
  methods : {
    remove() {
      // process the click on the Remove button
      this.$emit("remove", { id : this.element._id });
```

```
    },
    modify(event) {
      var value = event.target.value;
      this.input = false;
      this.$emit("modify", { id : this.element._id, value :
      value });
    }
  },
  emits : ["remove", "modify"],
  updated() {
    // check that refInput exists, and if so, give focus to
    // the input field
    if (this.$refs.refInput) this.$refs.refInput.focus();
  }
}

export default Element;
```

As the attribute transmitted for the creation of the `<Element>` component is named `element` and corresponds to an object `{ text, _id }`, we use `element.text` and `element._id` to display the text and use the identifier of the element (instead of the index).

You can check that the program still works, even if the connection with the server for insertion into the database has not yet been made.

> **Note**
> We have modified the code of the Vue.js program in order to adapt it to the use of the MongoDB database.

Let's now explain how the Axios library will allow the client and the server to communicate with each other, in order to update the MongoDB database.

Description of the Axios library for communicating between the client and the server

Now let's use Axios to insert the element into the database.

Axios offers four main methods for communicating between the browser and the server, with the JavaScript language. The server we are using here is a Node.js server, but Axios allows you to interact with any type of server. The four methods are those related to the types of HTTP requests one can make: GET, POST, PUT, and DELETE:

- `axios.get(url, options)`: This allows you to perform a GET type request.
- `axios.post(url, options)`: This allows you to perform a POST type request.
- `axios.put(url, options)`: This allows you to perform a PUT type request.
- `axios.delete(url, options)`: This allows you to perform a DELETE type request.

The `options` parameter allows you to specify additional parameters that will allow the server to perform its processing. For example, in the case of our application, we will indicate in this parameter the text of the list element that we want to store in the database.

> **Note**
>
> All these methods return a `Promise` object, which then allows you to continue with the `then(callback)` method. The `callback(response)` function is used to retrieve and analyze the server's response following the request being made.
>
> `Promise` objects were studied at the end of *Chapter 2, Exploring the Advanced Concepts of JavaScript*.

In each case, we will have to process the Axios request sent on the client side (in the `global-app.js` file associated with the `<GlobalApp>` component), then take it into account on the server side (in the `app.js` file, which receives the queries issued by Axios).

Now let's see how the POST request will allow us to insert elements into the database.

Using Axios with a POST type request (client side)

Now let's see how to use the `axios.post()` method to insert a new element into the `elements` collection, following the creation of a new element in the list.

> **Note**
> We are using the POST request here to insert the item, but other types of requests would work the same. However, using the POST request makes sense here because it follows the official recommendations for using **REpresentational State Transfer** (**REST**) requests.

Although only a few lines are added to each file, the full code is shown below each time, so you can see where the changes are located:

Adding a new element in the database, client side (global-app.js file)

```
import Element from "./element.js";
const GlobalApp = {
  data() {
    return {
      elements : []  // array of object { text, _id }
                     // (_id = document id in MongoDB)
    }
  },
  components : {
    Element:Element
  },
  template : `
    <button @click="add()">Add Element</button>
    <ul>
      <Element v-for="(element, index) in elements"
        :key="index" :element="element"
        @remove="remove($event)" @modify="modify($event)"
      />
    </ul>
  `,
  methods : {
    add() {
```

```
      var text = "Element " + (this.elements.length + 1);
      axios.post("/list", {text:text})      // pass object
                                            // {text:text} to
                                            // server
      .then((response) => {
        this.elements.push({text:text,
          _id:response.data.id});
      });
    },
    remove(params) {
      var id = params.id;
      // remove the element with this id from the elements
      // array
      this.elements = this.elements.filter(
      function(element) {
        if (element._id == id) return false;
        else return true;
      });
    },
    modify(params) {
      var id = params.id;
      var value = params.value;
      // modify the text of the element with this id in the
      // elements array
      this.elements = this.elements.map(function(element) {
        if (element._id == id) {
          element.text = value;
          return element;
        }
        else return element;
      });
    }
  }
}

export default GlobalApp;
```

The `axios.post("/list", {text:text})` method activates the `/list` URL on the server, using a `POST` type request. The `text` parameter is passed to the server so that it stores it in the `elements` collection.

In return for the call to the server, the latter returns a `response` object containing in `data.id` the identifier of the document created in MongoDB. This identifier and the element text are then stored in the `elements` array. Because the `elements` array is a reactive variable of Vue.js, its update causes the list to be re-displayed in the browser.

> **Note**
> Notice how the callback function is written in the `then(callback)` method. We use the form with `=>` (that is without using the `function` keyword) in order to preserve the value of `this` in the callback function. If you use the `function` keyword instead, the value of `this` is `undefined` and you can no longer access the `elements` variable through `this.elements`, which will cause an error.

The `POST` request was issued by the client (the browser), so it must now be processed by the server to insert a new element into the collection. Let's study how to proceed.

POST type request processing (server side)

Now let's see how the server handles the receipt of the `POST` request. It must create a new document in the `elements` collection of the database. The server's `app.js` file is modified to take into account the `POST` request on the `/list` URL:

Adding a new element in the database, server side (app.js file)

```
var createError = require('http-errors');
var express = require('express');
var path = require('path');
var cookieParser = require('cookie-parser');
var logger = require('morgan');

var indexRouter = require('./routes/index');
var usersRouter = require('./routes/users');

var mongoose = require("mongoose");
```

```
mongoose.connect("mongodb://localhost/mydb_test");

var listSchema = mongoose.Schema({
 text : String
});

var List = mongoose.model("elements", listSchema);

var app = express();

// view engine setup
app.set('views', path.join(__dirname, 'views'));
app.set('view engine', 'jade');

app.use(logger('dev'));
app.use(express.json());
app.use(express.urlencoded({ extended: false }));
app.use(cookieParser());
app.use(express.static(path.join(__dirname, 'public')));

app.use('/', indexRouter);
app.use('/users', usersRouter);

// creating a new element in the list
app.post("/list", function(req, res) {
  var text = req.body.text;
  List.create({text:text}, function(err, doc) {
    res.json({id:doc._id});   // send the MongoDB identifier
                              // in the response
  });
});

// catch 404 and forward to error handler
app.use(function(req, res, next) {
  next(createError(404));
```

```
});

// error handler
app.use(function(err, req, res, next) {
  // set locals, only providing error in development
  res.locals.message = err.message;
  res.locals.error = req.app.get('env') === 'development' ?
  err : {};

  // render the error page
  res.status(err.status || 500);
  res.render('error');
});

module.exports = app;
```

The `app.post("/list", callback)` method is used to receive and process the request to insert the new element into the `elements` collection.

The text sent in the Axios `text` parameter is received on the server in the `req.body.text` variable. The update of the `elements` collection is performed by the `List.create()` class method, to which we pass the `text` parameter. In the callback function associated with the `create()` method, we retrieve the identifier of the document created in `doc._id`.

We return this identifier in the response sent to the browser as a JSON object `{ id : doc._id }`. We use the `res.json()` method for this. This server return is processed in the `then(callback)` method when calling the `axios.post()` method previously seen (the `global-app.js` file).

If you run the preceding program, you'll see that the lines containing **Element X** are inserted one under the other on the page. But nothing says that the database has been updated. Let's verify the correct insertion using the tools available in MongoDB.

Verifying the correct operation of the insertion in the database

To verify the insertion in the database, just use the `mongo` utility, then type the command `db.elements.find()` to see the inserted documents displayed (assuming we have already connected the `mydb_test` database with the `db=connect("mydb_test")` command).

Assuming that three list items have been inserted, we get the following:

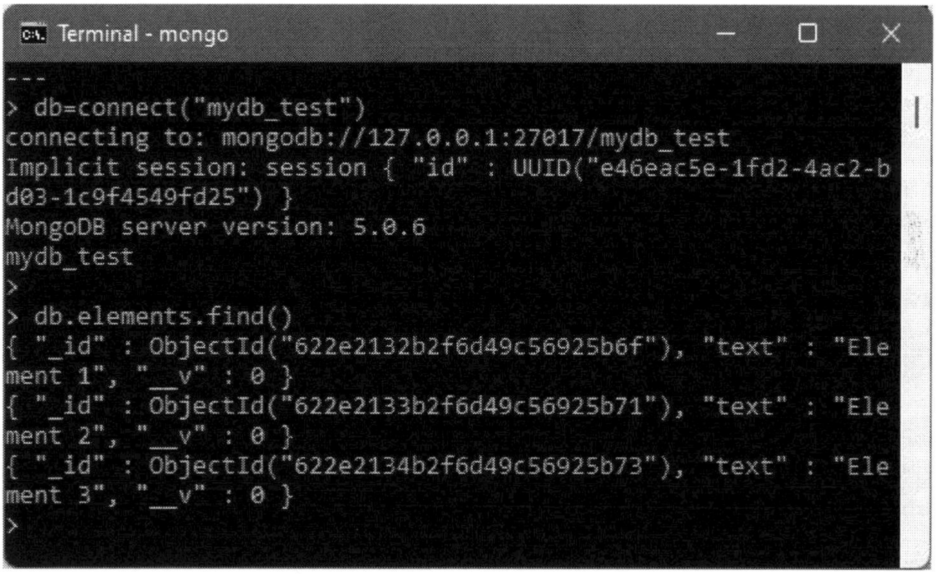

```
> db=connect("mydb_test")
connecting to: mongodb://127.0.0.1:27017/mydb_test
Implicit session: session { "id" : UUID("e46eac5e-1fd2-4ac2-bd03-1c9f4549fd25") }
MongoDB server version: 5.0.6
mydb_test
>
> db.elements.find()
{ "_id" : ObjectId("622e2132b2f6d49c56925b6f"), "text" : "Element 1", "__v" : 0 }
{ "_id" : ObjectId("622e2133b2f6d49c56925b71"), "text" : "Element 2", "__v" : 0 }
{ "_id" : ObjectId("622e2134b2f6d49c56925b73"), "text" : "Element 3", "__v" : 0 }
>
```

Figure 9.11 – Using the mongo utility to view the contents of the elements collection

The next step is to retrieve the information stored in the database to display the items in the list. The list should be viewed when the page is displayed at the start and will be updated as insertions, modifications, or deletions are made.

Displaying list elements

In this section, we deal with the first display of the page. Insertion has been seen previously, and modification and deletion are covered in the following sections.

> **Note**
> To display the list when the application starts, you must use the `created()` method or the `mounted()` method of the component, which are called in each Vue.js component when the component is created.

To retrieve the list of elements, we are going to use an HTTP `GET` request.

Using Axios with a GET type request (client side)

Here, we are going to make a `GET` type request with the `/list` URL to the server. The `axios.get("/list")` instruction is used to perform this request. We can use this instruction in the `created()` or `mounted()` method. Here, we choose to use it in the `created()` method:

Retrieving list of items, client side (global-app.js file)

```
import Element from "./element.js";
const GlobalApp = {
  data() {
    return {
      elements : []   // array of object { text, _id }
                      // (_id = document id in MongoDB)
    }
  },
  components : {
    Element:Element
  },
  template : `
    <button @click="add()">Add Element</button>
    <ul>
      <Element v-for="(element, index) in elements"
        :key="index"  :element="element"
        @remove="remove($event)" @modify="modify($event)"
      />
```

```
    </ul>
`,
methods : {
  add() {
    var text = "Element " + (this.elements.length + 1);
    axios.post("/list", {text:text})
    .then((response) => {
      console.log(this.elements);
      this.elements.push({text:text,
      _id:response.data.id});
    });
  },
  remove(params) {
    var id = params.id;
    // remove the element with this id from the elements
    // array
    this.elements = this.elements.filter(
    function(element) {
      if (element._id == id) return false;
      else return true;
    });
  },
  modify(params) {
    var id = params.id;
    var value = params.value;
    // modify the text of the element with this id in the
    // elements array
    this.elements = this.elements.map(function(element) {
      if (element._id == id) {
        element.text = value;
        return element;
      }
      else return element;
    });
  }
},
```

```
  created() {
    axios.get("/list")
    .then((response) => {
      this.elements = response.data.elements.map(
        function(element) {
          return { _id : element._id, text : element.text }
      });
    });
  }
}

export default GlobalApp;
```

The `axios.get("/list")` method makes the request to the server, then processes the response received in the `then(callback)` method. As before, the received `response` object contains the `data` property, which contains the response returned by the server (the `elements` field – see below).

As the server sends all the document fields of the `elements` collection, we filter the list received by the `map()` method in order to keep only the `_id` and `text` fields (we thus remove the `__v` field associated with the version number, which is unnecessary here).

Now let's see how to process the GET request on the Node.js server side.

GET type request processing (server side)

The `GET /list` request is received by the Node.js server through the `app.get("/list")` method defined in the `app.js` file. The processing will consist of reading the content of the `elements` collection and returning it in JSON form to the browser in the `elements` property. Each item in the returned collection has `_id`, `text`, and `__v` (for the version number of the document) fields:

Retrieving list of items, server side (app.js file)

```
var createError = require('http-errors');
var express = require('express');
var path = require('path');
var cookieParser = require('cookie-parser');
var logger = require('morgan');
```

```javascript
var indexRouter = require('./routes/index');
var usersRouter = require('./routes/users');

var mongoose = require("mongoose");
mongoose.connect("mongodb://localhost/mydb_test");

var listSchema = mongoose.Schema({
 text : String
});

var List = mongoose.model("elements", listSchema);

var app = express();

// view engine setup
app.set('views', path.join(__dirname, 'views'));
app.set('view engine', 'jade');

app.use(logger('dev'));
app.use(express.json());
app.use(express.urlencoded({ extended: false }));
app.use(cookieParser());
app.use(express.static(path.join(__dirname, 'public')));

app.use('/', indexRouter);
app.use('/users', usersRouter);

// creating a new element in the list
app.post("/list", function(req, res) {
  var text = req.body.text;
  console.log(text);
  List.create({text:text}, function(err, doc) {
    res.json({id:doc._id});
  });
});
```

```
// retrieving list of elements
app.get("/list", function(req, res) {
  List.find(function(err, elements) {
    res.json({elements:elements});
  });
});

// catch 404 and forward to error handler
app.use(function(req, res, next) {
  next(createError(404));
});

// error handler
app.use(function(err, req, res, next) {
  // set locals, only providing error in development
  res.locals.message = err.message;
  res.locals.error = req.app.get('env') === 'development' ?
  err : {};

  // render the error page
  res.status(err.status || 500);
  res.render('error');
});

module.exports = app;
```

The `elements` collection is read using the `List.find()` class method. We return the `{ elements : elements }` object in response to the browser, the use of which we saw earlier.

The list of items is now displayed each time the application is started. Just restart the server with `npm start`, then re-display the URL of the page, `http://localhost:3000`.

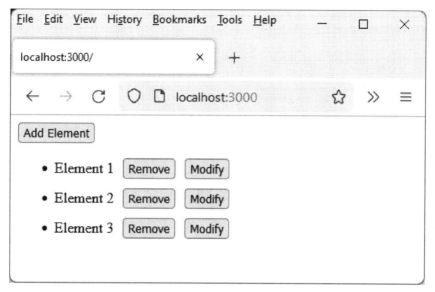

Figure 9.12 – The list of elements is displayed when the application starts

We have seen how to insert an element and retrieve the list of elements. Next, let's see how to modify an element in the list.

Modifying an element in the list

Here we show how to modify an element of the list, keeping this modification in the database. A `PUT` type request will be used for this.

Using Axios with a PUT type request (client side)

The `axios.put("/list", options)` method is used to perform a `PUT` type request to the server. We transmit to the server in the `options` parameter the new text of the modified element and its identifier in the database. The identifier and the new text will allow the item to be updated on the server:

Modifying an element, client side (global-app.js file)

```
import Element from "./element.js";
const GlobalApp = {
```

```
data() {
  return {
    elements : []  // array of object { text, _id }
                   // (_id = document id in MongoDB)
  }
},
components : {
  Element:Element
},
template : `
  <button @click="add()">Add Element</button>
  <ul>
    <Element v-for="(element, index) in elements"
    :key="index" :element="element"
      @remove="remove($event)" @modify="modify($event)"
    />
  </ul>
`,
methods : {
  add() {
    var text = "Element " + (this.elements.length + 1);
    axios.post("/list", {text:text})
    .then((response) => {
      console.log(this.elements);
      this.elements.push({text:text,
      _id:response.data.id});
    });
  },
  remove(params) {
    var id = params.id;
    // remove the element with this id from the elements
    // array
    this.elements = this.elements.filter(
    function(element) {
      if (element._id == id) return false;
      else return true;
```

```
      });
    },
    modify(params) {
      var id = params.id;
      var value = params.value;
      // modify the text of the element with this id in the
      // elements array
      this.elements = this.elements.map(function(element) {
        if (element._id == id) {
          element.text = value;
          return element;
        }
        else return element;
      });
      // modify the text of the element having this
      // identifier
      axios.put("/list", {text:value, id:id});
    }
  },
  created() {
    axios.get("/list")
    .then((response) => {
      this.elements = response.data.elements.map(
      function(element) {
        return {_id : element._id, text : element.text }
      });
    });
  }
}

export default GlobalApp;
```

The `then(callback)` method should not be used here because the server does not return any information for the browser.

Let's now see the management of the PUT request on the server side.

PUT type request processing (server side)

The server processes the PUT /list request in the app.js file. The processing consists of carrying out an update of the document of the collection having this identifier, with the text received from the browser:

Modifying an element, server side (app.js file)

```
var createError = require('http-errors');
var express = require('express');
var path = require('path');
var cookieParser = require('cookie-parser');
var logger = require('morgan');

var indexRouter = require('./routes/index');
var usersRouter = require('./routes/users');

var mongoose = require("mongoose");
mongoose.connect("mongodb://localhost/mydb_test");

var listSchema = mongoose.Schema({
  text : String
});

var List = mongoose.model("elements", listSchema);

var app = express();

// view engine setup
app.set('views', path.join(__dirname, 'views'));
app.set('view engine', 'jade');

app.use(logger('dev'));
app.use(express.json());
app.use(express.urlencoded({ extended: false }));
app.use(cookieParser());
app.use(express.static(path.join(__dirname, 'public')));
```

Modifying an element in the list   301

```
app.use('/', indexRouter);
app.use('/users', usersRouter);

// creating a new element in the list
app.post("/list", function(req, res) {
  var text = req.body.text;
  console.log(text);
  List.create({text:text}, function(err, doc) {
    res.json({id:doc._id});
  });
});

// retrieving list of elements
app.get("/list", function(req, res) {
  List.find(function(err, elements) {
    res.json({elements:elements});
  });
});

// modifying an element in the list
app.put("/list", function(req, res) {
  var id = req.body.id;
  var text = req.body.text;
  List.updateOne({_id:id}, {text:text}).exec();
  // don't forget exec()!
  res.send();  // close the connection to the browser
});

// catch 404 and forward to error handler
app.use(function(req, res, next) {
  next(createError(404));
});

// error handler
app.use(function(err, req, res, next) {
  // set locals, only providing error in development
```

```
    res.locals.message = err.message;
    res.locals.error = req.app.get('env') === 'development' ?
    err : {};

    // render the error page
    res.status(err.status || 500);
    res.render('error');
});

module.exports = app;
```

The text and the identifier are retrieved from the server in the `req.body.text` and `req.body.id` variables. The document with this identifier is updated in the database with the new text. The `List.updateOne()` class method allows this document to be modified, but since it does not use a callback function afterward, the `exec()` method must be used afterward for the update to be carried out in the database.

Also notice the `res.send()` instruction at the end of the processing. It closes the connection between the browser and the server. If the connection is not closed, the browser waits for the server's response, which would never come if the server sends nothing back to the browser.

Let's finish by explaining how to remove an item from the list.

Removing an element from the list

Finally, we will learn how to remove an element from the list. A `DELETE` type request will be used for this.

Using Axios with a DELETE type request (client side)

The `axios.delete("/list", options)` method is used to trigger a `DELETE` type request on the server. The `options` parameter must indicate the identifier of the element to be deleted from the collection.

However, unlike the previous `axios.get()`, `axios.put()`, and `axios.post()` calls, the `axios.delete("/list", options)` call requires that the `options` parameter be written in the `data` property (thus written as `{ data : options }`). If you don't follow this convention, it won't work.

Here are the instructions for performing a DELETE request with the Axios library:

Deleting an element, client side (global-app.js file)

```
import Element from "./element.js";
const GlobalApp = {
  data() {
    return {
      elements : []   // array of object { text, _id }
                      // (_id = document id in MongoDB)
    }
  },
  components : {
    Element:Element
  },
  template : `
    <button @click="add()">Add Element</button>
    <ul>
      <Element v-for="(element, index) in elements"
       :key="index" :element="element"
        @remove="remove($event)" @modify="modify($event)"
      />
    </ul>
  `,
  methods : {
    add() {
      var text = "Element " + (this.elements.length + 1);
      axios.post("/list", {text:text})
      .then((response) => {
        console.log(this.elements);
        this.elements.push({text:text,
        _id:response.data.id});
      });
    },
    remove(params) {
      var id = params.id;
      // remove the element with this id from the elements
```

```js
      // array
      this.elements = this.elements.filter(
      function(element) {
        if (element._id == id) return false;
        else return true;
      });
      axios.delete("/list", { data : {id:id} });
          // the options must be written in the data
          // property
    },
    modify(params) {
      var id = params.id;
      var value = params.value;
      // modify the text of the element with this id in the
      // elements array
      this.elements = this.elements.map(function(element) {
        if (element._id == id) {
          element.text = value;
          return element;
        }
        else return element;
      });
      axios.put("/list", {text:value, id:id});
          // modify the text of the element having this
          // identifier
    }
  },
  created() {
    axios.get("/list")
    .then((response) => {
      this.elements = response.data.elements.map(
      function(element) {
        return {_id : element._id, text : element.text }
      });
    });
  }
```

```
}

export default GlobalApp;
```

As mentioned before, we use the `options` parameter of the `axios.delete(/list", options)` method in the form `{ data : options }` so that the options are correctly passed by the DELETE method.

Let's now examine the processing performed by the server when receiving the DELETE request.

DELETE type request processing (server side)

The server receives the DELETE /list request using the `app.delete("/list, callback)` method. The callback function uses the identifier passed in the request to delete the corresponding document from the `elements` collection:

Deleting an element, server side (app.js file)

```
var createError = require('http-errors');
var express = require('express');
var path = require('path');
var cookieParser = require('cookie-parser');
var logger = require('morgan');

var indexRouter = require('./routes/index');
var usersRouter = require('./routes/users');

var mongoose = require("mongoose");
mongoose.connect("mongodb://localhost/mydb_test");

var listSchema = mongoose.Schema({
 text : String
});

var List = mongoose.model("elements", listSchema);

var app = express();
```

```js
// view engine setup
app.set('views', path.join(__dirname, 'views'));
app.set('view engine', 'jade');

app.use(logger('dev'));
app.use(express.json());
app.use(express.urlencoded({ extended: false }));
app.use(cookieParser());
app.use(express.static(path.join(__dirname, 'public')));

app.use('/', indexRouter);
app.use('/users', usersRouter);

// creating a new element in the list
app.post("/list", function(req, res) {
  var text = req.body.text;
  console.log(text);
  List.create({text:text}, function(err, doc) {
    res.json({id:doc._id});
  });
});

// retrieving list of elements
app.get("/list", function(req, res) {
  List.find(function(err, elements) {
    res.json({elements:elements});
  });
});

// modifying an element in the list
app.put("/list", function(req, res) {
  var id = req.body.id;
  var text = req.body.text;
  List.updateOne({_id:id}, {text:text}).exec();
  res.send();  // close the connection to the browser
```

```
});

// remove an element from the list
app.delete("/list", function(req, res) {
  var id = req.body.id;
  console.log(req.body.id);
  List.deleteOne({_id:id}).exec();    // don't forget exec()!
  res.send();   // close the connection to the browser
});

// catch 404 and forward to error handler
app.use(function(req, res, next) {
  next(createError(404));
});

// error handler
app.use(function(err, req, res, next) {
  // set locals, only providing error in development
  res.locals.message = err.message;
  res.locals.error = req.app.get('env') === 'development' ?
  err : {};

  // render the error page
  res.status(err.status || 500);
  res.render('error');
});

module.exports = app;
```

The `List.deleteOne({_id:id})` method is used to delete the document having this identifier in the collection. As we do not use a callback function in the `List.deleteOne()` method, we call the `exec()` method so that the deletion is performed in the database.

Also, notice the `res.send()` instruction at the end of the processing. It closes the connection between the browser and the server. If the connection is not closed, the browser waits for the server's response, which would never come if the server sends nothing back to the browser. In this case, you would see unexpected results by clicking several times on the **Delete** buttons in the list and reloading the list.

We have seen how to use MongoDB to insert, modify, and delete elements in a list, using a library such as Axios, allowing communication between the JavaScript code of the browser and the JavaScript code written for the server. And now, this brings us to the end of this chapter and the book.

Summary

Through this complete example, we have seen how to use JavaScript on both the client side (here, with Vue.js) and the server side (with Node.js and MongoDB).

The use of a single language to carry out all development simplifies learning and ensures great consistency throughout the application.

In addition, tools such as Vue.js, allowing the creation of reusable components, and modules such as Express and mongoose based on the MVC model, make it possible to properly architect JavaScript code, both on the client side and on the server side.

We also saw how the Axios library made it possible to communicate between the client and the server.

You now have everything you need to create reliable, robust, and well-structured client and server applications entirely in JavaScript.

Thanks

Thank you, dear reader, for purchasing and reading this book. It was written for the sole purpose of helping and guiding you. We hope it has been of great help to you.

If so, we ask you for a very small but extremely important contribution – to make our book knownto others by means at your disposal, in the hope that it can keep helping people like you. Thanks very much!

Index

Symbols

\<Element\> component
  using 174-176
\<input\> element
  \<span\> element, transforming
    into 183, 184
\<script\> tag
  and \</script\> tag, JavaScript code
    writing between 8-10
\<span\> element
  transforming, into \<input\>
    element 183, 184
$emit()
  using, to communicate with
    parent component 136-140
$event parameter
  used, for checking entered value
    is less than 100 130-132
  used, for entering only digits 132-134
  using 130

A

Ajax technology 277
alert() function
  versus console.log() method 11-13

app.js file
  defined routes, analyzing 226-229
  initial content 223-225
  route, adding 229
  route, processing directly 229
application
  splitting, into components 169-172
application components
  $emit(), using to communicate with
    parent component 136, 138-140
  assembling 134, 136
  props, using to communicate with
    child component 140-143
application screens
  displaying 166-169, 264-271
array
  about 55
  creating 55
  creating, with Array class 56
  creating, with square brackets
    [and] 55, 56
  elements, adding by index 64
  elements, adding with push()
    method 64-66
  elements, deleting from 68, 69
  elements, filtering 69

elements, filtering with
   filter(callback) method 69, 70
elements, filtering with
   map(callback) method 70, 71
items, adding 64
Array class
   used, for creating array 56, 57
array elements
  accessing 57
  accessing, by index 57-59
  accessing, with forEach(callback)
     method 61, 62
  accessing, with for() or while() loop 60
  deleting 66
  value, deleting 66, 67
arrays 6
attributes
  using, in component 114, 115, 117
Axios JavaScript library
  installing 277, 279
  reference link 277

C

callback function 61
callback parameter, of find(conditions,
    callback) method
  using 254, 255
cascade tests 29
characters
  accessing, in string 75
character string
  given format, checking 78-80
  modifying 77
  part, replacing with given format 80, 82
character strings 6
  about 72
  creating 72

literal, creating with backticks 73-75
literal, creating with double or
   single quotes 72, 73
charAt(index) method
  using 76
child component
  props, using to communicate
    with 140-143
class
  about 42
  constructor() method, using 50, 51, 53
  defining 42, 43
  methods 43
  methods, adding 47-49
  properties 43
  properties, adding 46, 47
  used, for creating object 43-45
classic effects, examples
  about 157
  move-down effect 160-163
  opacity effect 159, 160
  shrink effect 157-159
clearInterval() function
  using 87-89
collection
  about 237, 243
colors module
  features, using 212-214
  installing, in node_modules
    local directory 212
component
  attributes, using 114-117
  computed properties, defining in
    computed section 112, 114
  creating 103, 104
  inserting, from external file 107-110
  inserting, in application file 104-107
  methods, adding 110

methods, defining in methods
   section 111, 112
computed properties
   about 112
   defining, in computed section 112, 114
computed section
   computed properties, defining 112, 114
conditional tests
   writing conditions 25
console.log() method
   versus alert() function 11-13
constructor() method
   using 50, 51, 53
created() method 189
create(doc, callback) class method
   using 248-250
CSS class names
   using, for effect 154, 156
CSS code
   used, for changing appearance
      of list 177, 178

D

directives
   about 117
   using 117
   v-else directive 118, 119
   v-for directive 120
   v-if directive 118, 119
   v-model directive 123-125
   v-show directive 120
doc.save(callback) instance method
   using 245-247
Document Object Model (DOM) 188
documents
   about 237, 243
   creating 245

   creating, in MongoDB 243
   deleting, in MongoDB 260-262
   searching, in MongoDB 251, 252
   updating, in MongoDB 258-260
downloaded modules
   using, with npm command 210, 211

E

effect
   CSS class names, using 154, 156
   producing, on several elements 156
EJS 229
element
   adding, to list 173, 174
   deleting, from array 68, 69
   filtering, in array 69
   modifying, in list 183
   removing, from list 178-183
   value, deleting 66, 67
events
   managing 128-130
exec(callback) method
   using 255, 256
Express 210
   MVC pattern 222
   routes, using 223
   views, displaying 231-235
Express module 264
   installing 219-222
   used, for creating Vue.js
      application 272-274

F

file contents
   displaying, as strings 207, 208
   reading 206, 207

Index

filter(callback) method
  using 69, 70
forEach(callback) method
  used, for accessing element 61, 62
forEach() method
  versus for() loop 62-64
for() loop
  used, for accessing element 60
  versus forEach() method 62-64
for() statement
  processing loops, creating with 30, 32
functions
  for calculating the sum of first
    10 integers 38, 39
  for displaying the list of the
    first 10 integers 34-37
  used, for calculating the sum of
    first N integers 39, 40
  using 33

H

HTML page
  Vue.js, using 96, 97
HTTP Protocol
  using 169

I

input field
  exiting from 185, 186, 188
  focus, giving to 188, 189-191
inserted documents
  viewing, with mongo utility 250, 251
instance 42
internal Node.js modules
  file contents, displaying as
    strings 207, 208

file contents, reading 206, 207
non-blocking file reading,
  using 208, 209
using 206

J

JADE 228, 229
JavaScript
  multitasking 82
  variables, declaring 15
  variable types 5
JavaScript code
  specifying, in HTML file 8
  writing, between <script> and
    </script> tags 8-10
  writing, to external file 10, 11
JavaScript code written
  for browswer, versus for server 14
JavaScript Object Notation (JSON) 7
JavaScript program
  running, in browser 8
  running, on Node.js server 13

L

lambda function 107
list
  appearance, changing with
    CSS code 177, 178
  element, adding 173, 174
  element, modifying 183
  element, removing 178-183
list element, displaying
  about 292
  Axios, using with GET type
    request 292, 294
  GET type request, processing 294, 297

Index 313

list element, insertion
  about 280
  Axios library, communicating
    between client and server 285
  Axios, using with POST type
    request 286, 288
  correct operation, verifying
    in database 291
  POST type request, processing 288, 290
  text and index attributes, replacing with
    element attribute 280, 282, 284
list element, modifying
  about 297
  Axios, using with PUT type
    request 297, 299
  PUT type request, processing 300, 302
list element, removing
  about 302
  Axios, using with DELETE
    type request 302, 305
  DELETE type request,
    processing 305, 308

M

map(callback) method
  using 70, 71
methods
  defining, in methods section 111
methods section
  methods, defining 111, 112
model
  about 243
  creating 244, 245
Model View Controller (MVC) model 99
modules
  about 196
  creating 197

functionality, adding 201
  multiple functions, exporting 201-203
  so-called main function, using 205, 206
MongoDB
  about 237, 264
  documents, creating 243
  documents, deleting 260-262
  documents, searching 251, 252
  documents, updating 258-260
  installing 238, 239
MongoDB Community Edition
  installation link 238
MongoDB database
  connecting to 241, 242
MongoDB database structure 274, 277
mongoose module
  installing 240, 241
mongosh
  installation link 238
mongo utility
  about 238
  commands 239
  using 239
  using, to view inserted
    documents 250, 251
mounted() method 189
move-down effect 160-163
multitasking, JavaScript
  about 82, 83
  clearInterval() function, using 87, 89
  setInterval() function, using 86, 87
  setTimeout() function, using 83-85
MVC pattern
  in Express 222, 223
MVC pattern, in Express
  controller 222
  models 222
  views 222

N

Node.js http module
  using 216, 217, 219
Node.js server
  JavaScript program, running 13, 14
node_modules directory
  using 198, 199
node_modules local directory
  colors module, installing 212
non-blocking file reading
  using 208, 209
npm command
  downloaded modules, using with 210, 211
  using 210, 211
numerical values
  about 5
  Boolean values 6

O

object
  about 42
  creating, with class 43-45
  creating, without using class 45
  merging, with another object 53-55
  property values, modifying 49, 50
objects 7
opacity effect 159, 160

P

package.json file
  using 199-201
parent component
  $emit(), using to communicate with 136-140

Person class 43
processing loops
  creating 30
  using, with for() statement 32, 33
  using, with while() statement 30, 32
promises
  using 89-91
props
  using, to communicate with child component 140-143
push() method
  used, for adding element 64-66

Q

Query and Projection Operators
  installation link 252

R

reactive variables 99, 101, 103
reactivity
  using 99
regular expressions
  reference link 78
  using 78
REpresentational State Transfer (REST) 286
resources 226
route processing
  defining, with external file 230, 231
routes
  analyzing, in app.js file 226-228
  types 225, 226
routes, using with Express
  about 223
  app.js file, initial content 223-225

Index

routes, analyzing in app.js file 226-228
routes types 225, 226

S

schema
  about 243
  creating 243, 244
search conditions
  writing 252, 253
setInterval() function
  using 86, 87
setTimeout() function
  using 83-85
shrink effect 157-159
single-page application (SPA) 277
slice(start, end) method
  using 76, 77
square brackets [and]
  used, for creating array 55, 56
string
  characters, accessing 75
  characters, accessing with
    charAt(index) method 76
  characters, accessing with slice(start,
    end) method 76, 77
string literal
  creating, with backticks 73-75
  creating, with double or
    single quotes 72, 73

U

updated() method 189

V

variable declaration, JavaScript
  about 15
  const keyword, using 15-17
  let keyword, using 20-22
  uninitialized variable 23, 24
  var keyword, using 17-19
variable types, JavaScript
  arrays 6
  Boolean values 6
  character strings 6
  numerical values 5
  objects 7
v-else directive 118, 119
v-for directive
  about 120
  count in counts, using 120, 121
  (count, index) in counts, using 121, 122
  key attribute, using 122, 123
views
  displaying, in Express 231-235
v-if directive 118, 119
visual effects
  for element appearance 144
  for element disappearance 151
  using 143
visual effects, for element appearance
  CSS classes, example content 145, 146
  CSS classes, used by Vue.js 144
  CSS classes, using 146, 149, 150
visual effects, for element disappearance
  CSS classes, example content 151, 152
  CSS classes, used by Vue.js 151
  CSS classes, using 152, 154
v-model directive 123-125
v-show directive 120

Vue.js
  using, in HTML page 96, 97
Vue.js application
  creating 97, 99
  creating, with Express module 272-274

W

while() loop
  used, for accessing element 60
while() statement
  processing loops, creating with 32, 33
writing conditions, conditional tests
  about 25
  expressions, using 27-29
  forms 25-27
  nested test suites 29

Packt.com

Subscribe to our online digital library for full access to over 7,000 books and videos, as well as industry leading tools to help you plan your personal development and advance your career. For more information, please visit our website.

Why subscribe?

- Spend less time learning and more time coding with practical eBooks and Videos from over 4,000 industry professionals
- Improve your learning with Skill Plans built especially for you
- Get a free eBook or video every month
- Fully searchable for easy access to vital information
- Copy and paste, print, and bookmark content

Did you know that Packt offers eBook versions of every book published, with PDF and ePub files available? You can upgrade to the eBook version at packt.com and as a print book customer, you are entitled to a discount on the eBook copy. Get in touch with us at customercare@packtpub.com for more details.

At www.packt.com, you can also read a collection of free technical articles, sign up for a range of free newsletters, and receive exclusive discounts and offers on Packt books and eBooks.

Other Books You May Enjoy

If you enjoyed this book, you may be interested in these other books by Packt:

Real-World Next.js

Michele Riva

ISBN: 978-1-80107-349-3

- Get up to speed with Next.js essentials and learn how to build apps quickly
- Understand how to create scalable Next.js architectures
- Write unit tests and integration tests in your Next.js application
- Discover the powerful routing system and Next.js' built-in components
- Design and build modern architectures with Next.js using GraphCMS or any headless CMS

JavaScript from Beginner to Professional

Laurence Svekis , Maaike van Putten , Rob Percival

ISBN: 978-1-80056-252-3

- Use logic statements to make decisions within your code
- Save time with JavaScript loops by avoiding writing the same code repeatedly
- Use JavaScript functions and methods to selectively execute code
- Connect to HTML5 elements and bring your own web pages to life with interactive content
- Make your search patterns more effective with regular expressions

Packt is searching for authors like you

If you're interested in becoming an author for Packt, please visit authors.packtpub.com and apply today. We have worked with thousands of developers and tech professionals, just like you, to help them share their insight with the global tech community. You can make a general application, apply for a specific hot topic that we are recruiting an author for, or submit your own idea.

Hi!

I am Eric Sarrion, author of *JavaScript from Frontend to Backend*. I really hope you enjoyed reading this book and found it useful for increasing your productivity and efficiency in JavaScript.

It would really help me (and other potential readers!) if you could leave a review on Amazon sharing your thoughts on *JavaScript from Frontend to Backend*.

Go to the link below or scan the QR code to leave your review:

`https://packt.link/QUTSC`

Your review will help me to understand what's worked well in this book, and what could be improved upon for future editions, so it really is appreciated.

Best Wishes,

Eric Sarrion

Printed in Poland
by Amazon Fulfillment
Poland Sp. z o.o., Wrocław